NEW JERSEY DOMESTIC PARTNERS

PARTNERS
A LEGAL GUIDE

NEW JERSEY DOMESTIC PARTNERS
A LEGAL GUIDE

Stephen J. Hyland, Esq.

Distributed by

RIVERGATE
An Imprint of Rutgers University Press

No part of this publication may be reproduced, stored in a retrieval system or transmitted in any form or by any means, electronic, mechanical, photocopying, recording, scanning or otherwise, except as permitted under Sections 107 or 108 of the 1976 United States Copyright Act without either the prior written permission of the Publisher, or authorization through payment of the appropriate per-copy fee to the Copyright Clearance Center, 222 Rosewood Drive, Danvers, MA 01923, (978) 750-8400, fax (978) 646-8700. Requests to the Publisher for permission should be addressed to Stephen J. Hyland, c/o Hill Wallack, 202 Carnegie Center, Princeton, NJ 08543, (609) 924-0808, fax (609) 452-1888, E-mail: info@njdomesticpartnership.com.

The Author and Publisher, Stephen J. Hyland, makes available the information and materials in this legal guide (the Materials) for informational purposes only. While it is hoped and believed the Materials will be helpful as background matter, neither the Author nor the Publisher warrants that the materials are accurate or complete. Moreover, the Materials are general in nature, and may not apply to particular factual or legal circumstances. In any event, the Materials do not constitute legal advice and should not be relied on as such. Therefore, if you want legal advice, please consult a lawyer. The Author and Publisher disclaim any implied warranties, including warranties of merchantability and fitness for a particular purpose.

New Jersey Domestic Partners: A Legal Guide

Published by:

Stephen J. Hyland, Esq.
202 Carnegie Center
Princeton, New Jersey 08543
www.njdomesticpartnership.com

Copyright © 2004-2005 by Stephen J. Hyland. All rights reserved.

ISBN: 0-8135-3739-8

Printed in the United States of America

Library of Congress Control Number: 2005906383

DEDICATION

This guide is dedicated to Richard Leopold, my best friend, constant companion and domestic partner of over 18 years. Thank you for your encouragement and patience, your criticisms and careful editing, your love and kindness, and your cooking.

This guide is also dedicated to my parents, William F. Hyland, who taught me what it means to be a lawyer and Joan E. Hyland, who taught me to fight for what I believe is right.

ACKNOWLEDGMENTS

In writing the second edition of the New Jersey Domestic Partners: A Legal Guide, I want to acknowledge my colleagues in the New Jersey State Bar Association Committee on Gay, Lesbian, Bisexual and Transgender Rights, whose discussions on and off-line have contributed greatly to my understanding of many of the fine points of the New Jersey Domestic Partnership Act. In particular, I'd like to thank Peter Bergé for his very thorough review of the manuscript and for providing valuable suggestions for improvement.

I'd also like to acknowledge my partners and associates at Hill Wallack, whose support, breadth of knowledge and experience, and keen legal insight have helped me to better understand and interpret the Domestic Partnership Act and New Jersey law as it applies to same-sex couples. A special thanks goes to my colleagues, Henry T. Chou, who took time out of a busy schedule to edit the first draft, and Jae H. Cho, who helped pull together the glossary at the last minute.

WHO THIS BOOK IS FOR

This guide is primarily intended for same-sex couples and families who live in New Jersey, or who intend to live in New Jersey, whether or not they choose to register as domestic partners. It is my hope that this guide will help such couples understand their legal rights and responsibilities, whether provided by the Domestic Partnership Act or by other areas of New Jersey law. Even if a couple does not register as domestic partners, there are many issues covered in this book that can assist same-sex couples and families with planning their life in New Jersey.

To a lesser extent, this guide will be useful to opposite-sex couples who are considering registration, and who meet the requirement that both partners are at least 62 years of age.

This guide may also be useful to attorneys and other professionals practicing in areas that have been or will be affected by the DPA and the tremendous number of same-sex couples who desire some sort of formalization of their relationship. I hope it will help you extend your knowledge in this area.

CONTENTS

PREFACE

When the Domestic Partnership Act ("DPA") was signed into law by then Governor James McGreevey on January 12, 2004, New Jersey became the fifth state to provide legal recognition of same-sex couples. The Act, which went into effect on July 10, 2004, allows same-sex couples to register as domestic partners, thereby acquiring certain rights and responsibilities that have heretofore been reserved for legally married couples.

As the effective date of the Domestic Partnership Act approached, more and more attorneys began receiving inquiries from same-sex couples interested in registering their domestic partnership. Since there was little information available to the non-lawyer, and much misinformation about the effect of the Act, I began writing what, at the time, I thought would be a short guide to this new law. After many months of research and writing, the original guide had grown to over two hundred pages. In July 2004, shortly after the DPA went effect, I began privately printing and distributing the first edition. However, to make the guide as widely available as possible, I approached Rutgers University Press, who graciously agreed to take on distribution.

The year following the publication of the first edition has been a momentous one for the gay, lesbian, bisexual and transgendered (GLBT) community in New Jersey and elsewhere. On August 12, 2004, shortly after the Domestic Partnership Act he had signed went into effect, Governor McGreevey announced that he was a "Gay American." Although he resigned, it was notable that his resignation was the result of inappropriate use of his office and not his sexual orientation. New Jersey courts cautiously extended domestic partners a few more of the rights of marriage than had been provided by the Legislature in the Domestic Partnership Act. The worldwide GLBT community has seen marriage equality extended to same-sex couples throughout Canada and Spain, joining the Netherlands and Belgium as countries where same-sex couples can legally marry. In the United States, Connecticut became the fifth state providing legal protection for same-sex couples when it passed its civil unions act, and in May, over 5,000 same-sex married couples celebrated the first anniversary of marriage equality in Massachusetts. In addition, California's legislature passed a marriage equality law, although that state's governor has threatened to veto the law.

The year has not been without its disappointments. Those who vehemently oppose any recognition of GLBT rights continue their attempts to hold back marriage equality. Their efforts have resulted in a significant number of states now prohibiting same-sex marriage and, increasingly, any recognition of same-sex couples, including civil unions and domestic partnerships. Having tasted success, these allegedly "pro-family" forces have now turned their sights on adoption and parenting by same-sex couples. Fortunately, these efforts have not resonated well with New Jersey's residents, the majority of whom support equality for same-sex couples.

Similarly disappointing was the recent 2-1 decision in the New Jersey marriage case in which a New Jersey court of appeals upheld a lower court finding that there is no constitutional right to same-sex marriage in New Jersey. However, here is hope here that the appeal to the New Jersey Supreme Court will result in a reversal of this loss. If it does not, then expanded recognition of the rights and responsibilities granted under the New Jersey Domestic Partnership Act seems likely.

The intervening year has been personally momentous for me as well. Since the first edition of this guide, I have spent a great deal of time speaking, researching, writing, reading, and thinking about the implications of the Domestic Partnership Act, in particular, and the rights of same-sex couples in general. As a result, I have made extensive revisions to the guide to reflect changes in the law and my deeper understanding of it.

One final caveat: this book is about the rights of same-sex couples as the are currently recognized in New Jersey, not as I believe they should be. In many cases, I have speculated about the application of existing jurisprudence in areas where the Domestic Partnership Act is ambiguous. Where there is no guidance from the law or the courts, I have looked to related areas of the law in an attempt to make an educated guess about how a court would interpret a particular part of the law. For example, on much of what I have written regarding domestic partnership termination proceedings, I have drawn from rulings related to divorce. With few exceptions, I have refrained from suggesting that couples should base their lives on an expectation of future developments in the law relating to same-sex couples.

Legal guides in general are evolving documents that are nearly always a step or two behind the law. In a particularly fast-changing area such as domestic partnership and GLBT rights, it is impossible for a guide to be completely up to date. Therefore, if you have Internet access, you should periodically check the associated web site, www.njdomesticpartnership.com.

CHAPTER 1

INTRODUCTION

Same-sex couples are not a new phenomenon in New Jersey or elsewhere. For example, poet Walt Whitman spent his last years at his house on Mickle Street in Camden, New Jersey, cared for by a series of young male companions. Such couples, however, probably never considered that one day they might have any legal rights and responsibilities regarding each other. Indeed, until 1978, same-sex couples in New Jersey could still be prosecuted for sodomy.

Same-sex couples had traditionally lived without marriage and its associated rights, relying primarily on contractual or equitable rights in order to get some benefits of marriage. Even where couples had written contracts and wills to define and protect their partnership, these documents were often susceptible to challenges by hostile relatives, and courts were not adverse to set aside even the most carefully constructed documents if they contained any hint of the intimate nature of the couple's relationship.

For gay or lesbian parents, it was not uncommon for courts to deny them custody and visitation rights on the basis that the children needed to be "protected" from the homosexual lifestyle. Formal adoption by same-sex couples was simply unheard of in all states.

Couples who lived together often portrayed themselves as cousins or simply roommates, and took elaborate precautions to hide their relationship from family, coworkers, and neighbors. After World War II, many gays and lesbians congregated in big cities, such as New York or San Francisco, where same-sex couples could live together with fewer questions about their home lives.

At a time when homosexuals were frequent targets of the police, routinely purged from government or academic jobs, or threatened by exposure in the press, same-sex couples could not rely on the courts to protect them. Even judges who expressed sympathy to homosexuals did so out of pity, categorizing them as "unfortunate" but not "criminals or outlaws" as long as they were "well behaved." The idea that same-sex couples had rights equal to those of married heterosexuals was simply not considered by anyone at the time.

THE FIGHT FOR COUPLES RIGHTS

It wasn't until the emergence of the gay liberation movement in the late 1960s, when homosexuals began demanding equal rights, that the legal rights of same-sex couples were even considered. Even then, some members of the gay liberation movement, rather than supporting marriage rights for same-sex couples, were advocating the rejection of traditional heterosexual institutions like marriage.

Nevertheless, the first marriage equality cases were filed in the early 1970s with cases filed by couples in Minnesota,

Kentucky and Washington. In each case, state courts quickly rejected the couples' claims that the state prohibitions against marriage violated the United States Constitution. For much of the gay and lesbian community, the failure of these early marriage cases came as no surprise, and gay and lesbian rights organizations continued their focus on achieving basic equality in areas such as employment and housing, and on the decriminalization of homosexual acts. During this period there was little attention paid to the rights of same-sex couples, particularly among the men in "gay ghettos" such as New York's Greenwich Village or San Francisco's Castro District.

That same-sex couples had none of the basic rights of marriage associated with disability, health issues, death and inheritance became apparent in the 1980s, with the emergence of the AIDS epidemic. Suddenly, gay male partners who had lived together for years found themselves prevented from visiting a hospitalized partner, or stripped of their homes and property when a partner died without a will. For many gay men, the fear of infection caused a significant change in behavior, as well as a notable increase in the number of monogamous gay male couples.

Although unaffected for the most part by AIDS, many lesbian couples were shocked by the treatment of Karen Thompson, whose partner, Sharon Kowalski was severely injured in a 1983 automobile accident, leaving her severely paralyzed and impaired her ability to communicate. Upon learning that Thompson was Sharon's partner, Kowalski's parents forbade Thompson from seeing her partner, and convinced a Minnesota court to appoint their daughter's high school coach as her guardian. Only after a ten-year battle, at a cost of over $300,000, was Karen able to bring her disabled partner home.

Success and the Defense of Marriage Act

The recognition that same-sex couples were significantly unprotected, even in sympathetic states, helped to propel new attempts to extend marriage to same-sex couples. This time, however, the plaintiffs filed suit on the basis that the denial of marriage was a violation of state rather than federal constitutional protections and, as a result, the outcome was very different.

Hawaii - Reciprocal Beneficiaries

The first of these cases was filed in 1991 by three couples in Hawaii, after they were denied marriage licenses.[1] In a stunning decision in 1993, the Hawaiian Supreme Court ruled that, unless the State could show a "compelling reason" for limiting marriage to opposite-sex couples the denial violated the couples rights under the State's constitution. With that directive, the case was sent back for reconsideration by the lower court, which assigned the case to a trial judge on May 5, 1995 but then rescheduled the case for July 15, 1996, in order to receive the report of a legislative committee on sexual orientation and the law.

In shock, the United States Congress hastily introduced the Defense of Marriage Act (DOMA) May 1996, and late at night on September 21, 1996 the Act was signed into law by then-President Clinton. The Act was primarily passed to address the fear that same-sex couples from all over the United States would soon flock to Hawaii to marry, then return home, demanding that their states recognize their marriage under the Constitution's Full Faith and Credit Clause. See *Appendix B: Defense of Marriage Act*.

DOMA also prohibited federal recognition of same-sex couples by defining "marriage" to mean a "legal union between one man and one woman as husband and wife" and defining "spouse" as "a person

---

1.   *Baehr v. Lewin*, 74 Haw. 530, 852 P.2d 44 (Hi 1993)

of the opposite sex who is a husband or wife." As a result of its passage, the federal Defense of Marriage Act denied same-sex couples a total of 1,138 rights, benefits and privileges provided by the federal government to married couples. Equally panicked by the impending Hawaiian decision, a number of states passed similar laws, referred to as mini-DOMAs, designed to limit marriage to "one man-one woman."

On December 3, 1996, the Hawaiian court found that the State's marriage laws violated the equal protection clause of the Hawaiian Constitution and ordered the State to issue marriage licenses to the couples. However, the Hawaiian Supreme Court placed the order on hold while the Legislature feverishly negotiated two bills: an amendment to the Hawaiian Constitution limiting marriage to one man and one woman, and creating an alternate legal status for same-sex couples, called "reciprocal beneficiaries."

On April 29, 1997 both the Marriage Amendment and the Reciprocal Beneficiaries Bill were passed by the Legislature. Both represented significant compromises. Rather than limiting marriage to opposite-sex couples, the Amendment gave the Legislature the "power to reserve marriage to opposite-sex couples," leaving room for future legislative changes. The Reciprocal Beneficiaries Bill, on the other hand, provided a limited set of rights to anyone who was legally unable to marry, including close relatives as well as same-sex couples.

In the election of November 3, 1998, the Amendment was adopted and shortly thereafter, the court dismissed the Hawaiian marriage case. Although the outcome was a bitter loss for same-sex couples, the result was the first recognition of a legal status for same-sex couples that provided at least a few of the rights of marriage.

Buoyed by their initial success in the Hawaiian courts, GLBT rights advocates brought challenges in other jurisdictions, including an early loss in the District of Columbia[2] (1995) and successes in Alaska[3] (1998), and Vermont (1999). Although the Alaskan court found that the same-sex marriage ban was unconstitutional, an amendment to the Alaskan Constitution was quickly passed that limited marriage to "one man and one woman." However, in Vermont, the outcome was significantly different.

Vermont - Civil Unions

In *Baker v. State of Vermont*[4], the Vermont Supreme Court found that the State's refusal to issue marriage licenses to same-sex couples violated the "Common Benefits" clause of the Vermont Constitution. Rather than pass an amendment, however, the Court allowed the Legislature to pass a law that provided all of the privileges and responsibilities of marriage, but not the name, as an alternative for same-sex couples. As a result, Vermont enacted its Act Involving Civil Unions[5] in late 1999, and the Act was subsequently signed by then-Governor Howard Dean. For the first time, same-sex couples were legally provided all of the rights of marriage available under Vermont law. Although it represented an historic win, couples that register in Vermont are still denied all of the federal rights of marriage and only a few states currently recognize this legal status.

---

2.   *Dean v. District of Columbia*, 653 A.2d 307 (D.C. 1995)
3.   *Brause v. Bureau of Vital Statistics*, 1998 WL 88743 (Alaska Super. Ct. 1998)
4.   *Baker v. State*, 170 Vt. 194, 744 A.2d 864, (Vt. 1999)
5.   *Vt. Stat. Ann.* tit. 15. §§ 1201 *et seq.* and *Vt. Stat. Ann.* tit. 18, §§ 5160 *et seq.*

Massachusetts and Canada - Marriage Equality

Meanwhile, marriage proponents had greater success in Massachusetts and throughout Canada. On November 18, 2003, the Supreme Judicial Court of Massachusetts ruled in the case of Goodridge v. Department of Public Health[6] that seven same-sex couples could not be denied the right to marry, in a ruling that gave the State until May 17, 2004 to implement its decision. Like Vermont, the Legislature asked the Court for an advisory opinion as to whether civil unions would be an acceptable status. Unlike Vermont, however, the Massachusetts Court rejected that compromise, stating that "separate is seldom, if ever, equal." When the Legislature failed to act in time, the Court order came into effect, and marriage became a reality in Massachusetts, at least for its resident same-sex couples.

On July 21, 2005, marriage for same-sex couples became available throughout all of Canada, after the Canadian Parliament passed an act concerning civil marriage. The enactment of this national law followed five years of litigation in various provinces, beginning with Ontario, which granted marriage rights on June 10, 2003, followed by British Columbia on July 8, 2003, Quebec on March 19, 2004. Most other provinces followed suit, with the lone holdout, Alberta, conceding only when the national law passed.

Other States

Reacting to the historic wins in Vermont, Massachusetts and Canada, additional states passed their own defense of marriage laws or amendments, or in some cases by strengthening existing laws. Many of these laws not only prohibited recognition of same-sex marriage, but similarly prohibited recognition of civil unions, domestic partnerships, or any associated rights or obligations. Among the most onerous statutes passed was that of Virginia, which prohibited any "contract or other arrangement between persons of the same sex purporting to bestow the privileges or obligations of marriage."

Many of these same states have introduced laws prohibiting adoption by same-sex couples, including recognition of adoptions by same-sex couples in other states, as well as adoption and/or foster parenting by homosexuals. In some states, these efforts have been successful, particularly in Florida and Oklahoma.

The United States Congress, with the support of President Bush, reacted by introducing a federal Marriage Amendment in 2004, which would have prohibited recognition of any form of legal protection for same-sex couples, including marriage, civil union and domestic partnership. Although the Amendment failed to pass in 2004, it was reintroduced in the current session of Congress. At this time, the momentum seems to have gone out of the effort – for the time being, anyway.

Not all states have reacted so negatively to same-sex couples rights. Courts in Washington, New York, and California have ruled in favor of marriage equality for same-sex couples. In 2003, California replaced its prior domestic partnership registry with a comprehensive Domestic Partnership Act that provides all of the rights of marriage under California law. The California DPA went into effect on January 1, 2005. In 2004, Maine passed a limited domestic partnership registry providing some of the rights of marriage and in 2005, Connecticut enacted its Civil Union Act, which copied the Vermont Act, but which also limited marriage to opposite-sex couples.

Shortly before this guide went to print, the California Legislature passed a bill approving same-sex marriage. As I write this, Governor Schwarzenegger has yet to act on his threat to veto the bill. Clearly,

---

6.   *Goddridge v. Department of Public Health*, 440 Mass. 309, 798 N.E.2d. 941 (2003)

the final word regarding rights for same-sex couples has yet to be written.

SAME-SEX COUPLE EQUALITY IN NEW JERSEY

Although New Jersey was not the first among the 50 states to grant equality to same-sex couples, it has been far more liberal than most others. By the time the State abolished its sodomy law in 1978, its courts had begun recognizing that gays and lesbians, though "unfortunate" and "afflicted", nevertheless had many of the same rights as heterosexuals, so long as their "public behavior conform[ed] with currently acceptable standards of decency and morality."[7]

When it came to parenting, New Jersey laws have been quite liberal, based as they are on the "best interests of the child." Homosexuality is not a barrier to child custody, visitation, foster parenting, or adoption, and New Jersey is one of the few states that allow same-sex partners to jointly adopt a child. Since 1993, courts have allowed same-sex partners to adopt their partner's biological child, treating this as another form of "stepparent" adoption. In 2000, the state Supreme Court ruled that a former same-sex partner qualified as the psychological "parent" of her former-partner's child, even though she had not adopted the child, and was therefore entitled to seek joint legal custody of, and visitation with, the child. In 2005, a court ordered the State registrar to list two lesbians as the birth parents of a child born to one of them by artificial insemination.[8]

In June 2002, in a case entitled *Lewis v. Harris* seven same-sex couples filed suit against the State of New Jersey seeking equal marriage rights. The couples, each of whom was otherwise eligible to marry in New Jersey, sought to obtain marriage licenses but were refused on the basis that New Jersey's marriage laws only applied to opposite-gender couples. On November 5, 2003, the trial court granted the State's motion for summary judgment, thereby denying the couples' access to the over 850 rights and benefits.[9]

Several months before the trial court announced its decision in the *Lewis* case, two bills related to same-sex couples were introduced in the New Jersey Legislature. The first, entitled the "Family Equality Act," was introduced on June 5, 2003, provided limited recognition of same-sex and opposite-gender domestic partners. The second, a "Civil Unions Act," was introduced four days later and provided all of the rights of married couples to same-sex and opposite-gender couples. Both bills languished in committee until shortly after November 2003, when an appeal of the *Lewis v. Harris* decision was filed.

On December 15, 2003, after several feverish weeks of behind-the-scenes lobbying by a hard-working group of GLBT activists led by Laura Pople and Stephen Mershon, the Family Equality Act, (now entitled the "Domestic Partnership Act"), was passed by the Assembly and forwarded to the Senate. After passage in the Senate, the DPA was signed on January 12, 2004 by then-Governor James McGreevey in January 2004. Since its effective date of July 10, 2004 over 3,400 couples have registered their partnership.

On June 14, 2005, the appellate court upheld the decision of the trial court in *Lewis v. Harris*, ruling

---

7.   This quote is from a 1967 New Jersey Supreme Court decision permitting apparent homosexuals to congregate in bars. The case is *One Eleven Wines & Liquors, Inc. v. Division of Alcoholic Beverage Control*, 235 A.2d 12, 50 N.J. 329 (1967). In an interesting historical note, the Deputy Attorney General who argued that the ABC should have the right to revoke or suspend the liquor license of any bar serving "apparent homosexuals," was Stephen Skillman. Now a judge, Skillman wrote the majority opinion in the *Lewis* appeal rejecting equal marriage rights for same-sex couples.

8.   Two other courts subsequently refused to follow this decision so the matter remains undecided.

9.   *Lewis v. Harris*, 2003 WL 23191114 (N.J.Super. L. 2003)

that the State's restriction of marriage to opposite-gender couples in New Jersey was not unconstitutional.[10] In its opinion, however, the court concluded that "domestic partners may assert claims that the ... New Jersey Constitution entitle[s] them to addition legal benefits provided by marriage."

SUMMARY

The last words on domestic partnership and marriage equality have yet to be written in New Jersey. The *Lewis* appeal resulted in a 2-1 decision, giving the couples an automatic right to appeal to the New Jersey Supreme Court. It is expected that the Court will issue its opinion some time in 2006. Although a ruling in favor of the couples would be welcome, it could become irrelevant if either the New Jersey or Federal Constitutions are amended to ban recognition of same-sex marriage. Opponents of equality for GLBT persons and same-sex couples continue their efforts to derail gains made in other states, and in many states, these opponents have been successful.

Another question that remains is the fate of domestic partnership in New Jersey if the Lewis case succeeds in changing the marriage laws in New Jersey. When the California Legislature recently passed its law extending marriage rights to same-sex couples, it did not make any effort to repeal that state's Domestic Partnership Act, nor did it suggest that domestic partnership would be made equally available to opposite-sex couples. If marriage becomes available in New Jersey, perhaps domestic partnership will become another way for couples to legally commit to each other. Only time will tell.

In the following chapters, you and your partner will learn more about the Domestic Partnership Act, including the rights and obligations under the Act, your alternatives, and the extent of recognition of your rights under the DPA outside New Jersey.

---

10.   *Lewis v. Harris*, 378 N.J.Super. 168, 875 A.2d 259 (2005)

CHAPTER 2
THE DOMESTIC PARTNERSHIP ACT

Prior to the enactment of the Domestic Partnership Act, the only reliable way that you and your partner could create a legally-protected relationship in New Jersey was via contracts, such as living-together agreements, wills, and legal documents. For same-sex couples with children and couples who wanted to adopt, the Act provided no rights in addition to those already acquired from court recognition of parental rights.

Although the Domestic Partnership Act is certainly an improvement in that registered domestic partners are now specifically "entitled to certain rights and benefits that are accorded to married couples under the laws of New Jersey," only a few of the state's laws and regulations were actually modified by the Act. Because of this, there has been considerable confusion about what "rights and benefits" same-sex partners are now entitled to if they register.

RIGHTS AND OBLIGATIONS

Of the 60 sections that constitute the Domestic Partnership Act as passed, only section 2 actually defines the rights and benefits of registered couples. Of the remaining sections, one defines the obligations of partners to each other, four set up the requirements and procedures for establishing and terminating a domestic partnership, and approximately 35 are modifications to other laws to implement specifically enumerated rights. The remaining sections simply define the way the state and local registrar handle the records.

Registration Required

With certain exceptions, the rights and obligations provided to you and your partner require that you register your partnership. This requirement is not surprising, considering that unmarried heterosexual cohabitants in New Jersey are routinely denied marital rights as a way of encouraging marriage.

The primary exceptions to the registration requirement are found in three areas of law:

- **Emergency rights.** Unregistered partners are treated as registered in emergency medical situations, but only during the emergency. See *Rights of Unregistered Couples* in *Chapter 3: Rights and Obligations* for more information.

- **Equitable rights.** New Jersey courts have found that unmarried cohabitants may be entitled to a share of property acquired during the relationship, based upon their financial contribution, "sweat equity" or contributions made to the household. Unmarried cohabitants may also have claims for palimony. For further information, see *Property Settlement Agreements* in *Chapter 14: Separation, Termination and Nullification*.

Whether these exceptions continue to hold true depends upon future court interpretations of state and federal law and/or legislative changes to the law.

Prior to the Domestic Partnership Act, New Jersey courts would sometimes treat same-sex partners like married spouses because such couples were unable to legally marry. Because same-sex couples now have legal protection under the DPA, courts may withhold rights and obligations from unregistered couples in order to implement the State's policy encouraging formal partnerships.

Another reason you and your partner should register is that most rights and benefits available to registered partners will be available only from the date of registration. Thus, as new rights are granted to registered couples, it is very likely that they will be made retroactive to the date of registration. For example, in two cases where additional domestic partner rights have been recognized since the Domestic Partnership Act was passed, the courts have refused to extend the right further back than the date of registration, even though both couples had been together for many years prior to registration.

Other Rights And Obligations

The DPA is not meant to reduce or restrict any rights you and your partner may have, either individually or as a couple, under other applicable laws. This provision of the Act may well lead to court decisions that will more clearly define, and perhaps even expand the rights granted under the DPA.

Other rights and responsibilities, although not explicitly recognized in the Act, flow from decisions made in recent years by New Jersey courts, which have addressed issues such as "palimony," adoption, child support, and similar family law matters in the context of same-sex or other unmarried couples.

RECOGNITION OF YOUR RIGHTS

If you and your partner register as domestic partners in New Jersey, you should be aware that the rights extended to you under the Domestic Partnership Act are only recognized in New Jersey and, to an unknown extent, in those states that have enacted similar protections for same sex couples.

The extent to which your domestic partnership rights will be recognized in another state will depend on four things. First, does the state have a law that recognizes same-sex couples, other than in a marriage? Second, does the state prohibit recognition of all forms of legal same-sex partnerships? Third, does the state prohibit recognition of the "rights and benefits arising out of" legal same-sex partnerships? Fourth, does the state have laws that specifically prohibit or protect some of the parental rights that New Jersey has extended to same-sex couples?

Recognition of Other States Laws

Unlike many countries, the United States does not have a national law dealing with matters such as marriage, divorce, and family matters. Instead, each state is entitled to pass and enforce its own laws in all matters not found in the Constitution.[1] So long as each state's laws do not violate any federal Constitutional rights, the federal government is without authority to interfere.

One problem with allowing each state to pass its own laws regarding marriage and family life was getting each state to give equal recognition to the laws, judgments, and records of the other states. In order to avoid this problem, the drafters of the United States Constitution added a clause that requires each state to give "full faith and credit" to the public acts, records and judicial proceedings of every

---

1.   "The powers not delegated to the United States by the Constitution, nor prohibited by it to the States, are reserved to the States respectively, or to the people." U.S. Const. amend. X.

other state.[2] This "full faith and credit" clause makes it possible for a couple to marry in one state knowing that all other states will recognize the marriage.

Periodically, the Supreme Court has had to interpret the meaning of this clause in order to resolve conflicts between the states. In several cases, these conflicts have arisen in regard to changes in laws related to marriage. For example, when Nevada relaxed its divorce laws, residents of other states began flocking to that state to evade their own state's restrictions on divorce. Eventually, the Supreme Court decided that other states must recognize another state's divorce decree so long as it was legitimately obtained.

In other cases, the Supreme Court has found that marriages entered into in another state must be recognized in all states, except where they violate a particular state's public policy. For example, if one state forbids marriages between first cousins, and another state forbids these marriages, the second state may invoke the public policy exception and refuse recognition of the marriage.

When the Hawaiian Supreme Court ruled in favor of same-sex marriage, many other states feared that they might have to recognize such marriages. As a result, the United States Congress passed the Defense of Marriage Act, which prohibits recognition of same-sex couples in any federal law, regulation or entitlement, and which also created an exception to the Full Faith and Credit clause, allowing states to refuse recognition of same-sex marriages in other states. Although many believe the federal Defense of Marriage Act is probably unconstitutional, several federal courts have upheld the law.

Many states have also passed their own defense of marriage acts or amendments, particularly following the recognition of same-sex marriage in Massachusetts. Often these laws prohibit any legal recognition of same-sex couples or any rights and benefits arising out of such relationships. In some cases, these laws appear to prohibit any contracts or agreements between same-sex partners that provide the benefits of marriage. Not content with these restrictions, some states have begun restricting other rights for same-sex couples, particularly in the area of adoption and foster care.

It will be many years before the restrictions on recognition of same-sex couples are fully resolved among the states. However, you and your partner must remain aware of these laws and if you are moving to or even just visiting another state, you will need to take certain steps to ensure that your partnership is protected. The steps you should take to protect your rights will depend on the following:

- Whether your destination state has a civil union or domestic partnership act and, if so, whether it recognizes your New Jersey domestic partnership;

- Whether that state has passed a so-called "Defense of Marriage" act and, if so, whether the act prohibits domestic partnerships as well as same-sex marriage; and

- Whether you are relocating to that state, buying property in that state, or simply visiting.

In some cases, you and your partner will be able protect yourselves and your family with legal documents and agreements. In other cases, these limited forms of protection may be of questionable value and you should seriously consider avoiding visits to these states.

---

2.   "Full Faith and Credit shall be given in each State to the public Acts, Records, and judicial Proceedings of every other State. And the Congress may by general Laws prescribe the Manner in which such Acts, Records, and Proceedings shall be proved, and the Effect thereof." U.S. Const. art. IV, § 1.

States With Civil Union, Domestic Partnership or Reciprocal Beneficiary Laws

There are now five states in addition to New Jersey that extend some form of legal recognition to same-sex couples, other than marriage. These are Vermont, California, Hawaii, Connecticut and Maine. The laws they have enacted vary in the kinds of protection they provide and whether and to what extent they recognize New Jersey's Domestic Partnership Act.

Hawaii

The State of Hawaii enacted its Reciprocal Beneficiaries Law in 1991. The law does not recognize relationships entered elsewhere. So far, there is no case law to indicate whether Hawaii would even recognize a Vermont reciprocal beneficiary, the only other state with reciprocal beneficiary laws.

Vermont

The Vermont Civil Union law was enacted in 2001 and conveys nearly all of the rights and responsibilities afforded to married couples in Vermont. At the time the law was signed, no other U.S. state had enacted any form of legal protection for same-sex couples.

Since it was the first such law, the Vermont Civil Union Act did not reference legal relationships entered elsewhere. Thus, it isn't clear whether you and your partner can expect to receive any legal recognition for your registered domestic partnership without registering as a civil union.

California

The California Domestic Partnership Act was initially passed in 2001 and provided limited protection similar to that provided in New Jersey. In 2003, the California Legislature passed, and Governor Gray Davis signed, an updated DPA, which provides nearly all of the rights and responsibilities provided by the State to married persons.

The new Act, which took effect on January 1, 2005, recognizes civil unions and domestic partnerships that are entered into in another jurisdiction under laws that are "substantially equivalent" to the California Domestic Partnership Act.

If you registered in New Jersey as domestic partners, you and your partner can expect full recognition of your partnership in California, including all the additional rights and responsibilities given by the California law. If you relocate to California, you will not need to register there.

Maine

The Maine Domestic Partnership Act was enacted in 2004. It provides limited protection but does go further than the New Jersey DPA in that it places domestic partners on the same level as husbands and wives in regard to intestacy.

The Maine DPA does not explicitly extend recognition to civil unions or domestic partnerships entered into elsewhere. If you relocate to Maine, or if you own property in Maine, you may need to register locally in order to gain the protections in the act.

Connecticut

The Connecticut Civil Unions Act was enacted in 2005 and became effective as of October 1, 2005. Like the Vermont act on which it was modeled, the Connecticut Civil Unions Act conveys nearly all of the rights and responsibilities afforded to married couples in that state. As part of the act, Connecticut limited recognition of marriage to "one man and one woman."

The Connecticut act does not explicitly recognize civil unions or domestic partnerships entered in other states, although it does provide recognition of civil unions entered into in other countries. However, in September 2004, the Connecticut Attorney General issued an opinion that "out-of-state same-sex civil unions and certain domestic partnerships" would be recognized in the state. Although he did not specifically recognize New Jersey domestic partnerships, his statement that "out-of-state, legally authorized same-sex domestic partnerships may be recognized as civil unions in Connecticut, depending on how specific provisions of other states' laws compare." Presumably, this means that Connecticut, which limits civil unions to same-sex couples, will only recognize same-sex domestic partners who registered in New Jersey.

States With Defense Of Marriage Acts or Amendments

At least 36 states have some form of anti-gay marriage laws, and three have passed amendments to their state constitutions prohibiting same-sex marriages.

In most cases, these Defense of Marriage Acts add same-sex marriage to the list of marriages that are void and refuse to recognize such marriages if entered into in another state. In most of these states, you can expect no recognition of your legal status as registered domestic partners. However, most will uphold contractual relationships.

A new trend in anti-gay family legislation is seen in legislation passed in Utah, Virginia and Ohio, which have passed particularly draconian versions of Defense of Marriage Acts. These laws prohibit not only the recognition of same-sex marriage, they prohibit the recognition of civil unions or domestic partnerships entered elsewhere. In some cases, they even prohibit contracts between same-sex partners that would provide any of the rights of marriage.

If you relocate to any of these states you should consult with a knowledgeable local attorney to ensure that you're rights and responsibilities are protected, at least to the extent allowed by local law.

States With No Protection Or Prohibition

In states with no Defense of Marriage Act or other prohibition against same-sex partnerships, your New Jersey registration will not be recognized, unless these states later pass a similar law. On the other hand, these states are likely to uphold contractual relationships, and your New Jersey registration even though unrecognized, may help strengthen your case should you need to assert your contract rights.

Visiting Or Moving To Massachusetts

If you plan on visiting or moving to Massachusetts, you should be aware that Massachusetts, like most other U.S. states, does not recognize domestic partnerships, civil unions, or other marriage alternatives.

Although same-sex marriage is now legal in Massachusetts, nothing in the state's marriage laws recognize domestic partnership as either a barrier to or substitute for marriage. The only way to have your relationship recognized in Massachusetts is to be legally married in some other jurisdiction.

If you are moving to Massachusetts, you should be aware that you will need to be married legally in that state in order to gain recognition of your relationship. However, given that you will receive all of that state's benefits and obligations in return, you would be foolish to rely on your New Jersey registration.

If you choose to marry in Massachusetts after you have registered as a New Jersey domestic partnership, you will be asked on the Notice of Intention whether you have a state-created domestic partnership and, if so, if it has been terminated. This information is being collected for statistical purposes only and is not an impediment to a Massachusetts marriage. If you are in a registered domestic partnership with someone other than the person you intend to marry in Massachusetts, you should formally terminate the domestic partnership before you marry.

Federal Recognition

Unlike marriage, the U.S. government does not recognize the rights conferred by state civil unions or domestic partnerships. Furthermore, the Defense of Marriage Act makes many of the federal rights conferred on opposite-sex married couples inapplicable to these other forms of legal relationships. No one expects this to change in regard to domestic partnerships or civil unions.

As it is currently written, the proposed amendment to the U.S. Constitution that would prohibit same-sex marriage would similarly prohibit states from passing laws similar to New Jersey's Domestic Partnership Act or Vermont's Civil Union laws.

Immigration

The Domestic Partnership Act only requires you or your partner to have a residence in New Jersey. It does not require you or your partner to be a citizen or even a resident alien. However, because immigration is a matter of federal law, domestic partners do not have a right to sponsor their partner. Illegal immigrants in domestic partnerships run the risk of being deported.

Outside the United States

You and your partner may be planning a trip outside the United States. When you go, you need to recognize that your partnership will be protected in only a few countries.

In all other cases, you should consider bringing some documents, such as medical powers of attorney, that may support your right to make emergency decisions on behalf of your incapacitated partner. Each of you should carry these documents with your passport so that they can be readily produced should anything happen. However, these documents should not refer to each other as "partner," "spouse," or any term that might imply a same-sex relationship if you are traveling in countries with strong prohibitions or prejudices against homosexuals.

ALTERNATIVES TO NEW JERSEY DOMESTIC PARTNERSHIP

You are not required to register a domestic partnership in New Jersey any more than an opposite-sex couple is required to marry. Although registering a domestic partnership provides you with certain rights and benefits, it also carries with it some obligations that you or your partner may not wish to impose on your relationship. In particular, the Domestic Partnership Act places the weight of the law behind any agreements that you may have entered into with your partner, since the Act specifically allows you to contractually add to your rights and responsibilities.

One reason to consider an alternative is if it provides greater rights than you might otherwise obtain from a registered domestic partnership. Another reason is that the alternative provides greater freedom than a more formal legal status.

On the other hand, few of the alternatives provide you with any tax benefits under New Jersey law. If you and your partner own valuable assets, such as your home or other real or tangible property, you should be aware that you may lose the inheritance tax advantage conferred by the DPA if you choose one of its alternatives.

Available Alternatives

There are three alternatives to registered domestic partnership you and your partner should consider. First, you may attempt to marry in a jurisdiction that permits same-sex marriage, such as Canada or Massachusetts. Second, you may register in another jurisdiction that provides civil unions or domestic partnership. Finally, you could simply continue living together, as same-sex couples have done for many years.

Civil Marriage

Domestic partnership and the alternatives discussed below have significant limitations as compared to civil marriage. First, they attach a state-sanctioned second-class status to the same-sex couple. Second, they create a patchwork of laws that may or may not be recognized by other states the couple travel through or relocate in. Third, they have no effect on the many federal benefits of marriage, such as immigration, entitlement to benefits, or federal taxation. Finally, such laws are unlikely to be the useful basis of a challenge to the federal Defense of Marriage Act, which limits marriage for federal purposes to opposite-sex couples.

Furthermore, many couples see the rites of marriage as a more serious level of commitment to the relationship. Deeply committed couples want, and in many cases deserve, the additional respect that society attaches to a married couple. If you are among those couples that value marriage over all other forms of relationship, you may wish to consider entering civil marriage in Massachusetts, Canada, or elsewhere. However, in doing so, you should also consider problems associated with this alternative.

First, unlike opposite-sex marriage, a same-sex couple married in Canada or Massachusetts does not obtain automatic recognition of the marriage in New Jersey. In fact, the couple will most likely face a lengthy and expensive court battle for recognition with an uncertain outcome.

Second, there is a significant chance that the marriage may be rendered void by state and/or federal law. Massachusetts is attempting to amend its constitution to declare same-sex marriage invalid. There has been discussion, but no clear consensus on what the status of marriages entered between now and the year November 2006, the earliest date on which the amendment could go into effect. Furthermore, the Massachusetts governor has begun taking steps to invalidate marriages entered into by non-resident same-sex couples. The marriage could also be invalidated if the Federal Constitution was amended to invalidate same-sex marriage.

Third, the DPA recognizes civil unions and domestic partnerships entered elsewhere but there is no equivalent recognition to out-of-state or foreign marriages. Thus, a Vermont civil union would convey domestic partnership status on a couple, but a Massachusetts or Canadian marriage would not.

Finally, civil marriage may legally affect your ability to register as a domestic partner in New Jersey. As discussed above, the Act excludes a couple from registering as a domestic partner if either person (or both) is "in a marriage recognized by New Jersey law." On the other hand, if New Jersey law recognizes your marriage, you already have significantly more protection than you would receive from domestic partnership. Nevertheless, until New Jersey courts determine whether a marriage entered into in Massachusetts, Canada, or elsewhere is recognized in New Jersey, you should not rely on rights you may have acquired in those places.[3]

Civil unions or out-of-state domestic partnership

A second alternative to a New Jersey domestic partnership is to register in a civil union or another state's domestic partnership. Vermont's Civil Union law, which went into effect in 2000, and Connecticut's Civil Union Act, which became effective on October 1, 2005, provide all of the same benefits, protections and responsibilities as are granted to married couples under those states' laws. California's amended Domestic Partnership Act, which came into effect on January 1, 2005, similarly provides all of the rights and duties of married couples under California law. Notably, both the Vermont law and the California law allow non-residents to register.

The New Jersey Domestic Partnership Act specifically recognizes civil unions, domestic partnerships, and reciprocal beneficiaries entered into outside of New Jersey. However, the DPA does not grant any more rights to couples registered elsewhere than it does to couples that register in New Jersey. Registering in another state may be advantageous, however, if you own property in that state or plan to move or retire there.

Living Together

Many couples have lived happily together for years without any legal sanctioning of their relationship. Same-sex couples have been free to work out alternative relationships because of the inability to marry or enter some other form of legally recognized partnership. Unregistered partners are more easily able to terminate their relationship, since no formal court proceeding is required. Some couples believe that this freedom to leave has brought a greater level of commitment to the relationship. Others believe they should not enter relationships that mimic heterosexual norms.

If you do choose this alternative, it is particularly important that you and your partner develop a good set of agreements to establish each other's rights in the relationship. Many of these documents, such as a will, are documents that you will need to develop regardless of the legal form of your relationship. Others, such as visitation agreements, are more important in a non-formalized relationship, since there are no built-in protections for those who simply live together.

---

3.   In fact, two courts in New Jersey have already ruled that marriages entered into in Canada are not recognized in New Jersey.

CHAPTER 3
RIGHTS AND OBLIGATIONS

This chapter provides a brief overview of the rights and obligations same-sex couples now have in New Jersey. Most of these rights have been acquired as a result of the Domestic Partnership Act and most require you and your partner to register as domestic partners. This chapter also discusses the rights and obligations that are explicitly denied to domestic partners and those that are currently unrecognized. These rights and obligations are discussed in greater detail in later chapters of this guide.

RIGHTS OF REGISTERED DOMESTIC PARTNERS

The most important difference between the Domestic Partnership Act[1] as introduced, and the Act as signed by the governor is that the Legislative intent incorporated into section 2 of the law was substantially strengthened.[2] Thus, the Legislature clearly signaled its intent that same-sex couples are entitled to "certain rights and benefits that are accorded to married couples under the laws of New Jersey."

Although the Act modified only a few of the laws of New Jersey providing marital rights and benefits, it seems clear that the outer limits of the rights and benefits accorded to domestic partners have yet to be fully defined. Nonetheless, you and your partner should only count on those rights that are currently recognized under the Domestic Partnership Act.

Benefit Exclusions

Unless you work for the State of New Jersey it is not unlawful discrimination under the Law Against Discrimination if your employer does not allow you to enroll your domestic partner in your health benefits plan, even if the plan provider offers a domestic partnership benefits plan. Even if they do, your employer may also make you pay some or all of the premiums for your partner, even if they don't require this from married employees.

Opposite-gender domestic partners are specifically excluded from dependent domestic partner coverage under the State health insurance and pension benefits plan. The reason given for this last exclusion is that such couples have a legally recognized right to marry in New Jersey.

Recognized Rights

Once you and your partner register, you are entitled to at least the following rights and benefits enumerated in section 2

---

1.   At the time, it was called the "Family Equality Act".
2.   "All persons in domestic partnerships should be entitled to certain rights and benefits that are accorded to married couples under the laws of New Jersey. ... The need for all persons who are in domestic partnerships, regardless of their sex, to have access to these rights and benefits is paramount in view of their essential relationship to any reasonable concept of basic human dignity." Domestic Partnership Act, §2(d).

of the Domestic Partnership Act:

- **Protection from discrimination**. The DPA adds statutory protection for domestic partners to the New Jersey Law Against Discrimination, particularly in the area of housing, employment, and credit discrimination. See *Chapter 7: Discrimination*.

- **Health care and end of life issues**. The Act grants domestic partners hospital visitation and medical and end-of-life decision-making rights, as well as the right to make legal decisions on behalf of an incapacitated partner. See *Chapter 12: Health, Disability and End of Life Issues*.

- **Transfer inheritance tax exemptions**. Transfer of all property, including a decedent's share of jointly owned property, to the surviving domestic partner is now exempt from this tax. Certain pensions, annuities, retirement allowances or return of contributions payable to a domestic partner are also exempt. Previously, such transfers were subject to a 15% tax. See *Chapter 9: Money, Taxes and Insurance*.

- **Income tax exemptions**. A domestic partner may now claim a $1,000 New Jersey income tax exemption for a partner who does not file separately. See *Chapter 9: Money, Taxes and Insurance*.

- **Domestic partner benefits**. For State employees and retirees, domestic partners and married spouses and their dependent children are given equal access to State-provided health insurance and pension benefits. For other public employers, as well as private employers, this benefit is optional. See *Chapter 8: Domestic Partner Benefits*.

Although these enumerated rights and benefits were specifically implemented by the Act, it appears that the Act may provide substantially more rights than originally thought. Several months after the DPA went into effect, for example, two additional rights were recognized as a result of court challenges. These are:

- **Property tax exemption**. A court found that the property tax exemption provided to 100% disabled veterans must be provided to domestic partners who jointly own their home, at least while a disabled partner is alive. See *Chapter 9: Money, Taxes and Insurance*.

- **Loss of consortium**. A domestic partner may sue for loss of consortium, that is, the loss of a partner's "services, comfort, society and conjugal relations" resulting from the partner's injury.

Until the full extent of your rights are determined by the courts or by the passage of legislation or regulations, you and your partner should not assume you will have more than this set of rights.

Spousal Torts and Privileges

There are several common-law torts that allow one spouse to sue for emotional and financial losses that occur as a result of the accidental death or injury of the other spouse. Another form of spousal tort involves a civil claim made by one spouse against the other. Often these result from domestic violence or some other intentional or negligent act by the other spouse.

Loss of Consortium

Loss of consortium is a legal right to compensation for the temporary or permanent loss of a spouse's companionship. Lost income is a legal right to compensation for the loss of a deceased spouse's earnings. Emotional distress as a result of witnessing a loved one's death or injury, so called bystander liability, is another form of tort. All of these are based upon a close familial relationship ordinarily associated with marriage.

In the past, courts throughout the United States, including New Jersey, have refused to recognize these rights for unmarried couples in general, and same-sex couples in particular. In recent years, courts in some states have begun recognizing this and other rights for same-sex couples on the basis that the fact that the couple is legally unable to marry does not make them any less a couple.

After the tragic events of 9/11, when many gays and lesbians lost their spouse, courts in New York began extending the right to sue for lost income to same-sex couples who could demonstrate their long-term commitment to each other.

More recently, the New Mexico Supreme Court recognized that loss of consortium claims could be asserted by unmarried cohabitants if they can show they had an "intimate familial relationship." The New Mexico court based their decision, in part, on a New Jersey Supreme Court case that allowed bystander liability in the case of an unmarried, but engaged couple.

The Vermont Civil Union statute and the recent California Domestic Partnership Act explicitly extend this common-law tort to registered same-sex couples. Although the New Jersey Domestic Partnership Agreement does not define such a set of rights, a recent court decision may indicate a change in the law.

Recognizing that domestic partners have rights equivalent to married couples, an Essex County judge recently allowed a suit to be amended by one of the plaintiffs to include a claim for loss of consortium by the plaintiff's domestic partner. The court limited the period for which the partner could sue to that following the couple's registration. Thus it appears that a variety of common-law spousal causes of action may now be available to registered domestic partners.

Marital Privileges

Among the many benefits conferred upon married couples, but not on unmarried ones, are those referred to as "marital privileges." The most important of these is that one spouse may not be compelled to testify against the other.

In a recent New Jersey case involving a lesbian couple, one partner was compelled to testify against the other on the basis that this privilege was extended only to married couples. The couple tried to claim that the enactment of the Domestic Partnership Act, and the nature and duration of their relationship should allow the privilege to be extended to them. However, the judge rejected this in an unpublished decision.

Although you and your partner should not assume that this privilege will be extended to you after you have registered, it is very possible that the decision in this case would have come out in favor of extending the privilege had the couple been registered after the effective date of the DPA.

Excluded Rights

Under current interpretations of the Domestic Partnership Act, at least two of the "bundle of rights" provided to married couples in New Jersey are considered to be excluded from the rights granted to domestic partners. These are:

- **Property rights**. Property acquired by one partner during the domestic partnership is treated as individually owned by that partner unless specifically intended otherwise. For more information, see *Chapter 10: Property Rights*.

- **Parental rights and responsibilities**. The parent-child relationship is currently not affected by registration status. However, the courts in New Jersey have already recognized certain parental rights and responsibilities of same-sex couples. See *Chapter 11: Parenting*, for more information.

Although these particular rights are currently unavailable to you, the Act allows you and your partner to add rights and responsibilities in an agreement.

Unrecognized Rights

The currently recognized set of rights and benefits provided to you and your partner constitute about 1% of the approximately 850 "afforded to married couples" under New Jersey law. There are many other legal rights and benefits of marriage that have yet to be legally recognized. Some of the more important rights are:

- **Rights upon partner's death**. Unlike marriage, registration as domestic partners does not guarantee that you and your partner will be treated as next of kin when one of you dies. You are currently not entitled to any of the benefits given to a married spouse, such as rights to intestate or elective share of your partner's estate. Furthermore, there are other federal and state tax exemptions that only apply to married couples. See *Chapter 13: Estate Planning*.

- **Taxes**. You and your partner may not file joint state or federal income tax returns. You are also not exempted from taxable transfers to each other, such as the realty transfer fee paid when property is sold. See *Chapter 9, Money, Taxes and Insurance*.

- **Guardianship and incompetency**. You and your partner currently are not recognized as having a superior right over other family members when it comes to being named as guardian or to making many decisions on behalf of an incompetent partner. See *Chapter 12: Health, Disability and End of Life Issues*.

- **Family medical and bereavement leave**. Married couples are entitled to take paid and unpaid leave under federal and state law. Registered domestic partners have no such right under federal law and no recognized right under state law. See *Chapter 11: Parenting*.

Some of these rights and benefits can be approximated through the use of written agreements. Others await court recognition or changes in the law.

Rights of Unregistered Couples

Even if you are in an unregistered domestic partnership, whether by choice, through ineligibility, or because you haven't had time to do so, you and your partner are given some rights under the Domestic Partnership Act

In a medical emergency, unregistered domestic partners will be treated as registered, allowing one of you to accompany the other while being transported to the hospital. This emergency recognition also allows you to visit your partner in the hospital, just as any other family member is allowed.

In order to claim this emergency status, both of you, or one of you if the other is legally or medically incapacitated, must tell the emergency care provider that you are unregistered domestic partners. Although the Act specifically requires you to tell the provider that the two of you have met the requirements for establishing a domestic partnership other than registration, you are not required to show any proof of eligibility. This emergency recognition does not extend to any of the other rights or benefits you would otherwise have if you and your partner had registered.

In addition, the Act allows any individual or entity in the State, including your employer, a health care provider such as a hospital or your doctor, property owners such as landlords, and others to treat you and your partner as members of a domestic partnership, even if you haven't registered. The extent of this voluntary recognition is entirely up to the individual or entity, and the recognition can be withdrawn at any time.

There are two important things to know about this part of the Act. First, your private employer can extend domestic partnership benefits to unregistered couples and even opposite-sex unmarried couples, but is not required to do so. Second, if either you or your partner is employed by the State of New Jersey, or is otherwise covered by a State health or pension plan, you must be registered in order to obtain domestic partnership benefits. This is also the case if you are employed by a public employer, such as a municipality or school board, and your employer has passed a resolution defining the term "spouse" to include domestic partners.

Limits of Recognition

You and your partner must remain aware that the rights and benefits provided to you by the New Jersey Domestic Partnership Act are only available to you in New Jersey at this time. Most U.S. states do not have a domestic partnership or civil union law and, of those that do, only the new California law specifically recognizes your New Jersey partnership. Although it is likely that all of the states that do provide legal recognition for same-sex partners will recognize your registered domestic partnership, until it is clear that they do, you cannot afford to take chances.

You should also be aware that your domestic partnership is not recognized under federal law as a result of the federal Defense of Marriage Act. Until this law is abolished or found to be unconstitutional, rights under federal laws, such as bankruptcy protection, federal tax laws, and immigration are unavailable to you.

Finally, some states are passing legislation that prohibits the recognition of same-sex marriages, domestic partnerships, and civil unions, as well as the rights, benefits and obligations that arise from these legal relationships. Thus, there are certain documents you should prepare when you travel in order to protect your New Jersey rights to the fullest extent possible in these states.

At a minimum, when you travel outside of the state of New Jersey, you should always have with you the following:

- **Power of Attorney**. This document is used to name the person or persons who can make financial decisions on your behalf if you become legally incapacitated.

- **Hospital Visitation Authorization**. This document authorizes your partner to visit you in a health care facility.

- **Medical Proxy and Living Will**. A medical proxy authorizes you and your partner to make medical decisions on behalf of each other if you are legally incapacitated. In some states, this is called a "medical power of attorney." A living will, sometimes called an advance directive for health care, is your expression of the treatment you want if you are in a terminal condition or persistent vegetative state.

- **Disposition of Remains**. Unfair as it seems, in most states you have no right to claim your partner's remains, should he or she die.

Other documents you might want to take with you are rights of entry and possession (for example, your car), rights to travel with your partner's children, if any, and arrangements for any pets you may have.

OBLIGATIONS OF DOMESTIC PARTNERS

There are surprisingly few obligations specifically imposed by the Act. First, you and your partner are obligated to be responsible for each other's basic living expenses. Second, you and your partner must share a common residence. Third, you and your partner are obligated by any additional responsibilities you agree to in a contract between you.

The Domestic Partnership Act explicitly limits the obligations of domestic partners to those specified in the Act itself. As a result, it is unlikely that the New Jersey courts will impose additional obligations.

Basic Living Expenses

The requirement that domestic partners be "jointly responsible" means that you and your partner agree to provide for each other's "basic living expenses" should one of you become unable to do so. The DPA provides a somewhat narrow definition of "basic living expenses," defining it to mean the cost of basic food and shelter," including health care and other expenses that are paid "as a benefit because a person is another person's domestic partner."

This last provision could involve some significant costs, depending upon how it is interpreted. If may mean that the "other costs" are limited to paying for medical insurance and other benefits of employment. However, this provision could also be interpreted to mean that the benefit is provided by one partner to the other in recognition of their relationship, leading to demands for all sorts of benefits, such as fancy clothes, automobiles, educational expenses, and the like.

Common Residence

Although the "common residence" is primarily a pre-requirement for registration of a domestic partnership, there are several sections of the Act that appear to make this a continuing obligation.

First, the Act states in several places that partners are expected to "live together" and share a "common residence" and a "common mailing address." Furthermore, among the listed reasons for termination of a domestic partnership is that of "separation," where the partners have lived separately for at least 18 months. On the other hand, the Act recognizes that domestic partners might have separately owned residences and may not live together continuously.

The question of whether you and your partner meet this obligation is very fact-based. If you and your partner have multiple residences, you should review the discussion *Common Residence* in *Chapter 5: Eligibility* with regard to your particular living situation.

Contractual Obligations

You and your partner may agree to take on additional obligations or alter existing ones by contract, either written or oral, except that your agreement may not alter the requirements for creating a domestic partnership. This means, for example, that you cannot contractually agree that you will not be "jointly responsible for each other's common welfare" but you can define for yourselves what joint responsibility means. For more information, see *Modifying Rights and Obligations*, below.

Implied Obligations

Although the Domestic Partnership Act limits each partner's obligations to the other to those obligations specified in the Act, it would be misleading to think that the obligations are few. Some obligations are implied by other provisions of the Act.

For example, one reason stated for termination, "voluntary sexual intercourse" with someone other than your domestic partner implies that you are obliged to maintain an exclusive, monogamous relationship. Implied obligations may also be found on the flip side of rights and benefits.

Specific Exemptions

There are very few specific exemptions provided to domestic partners that are not similarly provided to married couples. The most important of these is joint liability for each other's debts.

Joint Liability for Debts

Under the Domestic Partnership Act, neither you nor your partner has any financial responsibility for payment of each other's separately incurred debts, whether accumulated prior to registration or after. Under the Act, you are only liable for jointly-contracted debts and debts that are contracted in your own name.

If you and your partner default on a joint debt, the creditor can seek repayment from either of you or both of you. If, on the other hand, your partner defaults on a separately incurred debt, the creditor can only seek repayment from your partner. However, the creditor can attach any property your partner holds title to, including your partner's share of joint property. See *Chapter 9: Money, Taxes and Insurance* for more information.

Termination of Obligations

If you legally terminate your registered domestic partnership, your obligations to each other cease on the date the judge grants your termination, unless you agree otherwise as part of a settlement agreement. However, if you fail to provide notice of the termination to any third parties who have previously been given a copy of your Certificate of Domestic Partnership, you may be sued for any expenses or other damages they incur. See *Post-termination Issues* in *Chapter 15: Termination Proceedings* for more information.

MODIFYING RIGHTS AND OBLIGATIONS

Whether or not you and your partner decide to register as domestic partners, you still need to use contractual and other legal means in order to obtain at least some level of the protection afforded to married couples by the laws of New Jersey.

However, even if you register as domestic partners, you and your partner cannot rely solely on currently recognized rights and responsibilities provided by the DPA. Instead, you should take the time to review your current situation with an attorney who has some understanding of the often-creative legal planning that must be used to recreate many of the legal rights and obligations granted to opposite-sex married couples.

Marital and Non-marital Agreements

Prior to the enactment of the Domestic Partnership Act, New Jersey law recognized only two categories of agreements between couples entering into a relationship: prenuptial agreements and non-marital cohabitation agreements.

Prenuptial Agreements

Prenuptial agreements, sometimes called antenuptial or premarital agreements, are agreements between prospective spouses made in contemplation of the marriage and intended to come into effect only when the couple marries. These agreements are statutorily recognized and enforceable in New Jersey under the "Uniform Premarital Agreement Act."

Although they cannot affect the right of child support, a prenuptial can legally address any or all of the following:

1. The rights and obligations of each party in any property either or both of them acquire;

2. The right to buy, sell, transfer, exchange, etc., or otherwise manage and control property;

3. The disposition of property upon separation, dissolution, death, or other events or non-events;

4. The modification or elimination of spousal support;

5. The making of a will, trust, or other arrangement to carry out the provisions of the agreement;

6. The ownership rights in and disposition of death benefits from life insurance;

7. The choice of law governing the construction of the agreement; and

8. Any other matter, including their personal rights or obligations, not in violation of public policy.

The formal requirements for a prenuptial are that they must be in writing, signed by both parties, and must have a statement of both parties assets attached to the agreement. Although prenuptial agreements can only be entered into prior to marriage, they can be amended or revoked during the marriage, but only in a written agreement signed by both spouses.

Courts can (and usually do) set aside prenuptial agreements if they find that one spouse executed the agreement involuntarily, or if the agreement is unconscionable at the time of enforcement, or if the spouse against whom the agreement is being enforced was not, before the agreement was signed, (1) given full and fair disclosure of the other spouse's earnings, property, and financial obligations, (2) did not voluntarily and expressly waive their right to disclosure, (3) did not and could not have knowledge of the other spouse's property or financial obligations, or (4) did not consult with independent counsel and did not voluntarily and expressly waive that opportunity to consult.

Cohabitation Agreements

Cohabitating unmarried partners, other than registered domestic partners, are not recognized under statutory law but written cohabitation agreements between unmarried adult cohabitants are enforceable, so long as they are not based on the provision of sexual services.

In the absence of written agreements, courts also can find that an "implied cohabitation agreement" exists if the partners' reasonable expectations and understanding about the financial and other arrangements are supported by evidence such as the amount of time they lived together, the services and financial contributed they provided to each other and their shared home, the pooling of income and other resources, the acquisition and titling of their home and other property, etc.

A key difference between prenuptial agreements and cohabitation agreements is whether there is consideration furnished. Prenuptial agreements are enforceable without consideration. Cohabitation agreements are not enforceable unless there is consideration.

Consideration

Consideration is a legal term meaning the "price bargained for and paid for a promise, goods, or real estate." In general, a contract is invalid if there is no consideration provided.

Consideration most often is financial in nature, but it can be something else, such as a promise to do something, or a promise to refrain from doing something you are entitled to do. No matter what the consideration is, it must be something that has value to the other party.

Domestic Partnership Agreements

A domestic partnership agreement, sometimes called a "living together agreement," is an agreement between you and your partner that sets out your rights and obligations toward each other. For unregistered partners, a domestic partnership is no different than a cohabitation agreement. Once you register, however, the enforceability of your agreement is strengthened because it gains the support of statutory law.

The contents of your agreement are entirely up to you and your partner. Your agreement may be as simple as declaring that you and your partner agree to share all expenses on an equal basis, own all property jointly, and undergo a certain amount of counseling for disputes that you cannot resolve informally. On the other hand, it may be quite complex, involving questions of child bearing and rearing, rights of economic or other contribution to the partnership, ownership of independently acquired property, and other important issues. See *Chapter 16: Legal Matters* for more on contracts and agreements.

Recitation of Consideration

Your agreement needs to recite the consideration for entering into your domestic partnership agreement to ensure that it is valid. If you have not registered and are executing this agreement in anticipation of registration as domestic partners, the consideration furnished is the act of registration. If you are executing this agreement after having registered as domestic partners, the consideration furnished is the modification of the statutory rights and obligations provided to you in the Domestic Partnership Act. For domestic partners who do not intend to register, the consideration for the agreement consists of the set of promises you recite in the agreement.

When to negotiate and execute

Ideally, you and your partner should negotiate and execute your agreement before you register as domestic partners. If you and your partner have been living together for some time and/or have already registered as domestic partners, your agreement will be valid but you should try to observe as many of the formalities of negotiation and execution as possible.

The formalities associated with executing your agreement are important particularly if you are executing this agreement before you have registered your partnership. Enforcement of your domestic partnership will take place in the Family Part of the Superior Court - Chancery Division and be decided by a judge who is most accustomed to enforcing prenuptial agreements. To avoid having the agreement set aside by the court, you should be prepared to demonstrate that both of you voluntarily executed the agreement, that before your partner signed the agreement:

1. You provided your partner with full and fair disclosure of your earnings, property and financial obligations; or

2. Your partner voluntarily and expressly waived, in writing, his or her right to disclosure of your property or financial obligations, beyond that which you provided; or

3. Your partner had, or reasonably could have had adequate knowledge of your property and financial obligations; or

4. Your partner consulted with his or her own lawyer or voluntarily and expressly waived, in writing, the opportunity to consult with independent counsel.

You and your partner should sign and date two copies of your domestic partnership agreement - one for each of you. This document must be notarized or signed by an attorney in New Jersey, and each of you should keep a copy in your own files.

Modifying or revoking your agreement

In order to be consistent with the laws governing prenuptial agreements, if you and your partner want to modify or revoke your agreement after you have registered, your modifications or revocation should be made in writing and signed by both of you. Each partner should have the revocation or modifications reviewed by their own attorney prior to signing.

Limiting future rights and responsibilities

When the State of California passed its Domestic Partnership Act in 2003, it expanded the rights and responsibilities of domestic partners to encompass nearly all those provided to married couples. These expanded rights were retroactively applied to couples that had registered under the prior law. This created a dilemma for some couples that had registered as domestic partners under the prior act but didn't want to take on these expanded rights and obligations. Thus, the State sent notices to all registered domestic partners, giving them an opportunity to "opt-out" of the expanded act by terminating their partnership.

A similar problem will arise in New Jersey as the courts and/or the Legislature expand rights and obligations of registered domestic partners. The easiest way for you and your partner to limit expansion of your obligations is to incorporate these limits in a valid contract, such as a "living together" or "domestic partnership" agreement. Then, if you agree to new obligations, you can modify your agreement.

Open relationships and sexual infidelity

The Domestic Partnership Act defines "voluntary sexual intercourse between a person who is in a domestic partnership and an individual other than the person's domestic partner" as a legal cause for immediate termination of the partnership. Same-sex couples that view traditional concepts of monogamy as old-fashioned and restrictive may want to establish a way of legally circumventing this prohibition, perhaps by including language allowing such liaisons in their domestic partnership agreement.

Since the DPA allows registered partners to contractually "modify the rights and obligations to each other," it would seem that you and your partner could disclaim this as a reason for termination in some form of written agreement. However, it is unlikely that such a provision would be upheld in court.

Although, as a general rule, you are entitled to contractually disclaim a statutory right, New Jersey courts have generally refused to enforce agreements where the waiver is against public policy. In enacting the Domestic Partnership Act, the Legislature expressly stated that it was encouraging "committed relationships" between same-sex couples. That the State expects these committed relationships to be exclusive is further evidenced by the inclusion of sexual infidelity as a cause for termination. Because the DPA appears to set a policy favoring monogamous domestic partnerships, this disclaimer would not be upheld and could be used to invalidate the entire agreement.

Another reason for not including an "open relationship" clause in a domestic partnership agreement is that it reduces the likelihood that the agreement would be upheld if you needed to enforce it in a state that did not recognize domestic partnerships.

CHAPTER 4
BEFORE YOU REGISTER

Unlike living together, registering as domestic partners places you and your partner in a legal relationship that can only be terminated by a judge in court proceedings that are very similar to a divorce. And unlike marriage in New Jersey, there is no waiting period required before you take this important step. When you and your partner register, you will show proof of eligibility, fill out a form, swear to its contents, and receive a certificate of registration. The entire process takes just minutes whereas ending a domestic partnership can take many months. You and your partner should take time to consider your current relationship, the level of your commitment to each other, the alternatives to registration, and your expectations before proceeding with registration.

There is another, important reason for careful planning. Sometime in 2006, the New Jersey Supreme Court will announce its decision regarding the right to marry. If equal marriage rights for same-sex couples becomes a reality, the planning you do now will be essential in making the transition from registered domestic partnership to marriage. Although you should not put your plans to register on hold until the marriage issue is decided in New Jersey (and the United States), you should certainly prepare for the possibility that you may be able to or even required to change your legal status from domestic partnership to civil marriage in the near future.

EVALUATE YOUR CURRENT COMMITMENT

Although it is tempting for you and the love of your life to rush out to register, you should carefully evaluate your current situation, particularly if you and your partner jointly or separately own valuable assets, such as automobiles, your home, or your furnishings. You also need to consider legal matters that are not currently recognized under the New Jersey Domestic Partnership Act, such as inheritance rights, parenting and custody issues, insurance needs, property ownership, and other matters.

A good estate-planning attorney, particularly one who is experienced working with same-sex couples, can assist you with the additional documents you should execute prior to registration, including a living-together or domestic partnership agreement, support agreements, wills, declarations of guardianship, and the like. See *Modifying Rights and Obligations* in *Chapter 3* for more information on the kinds of agreements and documents you and your partner should prepare.

If You Are A New Couple

If you have only recently become a couple, or have only recently begun living together, your personal and financial lives may not have intertwined. You and your partner need to have a clear understanding, as you enter into the relationship, what property belongs to each partner, particularly if one or both of you have substantial assets. Doing so at this time will help you avoid needless arguments and emotional distress should your partnership happen to fail.

You and your partner should get together and make a list of your individual assets. This may not be the most romantic thing you and your partner can think of doing, but it is an essential first step in developing a domestic partnership agreement. You will also need this list of assets to develop your will and other estate planning documents.

You and your partner should also make a list of each partner's responsibilities, particularly when it comes to issues such as financial support of the household, financial management, and responsibility for any children. This list is necessary to develop a living-together agreement.

Finally, you and your partner should determine how you would handle ownership of assets you acquire after you register, such as a home or other real property, big-ticket items such as appliances and automobiles, savings, and other investments. You should also decide whether these items will be financed by loans in one partner's name or in both partner's names.

If you and your partner are not currently living together, you will need to obtain one or more of the documents necessary to prove "joint responsibility" in order to register your domestic partnership. These proofs, discussed in *Chapter 6: Registering Your Domestic Partnership* will need to be prepared prior to registration with the local registrar. Of the proofs enumerated in the Domestic Partnership Act, the easiest to establish are a joint bank account, designation as an insurance beneficiary, and a will. You will also have to establish that you have a common residence, by either signing a lease or purchasing a residence.

If You Have Been Together For Some Time

If you and your partner have lived together for some period of time, your personal lives and financial lives have already become difficult to separate. You should nonetheless review the suggestions in the previous section and prepare similar lists of assets and responsibilities in order to prepare the documents you should have going into the domestic partnership.

One area that may be difficult to sort out, particularly if you and your partner have been living together over a period of many years, is the ownership of individual assets. Unless you and your partner are scrupulous record keepers, it may be difficult to establish who bought what piece of property and when. To minimize arguments, it may be simpler for you both to designate most or all of the assets you have acquired as "joint property" to be equally divided should you decide to terminate your partnership.

Another way to look at your assets, particularly if you have children or other potential legal heirs, is to determine what assets you have that you would want to leave to those heirs in your will. You may also want to isolate assets that are family heirlooms, such as silver that has been given to you or your partner by a parent, and designate these as separate.

If you or your partner currently hold separate title to your home or other real property, you should consider whether you want to change the title to joint ownership with a right of survivorship. If you currently hold joint title to any property, you should also ensure that the property is held with a right of survivorship, if desired, since the DPA does not adequately protect your inheritance rights.

If You Are Currently Married, Or In Another Legal Relationship

A person who is currently in a marriage recognized in New Jersey, or a member of another domestic partnership is prohibited from entering into a registered domestic partnership. If either you or your partner had been previously married, or in a prior domestic partnership or civil union with someone else, you should be prepared to demonstrate that you have been granted a legal divorce (if you were married) or your domestic partnership has been terminated at least 180 days prior to filing your new affidavit. If, however, your prior marriage or domestic partnership ended because of the death of your spouse or partner, you are not bound by the waiting period.

It is currently unclear how a marital support agreement would be affected by domestic partnership registration. Some divorce agreements provide spousal support only so long as the recipient remains unmarried or is not cohabiting with another person of the opposite sex. Whether a New Jersey court would rule that spousal support should end when a domestic partnership is entered into is unknown at this time, but you can expect the issue to be raised by the ex-spouse paying such support. If you or your partner is receiving spousal support and/or child support from a prior marriage, you should consult with a qualified attorney before registering your partnership.

Another notable oversight in the Domestic Partnership Act is the failure to amend the New Jersey marriage laws to define the existence of a domestic partnership as an impediment to marriage. Thus, it is currently legal for a person to be both a member of a registered domestic partnership and a recognized marriage to another person, so long as the domestic partnership predates the marriage.

DOCUMENTS YOU SHOULD PREPARE

There are a number of documents you should prepare to protect your interests and those of your partner. At a minimum, you and your partner should prepare a living together or partnership agreement prior to registration of your domestic partnership. The primary reason for preparing these agreements before registration is to ensure that, should your domestic partnership terminate for some reason, distribution of assets would take place in an agreed manner. Otherwise, a judge will do this distribution for you. See *Chapter 15: Termination Proceedings* for more information about termination proceedings.

You and your partner should also prepare your wills and related estate-planning documents, as well as execute documents such as a guardianship directive, property transfer agreements, living wills, and any documents that may alter or enhance your rights and responsibilities in the domestic partnership. If you have previously prepared such documents, you should have them reviewed by your attorney to ensure they are consistent with the change in your legal status that registration brings.

If you and your partner have not already done so, you will need to establish one or more of the proofs of "joint responsibility" you will be required to show when you register your domestic partnership. These proofs, discussed in *Chapter 6: Registering Your Domestic Partnership* will need to be prepared prior to registration with the local registrar. Of the proofs enumerated in the Domestic Partnership Act, the easiest to establish are a joint bank account, designation as an insurance beneficiary, and a will.

SUMMARY

If you and your partner are seriously considering registering in New Jersey as domestic partners, you should evaluate the following:

- Is domestic partnership better for you and your partner than alternatives such as marriage, civil union, or simply living together?

- Do you and your partner currently meet the legal requirements for a registered domestic partnership?

- Do the financial advantages outweigh any financial penalties?

- Are you and your partner willing to fulfill all your obligations under the Domestic Partnership Law?

- Will you and your partner continue to maintain a residence in New Jersey for at least the foreseeable future or, if you may have to move, will you be relocating to a state that may recognize your registration?

- If you no longer reside in New Jersey, are you or your partner enrolled in a New Jersey sanctioned retirement or pension plan?

- Do you and your partner sincerely want a legal status that will require a judge's order to terminate?

If you answer yes to all of these questions, then you should determine what additional agreements and legal documents you should put in place to protect and add to your domestic partnership rights. You and your partner should:

1. List your individual and shared assets

2. Decide if you need a domestic partnership agreement

3. Meet with estate planning attorneys to draft wills and similar documents

4. Meet with a real estate attorney if you need to change the title of your home or other property

5. Make certain you have at least one of the required proofs of financial responsibility

6. Obtain the Certificate of Domestic Partnership

Remember, unlike marriage in New Jersey, which requires a couple to obtain a marriage license in advance of the actual wedding, a registered domestic partnership is entered into at the moment a clerk accepts your affidavit. Like marriage, however, once entered into, you and your partner will find domestic partnership hard to end, should your relationship fall apart. You should consider your decision to register with at least the same level of thought as you would a marriage.

CHAPTER 5
ELIGIBILITY

In order to register as domestic partners, you and your partner must determine your eligibility. The eligibility require-ments are clearly set out in the Domestic Partnership Act in section 4, but some may be a little vague. This chapter should help you decide if you are eligible and, if you are not, help you understand how you can correct some of the more common problems.

ELIGIBILITY REQUIREMENTS

To be eligible to enter a legally recognized domestic partnership in New Jersey, you and your partner must meet the fol-lowing criteria, prior to or at the time of registration:

- You must demonstrate that you "have a common residence" and are otherwise "jointly responsible" for each other's "common welfare."

- You must agree to be jointly responsible for each other's basic support.

- Neither of you may be in a marriage "recognized by New Jersey law" nor a member of another domestic part-nership.

- You are unrelated to each other by blood or "affinity up to and including the fourth degree of consanguinity."

- You must both be members of the same sex, unless you are both at least 62 years of age.

- You must have chosen to "share each other's lives in a committed relationship of mutual caring.

- Both of you must be at least 18 years of age.

- You must jointly file an Affidavit of Domestic Partnership; and

- Neither of you may have been a partner in another domestic partnership that was terminated less than 180 days prior to filing the Affidavit, unless the prior domestic partnership ended as a result of the death of a partner.

See *Section 4 (b)* in *Appendix A: Domestic Partnership Act*, for the exact requirements for registration.

Common Residence

The requirement that you "have a common residence" generally means that you and your partner must share a place to live in New Jersey at the time of registration.

Common residence does not mean that your primary residence (called domicile) is in New Jersey; many people have more than one residence, such as a winter home in Florida or a summer home at the New Jersey shore. It is apparently enough under the Act that you and your partner live, at least part of the time, in New Jersey.

The common residence requirement also does not mean that you and your partner must jointly own or lease the residence. It also does not matter if one or both of you have additional residences that you do not share, or if one of you must reside temporarily elsewhere, on either a short-term or long-term basis, for reasons such as medical care, attending school, taking a sabbatical, employment, or incarceration, so long as there is an intent to return to your shared residence.

Non-residents of New Jersey

Non-residents of New Jersey may not register as domestic partners, with one exception. If either you or your partner is a member of a New Jersey-administered retirement system, you are not required to share a common-residence in New Jersey. This means that if either you or your partner is a State employee or retiree, for example, you could register even if you lived in Pennsylvania or New York. To register, you will need to show proof that you are a member of the appropriate retirement system. See *Appendix D: Certificate of Pension Membership*, for an example form of proof.

Note that if you are an eligible non-resident, a part-time resident of New Jersey, or if you relocate to another state, you may find that the other state of residence does not recognize your domestic partnership. If you are in this category, you should take the time to meet with an attorney in that state to ensure that your rights outside of New Jersey are protected.

Joint Responsibility

The requirement that you be "jointly responsible" means that you and your partner agree to provide for each other's "basic living expenses" should one of you become unable to do so. The DPA provides a somewhat narrow definition of "basic living expenses", defining it to mean the cost of basic food and shelter," including health care and other expenses that are paid "as a benefit because a person is another person's domestic partner."

This definition of basic living expenses could involve some significant costs, depending upon how it is interpreted. It may mean that the "other costs" are limited to paying for medical insurance and other benefits of employment. However, this provision could also be interpreted to mean that the benefit is provided by one partner to the other in recognition of their relationship, leading to demands for all sorts of benefits, such as fancy clothes, automobiles, educational expenses, and the like.

You and your partner may want to consider discussing this requirement and incorporating your understanding of "basic living expenses" into a living together or other domestic partnership agreement, since a court will otherwise interpret this provision. After all, you and your partner may have vastly different ideas about the meaning of "basic living expenses" and a difference of opinion could lead to significant rancor.

You should also be aware that, unless you and your partner specifically obtain a loan in both names, you and your partner are not jointly responsible for each other's debts. See *Obligations of Domestic Partners* in *Chapter 3* for more information on financial obligations.

Unrelated Individuals

One requirement for registration under the Domestic Partnership Act is that you must be unrelated to each other "by blood or affinity up to and including the fourth degree of consanguinity." This creates a conflict with the provision found elsewhere in the Act that recognizes certain relationships entered in other states.

Consanguinity

Consanguinity is generally used to refer to someone related by blood. Simply stated, individuals who are first cousins or more distantly related meet the requirement of not being related to the fourth degree of consanguinity.

The DPA specifically recognizes reciprocal beneficiary relationships as equivalent to a registered domestic partnership. Both Hawaiian and Vermont law allow two closely-related persons, such as two sisters, to register as reciprocal beneficiaries. Their registration, however, would probably not be recognized in New Jersey since it violates this eligibility criteria. See *Out-of-State Registrations*, below.

Current or Previous Marriage or Domestic Partnership

Neither you nor your partner may be in a marriage "recognized by New Jersey law" or in a domestic partnership with someone else. If either of you were in a domestic partnership with another partner, that prior partnership must have been legally terminated at least 180 days before you and your new partner register your domestic partnership. However, if your prior partner died, the 180-day restriction no longer applies.

Since the DPA explicitly recognizes civil unions, domestic partnerships, and reciprocal beneficiary relationships entered in other states, the 180-day restriction appears to be applicable to legal relationships formed in other states. Thus, if either of you have previously registered in a civil union, domestic partnership, or affinity relationship in another state, you must wait at least 180 days before registering your new partnership. See *Recognition of Your Rights* in *Chapter 2* for more information.

If you and your partner were previously joined to each other in an out-of-state civil union, domestic partnership, or affinity relationship, you do not need to register your partnership in New Jersey in order for it to be recognized. In fact, you should probably not register in New Jersey since it is unclear whether doing so would terminate your registration elsewhere and, perhaps even limit your rights in those states. The New Jersey Domestic Partnership Act specifically recognizes these out-of-state registrations as equivalent to a New Jersey registration.

If one (or both) of you, on the other hand, was previously in such an out-of-state legal relationship, and that relationship has not been legally terminated, you will be able to initiate a termination proceeding in New Jersey. For information on terminating out-of-state civil unions or domestic partnership see *Chapter 14: Separation, Termination and Nullification.*

If you have been previously married or in another legally recognized relationship, and that marriage or other relationship has been legally terminated via a divorce or similar proceeding, you will be required to show the clerk a certified copy of your divorce or termination decree, which must show that the divorce or termination was granted at least 180 days prior to the day you register your new partnership.

This would apply to you even if you were divorced from a legally recognized same-sex marriage in Massachusetts, Canada, or elsewhere to someone other than your current partner, since it is now clear that New Jersey law does not recognize a same-sex marriage entered elsewhere.

Sex And Age Restrictions

In addition to the other eligibility requirements, the Domestic Partnership Act imposes some age and sex-related restrictions on partners. Domestic partners must be of the same sex and, therefore, unable to enter a marriage recognized in New Jersey, or they may be of opposite sex and at least 62 years of age.

This latter category is directed at opposite sex couples that are unwilling to marry for reasons such as a desire to maintain separate property or retirement benefits. If you and your partner fit this category, you should consult with a qualified estate planning or elder law attorney in order to determine if domestic partnership makes sense in your situation.

If you and your partner are of the same sex, both of you must be at least 18 years of age. Unlike the marriage laws, a parent may not give their consent in order for minor to enter a domestic partnership, nor may a legally emancipated minor enter a domestic partnership.

OUT-OF-STATE REGISTRATIONS

If you and your partner entered into a California or Maine domestic partnership, a Vermont or Connecticut civil union, or a Hawaiian reciprocal beneficiary relationship, your status is recognized in New Jersey under the Domestic Partnership Act and you do not need to re-register in New Jersey. Furthermore, if you have registered out-of-state, registration in New Jersey may be interpreted as a termination of your prior partnership. Whenever you are required to show proof of your relationship by providing a copy of your Certificate of Domestic Partnership, you may substitute a copy of that state's official confirmation of your legal relationship. You may need to send a copy of Section 6 (a) of the Act in order to prove that your out-of-state registration is valid.

Registration in a Local Registry

In some states without legal recognition of same-sex couples, certain counties or municipalities have local domestic partner registries that allow you to obtain certain benefits. For example, New York City and certain counties in the state of New York allow same-sex couples to register as domestic partners.

Although New Jersey recognizes such registrations as equivalent, other states do not. For example, when the Connecticut Attorney General issued his opinion that the state would recognize out-of-state civil unions and domestic partnerships, it specifically ignored local registries, implying that it would only be required to recognize state registration.

To be safe, you should register in a state in which you are eligible in order to achieve recognition in the widest number of localities in the United States.

Recognition of Same-Sex Marriage

There is one noteworthy exception to the recognition provision – it does not mention marriage. In fact, marriage is listed in Section 2 (b) as a barrier to registration in New Jersey, but only if the marriage is "recognized in New Jersey."

In a recent decision involving property rights, however, a New Jersey tax court specifically ruled that a same-sex marriage entered into in Canada was not a marriage recognized in New Jersey. Therefore, if you and your partner were married in Canada, your marriage is not an obstacle to registration in New Jersey. Although the question of recognition of same-sex marriages validly entered into in Massachusetts has yet to be decided, a marriage in that state would not be an obstacle to registration in New Jersey. Similarly, since Massachusetts does not recognize domestic partnerships, civil unions or reciprocal beneficiaries, your registration in New Jersey will have no effect on your rights in Massachusetts.

Until the question of same-sex marriage recognition is firmly decided in New Jersey, you and your partner should register in New Jersey to protect your rights in this state.

CHAPTER 6
REGISTERING YOUR DOMESTIC PARTNERSHIP

If you have decided whether registration is right for you, determined that you are eligible, assembled the proofs of eligibility needed, and have prepared a domestic partnership agreement, you can proceed with registration.

REGISTRATION PROCESS

The registration procedure is fairly quick and painless.. You and your partner will execute an Affidavit of Domestic Partnership (in quadruplicate) then file it with a local registrar. The local registrar will stamp the Affidavit with the date of receipt and the name of the district in which it is filed, then return two copies to you.

After you have filed the Affidavit and paid a fee of $28, the local registrar will complete a Certificate of Domestic Partnership, and will issue two copies of this to you along with two copies of the Notice of Rights and Obligations of Domestic Partners. The local registrar will retain a copy of the Affidavit and the Certificate for its files, and forward the originals to the State registrar's office in Trenton.

The Act specifies that the local registrar, who is either the city clerk or the registrar of vital statistics, shall do the actual registration. The local registrar is required to verify the validity of the domestic partnership, issue a domestic partnership certificate, and record a local copy.

WHERE TO REGISTER

The DPA requires you to register with a local registrar, who is either the city clerk in first-class cities, or the registrar of vital statistics in most other municipalities. Unless the regulations require otherwise, you may register with any local registrar in any municipality in New Jersey. The New Jersey Department of Health and Senior Services maintains a list of local registrars on its web site at http://www.state.nj.us/health/vital/regbycnty.shtml.

Unlike the New Jersey marriage laws, which specify the local registrar to be used, the DPA does not require you to register in the town in which you have your residence. Although this may have been an unintentional oversight, the lack of a specified registration locale is useful if you and your partner are not comfortable self-identifying as a same-sex couple in your community. You may, for instance, feel more comfortable registering elsewhere in the State.

Proof Of Joint Responsibility

The Domestic Partnership Act requires you to show that you and your partner have a common residence and that you are jointly responsible for each other. In order to demonstrate this, you are required to show one or more of the following forms of proof:

- A joint deed, mortgage or lease;

- A joint bank account;

- Designation by one partner of the other as one of your primary beneficiaries in a will;

- Designation by one partner of the other as one of your primary beneficiaries of an insurance policy or retirement plan; or

- A joint title to a motor vehicle.

Additional Proofs

If you were in a marriage recognized in New Jersey, you must prove that your prior marriage was legally dissolved by providing a certified divorce decree. If you are merely separated, but not legally divorced, you may not register in a domestic partnership and any attempt to do so will render your domestic partnership void *ab initio*, that is, completely invalid from the date of registration, even if you are later divorced. Similarly, if you were in a prior registered domestic partnership, civil union or reciprocal beneficiary relationship that has ended, you must show proof that your marriage or prior relationship has been legally terminated at 180 days prior to your registration.

If your prior marriage or domestic partnership ended as a result of your spouse's or partner's death, there is no waiting period required. However, you should be prepared to show proof in the form of a death certificate.

What happens after we file?

After you and your partner file your Affidavit of Registration with the local registrar, the law requires the local registrar to take the following steps:

1. On the tenth day of each month, the local registrar must file all such certificates with the State registrar.

2. The State registrar then updates the State registry.

The State registrar is also responsible for revising records when a domestic partnership is legally terminated or when a record needs to be corrected.

THE AFFIDAVIT OF DOMESTIC PARTNERSHIP

At the time of registration, you must file an Affidavit of Domestic Partnership that specifies you and your partner's names, ages, common mailing address, and contains a statement that you meet the requirements for domestic partnership at the time you sign the affidavit and that you intend to enter such a partnership. Each partner must appear together in the presence of a notary public (usually the registrar) to sign and swear to the Affidavit. At this time, you can obtain a form only at a local registrar's office.

You will be required to provide the following information:

- Each partner's full name, date of birth, age, and sex
- The full address of your common residence, including your county

The affidavit form is in four parts, two of which are retained by the registrar. The other two copies are returned to you at the time you register. For a sample affidavit, see *Appendix C: Affidavit of Domestic Partnership*.

CAUTION: filing an affidavit of domestic partnership that is intentionally false or misleading can subject you to a suit under the New Jersey Penalty Enforcement Act. The violation can lead to a penalty of up to $1,000, so you should be sure that when you and your partner submit the affidavit, the information it contains is correct.

CERTIFICATE OF DOMESTIC PARTNERSHIP

At the time you register, the local registrar will complete a Certificate of Domestic Partnership, which contains your full names, the date of registration, a statement that you and your partner are members of a registered domestic partnership recognized by the State of New Jersey, and a statement that you and your partner are entitled to all the rights, privileges and responsibilities that law provides. The registrar will then provide you with two copies of the Certificate, which bear an official state seal, and a copy of the Notice of Rights and Obligations of Domestic Partners. See *Appendix E: Notice of Rights and Obligations*.

You and your partner should keep these Certificates and your file-stamped copies of the Affidavit, with your other valuable papers in a fireproof safe or safe deposit box.

Obtaining Copies of the Certificate

At the time you register your domestic partnership, the local registrar will provide you with two copies of the Affidavit and the Certificate. For a nominal fee, the clerk can provide you with additional copies at the time you register, or you can request additional copies at a later date, either in person at a local registrar or by filing a request in person or by mail with the State registrar in Trenton. See *Appendix F: Application for Certification*.

Are my registration records private?

Access to your registration record information is considered private under several recent regulations. In order to obtain information about a particular registration, you must prove your identity and specify your relationship to the persons in the record. In some cases, you may need to obtain a court order.

Be sure to keep track of the date you registered. You may not think of this date as your "anniversary," but in order to obtain a copy of your certificate, you will need to provide both the date and the location where you registered. If you don't have all of these items, the clerk will not issue you a copy.

Making Changes to Your Certificate

If there are any corrections that need to be made to your certificate, you must first obtain a copy of your certificate then submit the changes to the state registrar. The exact procedure for making changes has not yet been set, so you should first check with the New Jersey Department of Health and Senior Services for further guidance.

CHANGING YOUR NAME

You and your partner may wish to change your name to reflect your status as a couple. Although this is not addressed in the Domestic Partnership Act, the courts in New Jersey have upheld the right of a person in a same sex relationship to change their name to that of their partner.

In order to change your name, you and/or your partner must begin by filing a complaint in the Superior Court, along with a sworn affidavit that states your current name, social security number, criminal history, if any, and including a statement that the change is not for avoiding either civil or criminal liability or perpetrating criminal or civil fraud. Although the judge has broad latitude in granting or rejecting the name change, the mere fact that you are doing so to present yourself as a couple is not sufficient reason to reject the change.

There are three basic steps to changing your name:

1. Fill out the appropriate forms and file them with a filing fee at the Superior Court in your county. The forms are obtained from the court, and consist of the complaint, an order for a hearing, a proposed final judgment, and a case information statement.

2. When the court returns the documents to you, it will set a hearing date and time and a docket number. You must then publish the date and time of the hearing in a newspaper at least two weeks before the hearing date. The court will provide the name of the paper you must use. You will also need to notify any other interested parties.

3. After the court hearing, the court will issue a final judgment granting your name change. You must then publish the final judgment in the newspaper and notify the New Jersey Department of Treasury, the Registrar of Vital Statistics, and the Division of Motor Vehicles. You must also notify the Social Security Administration and other federal agencies, as appropriate. Finally, be sure to notify all interested parties including creditors, banks, schools, etc.

If you change your name after you have registered, you will need to make corrections to your certificate of domestic partnership. Therefore, if you and your partner intend to change your names to reflect your status as a couple, you should do so before you register to save yourself and extra step.

CHAPTER 7

DISCRIMINATION

By registering as domestic partners, you and your partner gain certain protections from discrimination on the basis of domestic partnership in important areas such as employment, housing and credit. These rights are protected under two laws, the New Jersey Law Against Discrimination, and the New Jersey Civil Rights Act.

The Law Against Discrimination and the Civil Rights Act are generally enforced by the Attorney General through the Civil Rights Division of the Department of Justice. However, in certain cases, you may bring a private cause of action in New Jersey.

THE NEW JERSEY LAW AGAINST DISCRIMINATION

New Jersey has one of the strongest anti-discrimination laws in the country, known as the "Law Against Discrimination" (LAD). Even though the Law Against Discrimination already prohibits discrimination on the basis of "affectional or sexual orientation," the Domestic Partnership Act amended certain sections of the law to prohibit discrimination on the basis of domestic partnership.

As a result of this amendment, you and your partner are protected from discrimination in many critical areas, such as housing, employment, or extension of credit. However, these protections are only provided to you and your partner if you have registered as domestic partners. See *Appendix G: Law Against Discrimination*.

Employment

Under the LAD as amended by the Domestic Partnership Act, it is now unlawful for an employer to discriminate against you on the basis that you are a partner in a registered domestic partnership. For same-sex couples, this protection adds to the earlier prohibition against discrimination on the basis of affectional or sexual orientation.

An employer may not refuse to hire you or bar you from future employment, nor may your current employer discharge you, or require you to retire on the basis that you are in a registered domestic partnership. Furthermore, employers may not discriminate against you in regard to your compensation, or in regard to any other terms, conditions, or privileges of employment because you are in a registered domestic partnership.

Labor unions are also prohibited from discrimination on the basis of domestic partnership. Thus, a union may not exclude or expel from membership someone on the basis of domestic partnership status. Furthermore, a union or other such organization may not discriminate on that basis in any of its programs, such as apprenticeships or other training programs, nor may unions boycott employers who do not discriminate on the basis of domestic partnership status.

It is also a violation of LAD for an employer or employment agency to discriminate against domestic partners when providing applications, advertising jobs, or otherwise printing or circulating any information regarding employment.

Finally, it is illegal to take any form of reprisal against someone who has opposed attempts to discriminate against someone on the basis of domestic partnership status, or because that person has filed a complaint, testified in regard to, or cooperated in an investigation of discrimination on the basis of domestic partnership. In addition, anyone who attempts to coerce, intimidate, threaten, or otherwise prevent someone from exercising their civil rights in this (or any other) regard is in violation of LAD.

Exemptions

There are several exceptions, however. It is not unlawful for a religious organization to discriminate against you if it is following the tenants of its religion. Thus, a church that opposed domestic partnership for religious reasons would be exempt if it discriminated in employment based upon that opposition.

Unfortunately, the Act also exempts a private employer in regard to the provision of domestic partner health benefits. It is specifically not a violation of the LAD for your employer to refuse to provide domestic partnership benefits, nor is it a violation if your employer to require you to pay part or even all of the cost of coverage for your dependents. However, it would most likely be a violation of the Law Against Discrimination if your employer refused to provide these benefits on an equal basis with married couples, other than passing on the cost of the premiums.

Public Accommodations

It is unlawful for the owner or employees of any restaurant, hotel, bar, casino, or other place of public accommodation to refuse, withhold from or deny any accommodations on account of domestic partnership status. It is also unlawful for such a place to advertise that it discriminates or to refuse the patronage of someone in a domestic partnership.

Interestingly, it is unlawful for a private club or association to discriminate against its members on the basis of domestic partnership status. Thus, if you are a member of a country club that offers a discount or special membership to its married members, the club must now offer the exact same discount to you and your registered partner.

Housing

The DPA now makes it unlawful to discriminate on the basis of domestic partnership status in the sale or rental of housing. This prohibition is extended to all aspects of housing, including advertising, application forms, circulars, etc. This prohibition extends to anyone involved in real estate transactions, including real estate agents, landlords, superintendents, mortgage brokers, or other financial institutions.

This prohibition extends to 55+ and active adult communities, as well as senior housing. If one of you is qualified to live in age-restricted housing, and the other partner is not, it is illegal for such a community to prevent both of you from living in the community if the bylaws would allow a married couple with a similar age difference to live there.

Credit and Contracting

The Law Against Discrimination, as modified by the DPA, also prohibits discrimination in matters of credit on the basis of domestic partnership status. In addition to mortgages and other real estate-related financing, it is unlawful to refuse to do business with someone because they are in a registered domestic partnership.

It is also unlawful to boycott someone or some organization as a result of domestic partnership status or because that organization recognizes domestic partnerships. It is not unlawful, however, to discriminate in collective bargaining or similar agreements.

Since the Domestic Partnership Act does not make one partner responsible for the debts contracted solely in the other partner's name, it would probably be a violation of the Law Against Discrimination for a lender to refuse to extend credit to one partner unless both cosigned.

NEW JERSEY CIVIL RIGHTS ACT

In addition to the Law Against Discrimination, New Jersey passed the New Jersey Civil Rights Act in 2004. This Act applies to any person who has had any of the substantive due process or equal protection rights, privileges or immunities secured by the Constitution or laws of the United States, or any substantive rights, privileges or immunities secured by the Constitution or laws of New Jersey may bring a complaint under this new Act. See *Appendix H: Civil Rights Act*.

Suits against private individuals or companies must be brought to the attention of the Division of Civil Rights (see below). Suits against state or local public agencies, including denial of rights by public employees, may be brought in New Jersey state court in a private cause of action.

HOW TO FILE A DISCRIMINATION COMPLAINT

If you or your partner believe you have been discriminated against as a result of your domestic partnership status, or on any other basis, you need to file a complaint with the Division of Civil Rights, within the Office of the New Jersey Attorney General. Your complaint must be filed with one of the five regional offices within 180 days of the act or acts of discrimination.

Following the filing, the Division will investigate your complaint to determine whether there is probable cause to take further action. If so, a Deputy Attorney General may litigate your complaint in a hearing before an Administrative Law Judge. If, as a result of the investigation and hearing, a determination has been made that your rights were violated, the Director of the Division of Civil Rights will take action to rectify the discrimination. This action may include fines, damages including pain and suffering, and awarding of attorney fees, as well as remedial action to correct the problem.

If the Division has not responded to your complaint with a probable cause finding within 180 days of filing, you may proceed with the matter on your own, or with the assistance of private counsel in the Office of Administrative Law.

Instead of filing a complaint with the Division of Civil Rights, you may file a complaint in New Jersey Superior Court, where you are entitled to a jury trial. However, if you take this route, you may not file a complaint with the Division, and you take a further risk that, if you lose, the other side's attorneys' fees could be assessed against you.

If you are a member of a union, there may be additional rights available to you under your collective bargaining agreement. If you are being discriminated against in work-related matters, such as pension benefits, you should review your rights under your union contract, and you should discuss the problem with your union representative or shop steward. If your union refuses to help with your complaint, its actions could constitute discrimination that is actionable under the Law Against Discrimination.

If you believe you have been discriminated against, it is vitally important that you document the incident or incidents as completely as possible, as well as obtain the names and addresses of any persons or entities that you believe discriminated against you. The more information you can supply, the more likely your complaint can be quickly and effectively addressed. It is also important that you do not delay the filing of your complaint, since the filing deadlines are strictly enforced.

CHAPTER 8
DOMESTIC PARTNER BENEFITS

The Domestic Partnership Act has extended a limited set of rights to domestic partner benefits such as health insurance and pension benefits. The extent of these rights will depend upon whether you are a State employee, an employee of some other public agency, or a private employer.

HEALTH INSURANCE

The Domestic Partnership Act addresses the area of health insurance benefits for domestic partners in three ways. First, it extends coverage to the domestic partners of State employees on the same basis as married couples. Second, it provides a means by which domestic partner benefits may be provided to employees of public agencies other than the State, such as schools and municipalities. Finally, it encourages private firms to offer these benefits by requiring all providers to make available domestic partnership benefits as a prerequisite to approval or renewal by the Insurance Commissioner.

Insurers must begin making coverage available

The Domestic Partnership Act requires all health insurers doing business in the State, including hospital service corporations, medical service corporations, health service corporations, HMOs, dental service plans, and the like, to begin making domestic partner coverage available to all customers. The Act requires these insurers to begin making domestic partnership coverage available as a prerequisite to doing business, or continuing to do business in New Jersey. This does not mean, however, that your employer is required to provide you with such benefits, only that such benefits will eventually be available in all plans offered in New Jersey.

COBRA

If you or your partner is employed by the State, or by a public agency that is participating in the State Health Benefits Program (SHBP), your benefits are included within its COBRA program. However, if a public employer other than the State later rescinds domestic partnership benefits, the change is not considered a COBRA event.

If you leave a private employer that has extended you domestic partner benefits, you are not guaranteed that your partner will be eligible for continuation of those benefits under COBRA. Federal law allows an employer to provide greater coverage than required by the COBRA regulations so continuation of these benefits will depend entirely on what plan your employer has at the time you leave.

PENSION BENEFITS

If you or your partner is a member of one of the New Jersey public employee retirement plans, you may be entitled to the same pension rights as those afforded to opposite-sex married couples. You are also eligible if you have entered into a civil union or domestic partnership in another jurisdiction, such as Vermont or California.

Available Plans for Public Employees

The plans that have been modified to allow domestic partner benefits are the Public Employees' Retirement System (PERS), the New Jersey Teachers Pension and Annuity Fund (TPAF), the New Jersey Police and Firemen's Retirement System (PFRS), the New Jersey State Police Retirement System (SPRS), and the Judicial Retirement System (JRS).

The Alternate Benefits Program (ABP), available to the employees of many of New Jersey's community colleges, has not been included in the DPA, nor are members of the Consolidated Police and Firemen's Pension Fund, the Prison Officers' Pension Fund, or the Volunteer Emergency Worker's Survivors Pension.[1]

The benefits provided to same-sex domestic partners are limited to the State component, as a result of limitations imposed by federal tax law. The benefits provided also differ depending on the plan. See *Appendix I: Pension Benefits Frequently Asked Questions* for more information.

PERS and TPAF members

If you are a PERS or TPAF member, the only benefit extended by the DPA is that of Accidental Death, which provides a pension to your domestic partner if you are accidentally killed during the performance of your duties while at work. The benefit paid is subject to federal taxes, but not state tax.

Your regular PERS or TPAF retirements are unaffected, since you can already name your partner as the beneficiary of your pension benefits. However, the IRS does impose some restrictions on your beneficiary.

PFRS and SPRS members

If you are a PFRS or SPRS member, your registered partner will be eligible to receive the statutory survivor's benefit, as your "widow" or "widower."

If you are the surviving spouse or partner of a PFRS or SPRS member and are receiving the statutory survivor's benefit, you will lose this benefit once you register in a new domestic partnership. At this time, this will only affect the widow or widower of a PFRS or SPRS member who subsequently registers in a domestic partnership benefit. This loss of benefit does not apply to benefits received as a result of an accidental death in the line of duty.

JRS members

If you or your partner is a member of the New Jersey judiciary, your statutory survivor's benefits will not be awarded to your surviving domestic partner, as your "widow" or "widower."

As with PFRS and SPRS beneficiaries, the survivor's benefit is lost if you remarry or register in a new domestic partnership.

---

1.   Legislation has been introduced to include domestic partners in several of these plans. You should check the web site, http://www.njdomesticpartnership.com periodically for updated information on legislation.

STATE EMPLOYEES

If you or your partner is an appointed, elected, or full-time employee of the State of New Jersey, including the Executive, Judicial, or Legislative branches, Rutgers University, New Jersey Institute of Technology, UMDNJ, other state colleges and universities, or an employee of any subsidiary or other corporation of the Delaware River Port Authority, formerly employed by the South Jersey Port Corporation, you will be able to get domestic partnership health and pension benefits.

Health Insurance

Your covered dependents now include your registered domestic partner and, as a result of a recent decision by the New Jersey Division of Pensions and Benefits, your domestic partner's children can be added to the employees coverage if they are single, under the age of 23, live with you, and are substantially dependent upon you for support. You will have to file an Affidavit of Dependency in order to add them. See *Appendix K: Affidavit of Dependency.*

The State pays one hundred percent of the premiums for your partner and any eligible dependents. You should be aware, that this has federal tax implications that you'll need to consider. See *Tax Treatment of Benefits* in *Chapter 9: Money, Taxes and Insurance,* for more information.

Pension benefits

The benefits available to you as a State employee will depend upon what plan you are participating in. See your plan administrator for more information.

Eligibility and Enrollment

In order to demonstrate eligibility, you must provide your employer with a copy of your Certificate of Domestic Partnership, or a valid form of certification, if you and your partner are members of a civil union or domestic partnership entered in another jurisdiction. The health benefits are not available to opposite-sex domestic partners, even if registered.

If you are employed by the State or by another participant in the SHBP, you enroll your domestic partner and his or her qualified dependent children by filing an SHBP application, with a copy of your Certificate of Domestic Partnership or other proof attached. You must file this within 60 days of registration of your domestic partnership; otherwise, you will be required to wait until the next regular open enrollment period. See *Appendix J: NJ State Health Benefits Application* for an example of the required application.

The pension benefit changes apply to State employees immediately upon registration by a same-sex couple as domestic partners.

If You Are Retired

If you are a State retiree, you may also add your registered domestic partner to your coverage. If you were employed by a public employer, other than the State, who is a participant in SHBP, you will only be able to add your partner to your coverage if your former employer passes the required authorizing resolution or ordinance. In all other cases, it is up to your former employer as to whether domestic partner benefits are made available to retirees.

As you would expect, there are tax implications for retirees with domestic partnership benefits. See

Chapter 9: Money, Taxes and Insurance for more information.

Medical Savings Plans (Tax$ave)

Many employees have set up medical savings plans under IRS Section 125 (Tax$ave) plan in order to use pre-tax dollars to pay for medical expenses and benefits. Because Tax$ave is a federal program, you will not be able to use these funds for payment of your partner's health premiums, unless you can demonstrate that your partner qualifies as your dependent for federal tax purposes.

OTHER PUBLIC EMPLOYERS

If you work for a public employer other than the State of New Jersey, such as a municipality or school board, your employer may offer you domestic partner health and pension benefits, but it is not required to do so. If your employer does decide to offer such benefits, its governing body must pass a resolution or ordinance authorizing the benefits.

A public employer can later rescind its decision to offer these benefits; if it does so, the change will take place at some date set by the governing body.

Health Insurance

If your public employer participates in the State Health Benefits Program (SHBP), it may choose to extend domestic partnership benefits by adopting a resolution providing that the term "dependents" shall include domestic partners. See *Appendix L: State Health Benefits Program Resolution* for a copy of the resolution, which must be passed at a regular meeting by your employer's governing body.

As with State employees, you may enroll your partner's children if they are qualified. You enroll your domestic partner and his or her qualified dependent children by filing an SHBP application, along with a copy of your Certificate of Domestic Partnership attached. See *State Employees*, above. If you registered your domestic partnership before your employer adopted the Health Benefits Resolution, you have 60 days following your receipt of notice that resolution was adopted in order to enroll.

If your public employer is one of the many that do not participate in the SHBP, your employer may offer these benefits on the same basis as private employers, but is not required to do so.

Unlike the State, however, other public employers can require you to pay some or all of the premiums for your dependents. Any portion of your dependent domestic partnership premium that is paid by your employer is considered taxable federal income. See *Tax Treatment of Benefits* in *Chapter 9: Money, Taxes and Insurance*, for more information.

Unfortunately, if your employer refuses to extend health benefits to your domestic partner or his or her dependents, there is little you can do. The DPA specifically exempted employers other than the State from any violation of the Law Against Discrimination if they fail to provide health benefits for domestic partners.

Pension Benefits

Other public employers, such as school boards, counties, or municipalities, may also extend pension benefits to their employees if they are participants in one of the authorized plans.

In order to begin offering pension benefits, the governing body of the agency must pass a resolution or ordinance extending the benefits to its employees and retirees, and then file this with the Division of Benefits and Pensions. See *Appendix M: Pension Resolution* for a sample resolution for extending benefits.

Unlike the provision of health benefits, however, failing to provide pension benefits to same-sex domestic partners may result in a violation of the Law Against Discrimination. Although your employer may initially refuse to adopt these benefits, it may be required to in the near future, and the threat of litigation may be sufficiently persuasive.

PRIVATE EMPLOYERS

If you work for any other employer, your employer is not required to provide you with domestic partnership benefits, although the soon-to-be universal availability of such benefits means that you may have success lobbying your employer to add domestic partnership benefits.

Private employers can require you to pay some or all of the premiums for your dependents. Any portion of your dependent domestic partnership premium that is paid by your employer is considered taxable federal income.

As is the situation with public employers other than the State, your employer may refuse to provide health benefits to your domestic partner and his or her dependents without violating the Law Against Discrimination.

The availability of pension benefits will depend upon your employer's policies. The Domestic Partnership Act does not require these benefits to be added.

Many private employers, however, already allow you to designate a domestic partner as your beneficiary. Some benefits, however, are subject to restrictions imposed by federal law. If you work for a private employer, you should check with your employee benefits representative to see what is available.

Benefit Exclusions

Unless you work for the State of New Jersey is not unlawful discrimination under the Law Against Discrimination if your employer does not allow you to enroll your domestic partner in your health benefits plan, even if the plan provider offers a domestic partnership benefits plan. Even if they do, your employer may also make you pay some or all of the premiums for your partner, even if they don't require this from married employees.

Opposite-gender domestic partners are specifically excluded from dependent domestic partner coverage under the State health insurance and pension benefits plan. The reason given for this last exclusion is that such couples have a legally recognized right to marry in New Jersey.

CHAPTER 9

MONEY, TAXES AND INSURANCE

Same-sex couples have many of the same financial needs and responsibilities as opposite-sex couples. However, they are treated very differently when it comes to financial issues such as taxation, insurance, debts, and pooling of income and assets because same-sex couples lack certain legal protections and exemptions provided to married couples. Some of the ways in which same-sex couples (and unmarried cohabitants) are discriminated against in state and federal law include:

- **Gifts and property transfers to partner**. Taxable under state and federal law.

- **Inheritance**. No unlimited marital deduction.

- **Income tax**. Must file independently.

- **Social security and veteran death benefits**. None.

- **Retirement**. Death benefits immediately taxable.

- **Domestic partner benefits**. Taxable income.

For same-sex couples living in New Jersey, registration in a domestic partnership can help alleviate some of the state law discrimination, such as the tax on inherited transfers, but it does not affect the way they are treated under federal law. Until the federal Defense of Marriage Act is repealed or found unconstitutional, same-sex couples will continue to be disproportionately effected by federal discrimination.

YOUR FINANCES

For many couples, same-sex or opposite-sex, financial matters can lead to disagreement and, as a result, they avoid discussion until some financial crisis emerges, such as a sudden illness or a loss of a job. The pressure that results from these problems can often drive couples apart. The best way to avoid these unintended consequences and ensure a secure future together is to develop a financial plan as a couple.

Your status as a same-sex couple makes it even more important to plan your finances, since you will pay more in taxes and have less opportunity to shelter your income than a similarly situated married couple. The specifics of planning will depend upon your current financial situation, your financial goals, and whether you choose to register.

Whether or not you register, you and your partner need to decide your shared financial obligations, your contributions to your partnership, how you will divide up financial responsibilities such as paying bills, and set financial goals such as saving for a new house. You also need to decide to what extent you will keep separate accounts and joint accounts. Once you have made these decisions, you should consider formally acknowledging these decisions in a written agreement. First, however, it helps to have some understanding of the different ways married couples and domestic partners are treated when it comes to income, assets and debts.

Assets, Liabilities, Net Worth and Equity

Assets are those things that you own, such as your home, your car, your checking and savings accounts, the contents of your home, and the cash in your pocket. Income is a form of asset to the extent that it is earned. For most individuals, most if not all income comes from work or from a pension or other retirement benefit. Some income may also come from investments you have made or from property you own. For some lucky individuals, income comes from a trust of which they are beneficiaries.

There are several ways that assets are classified. Tangible assets are those that have a physical existence, such as a house, cash, or a stock certificate. Intangible assets are less common but include things like patents, trademarks or copyrights. Cash and assets that can be readily exchanged for cash are referred to as liquid assets.

You acquire assets by exchanging one asset you own for another, such as paying cash for a book; by investing assets, such as depositing cash in an interest-earning account; by doing some work in return for income; or by taking on a debt, such as a mortgage. You may also receive an asset as a gift or through inheritance. Often, you acquire an asset through some combination of these methods, such as buying a house with a down payment in cash and taking on a mortgage for the balance.

Liabilities are those debts that you owe, such as mortgages, credit card debts, student loans, or promissory notes. Liabilities are either secured, which means they are attached to a particular asset, or unsecured. The most common secured liabilities are mortgages and auto loans; the most common unsecured debts are credit card balances.

Your net worth is equal to the value of your assets minus the amount of your liabilities, but this is only one measure of your present financial situation. Another important measure is equity, which is usually measured in terms of individual assets. The equity in a particular asset is equal to the current value of that asset minus any liabilities secured by that asset. For example, the equity in your house is equal to the value of your house minus the balance of your mortgage or other home loans.

Marriage vs. Domestic Partnership

For married couples in New Jersey, most assets acquired during the marriage are considered marital property in which each spouse has equal ownership, even if individually acquired by only one spouse. The major exceptions to this rule are property owned by one spouse before the marriage, gifts to one spouse, and inherited assets. Even these assets can become marital assets if, for example, they are acquired in anticipation of the marriage, or if they appreciate in value through the efforts of both spouses.

For domestic partners, on the other hand, any asset acquired by one partner during the partnership is currently treated as that partner's individually owned asset, unless both partner's intend otherwise. However, like all rights and obligations, the ownership of assets acquired during your domestic partnership can be modified in a valid contract signed by you and your partner.

Liabilities are also treated differently for domestic partners. In a marriage, spouses are each liable for the debts of the other spouse incurred during the marriage, at least to the extent that the debt arises from "necessary expenses" of the marriage. Domestic partners, on the other hand, are specifically not responsible for each other's individual debts incurred during the domestic partnership unless both agree. However, a creditor can try to satisfy the debt from your partner's share of joint property. See *Judgments Against Domestic Partners*, below.

One area married couples really get different treatment is in regard to equity. Each spouse has equal ownership in all marital assets, regardless of individual contribution. Thus, for all purposes, married spouses have one-half of the equity in joint property. If you and your partner own assets jointly, however, your individual equity will vary depending on your percentage of contribution, and in some circumstances, you must be able to prove the amount of contribution. For more information, see *Financial Record Keeping*, below.

Judgments Against Domestic Partners

If you and your partner are found jointly liable on a debt or in a civil suit, the court will issue a judgment against both of you. In this case, the judgment holder is entitled to collect the judgment from any property you own individually or jointly.

If, on the other hand, a creditor or other party obtains a judgment against your partner individually, the creditor can collect the judgment by filing a judgment lien against any real property your partner has in the state, and executing the judgment against any assets your partner owns individually. If your partner's individually owned property is insufficient to cover his debt, the creditor can then seek repayment from your partner's share of any jointly owned assets.

Although jointly owned property is only subject to a judgment to the extent of the individual debtor's share, a judgment against one partner can create great difficulties for both partners. Jointly owned and titled property, such as a home or car, may be exempt from seizure but the judgment holder can file a lien that will "cloud" the title, making it difficult or impossible for you to refinance or sell the property without repaying your partner's debt. Furthermore, unless each partner's percentage of ownership in an asset is clearly stated, the creditor may presume that the debtor owns all of the equity and require you to prove otherwise.

With untitled property such as personal property, it may be extremely difficult to show that a particular piece of property belongs entirely to the non-debtor partner and is therefore not subject to seizure. Judgments are routinely collected in New Jersey by sending a county sheriff around to seize personal property from the debtor, after which the property may be sold to satisfy the debt. The only way to prevent seizure and sale of particular items is to be able to show the sheriff and/or a court that the debtor partner has no ownership rights in the asset.

Jointly held financial accounts, such as checking accounts or broker accounts, are also subject to a judgment. A judgment creditor can force the financial institution to freeze most of the funds held in the account while they seek an order to turnover the funds.

If you or your partner have accumulated significant debts prior to registering, if either one of you has a history of defaulting on debts, or if either one of you expects to be sued for some reason, you should take steps to identify and protect your individual assets so that they are not subject to a judgment against the other partner. For more information on protecting your personal assets, see *Chapter 10: Property Rights*.

Modifying Financial Obligations

Although the Domestic Partnership Act imposes certain financial obligations on you and your partner, you may alter these obligations and even add additional ones in a valid contract between you. You may also agree to take on certain debts of your partner, or refuse to be jointly responsible for any debts. Although most of these issues should be addressed in your domestic partnership agreement, you may execute a separate financial agreement.

However, you should be aware that if you take on a debt in your own name for purposes of providing some or all of your partner's "basic living expenses," you may want to consider adding a clause that allows you to seek contribution from your partner for that portion of any debt you incur.

Your agreement should address the issues of contribution toward household expenses, joint liability for debts and judgments, and whether or not support will be continued during any period of separation or after termination. You should also include a clause the defines "basic living expenses" and other household expenses for which you agree to be "jointly liable." If you and your partner have children, you may want to address their financial support but you cannot limit your obligation if you are a legal parent.

Equalizing Differences in Income and Ownership

In many cases, there are significant differences between each partner's current finances. This difference may be short-term, as where one partner is between jobs, or they may be on-going, such as when one partner has a high-paying job and the other earns substantially less. In addition to the tensions that these differences cause in the relationship, these can create tax and estate problems, particularly when purchasing joint assets.

The problem arises most frequently when domestic partners purchase their first home together. In many cases, the partners are unable to equally contribute to the down payment, but jointly qualify for the mortgage. In order to close, one partner contributes most or all of the down payment but both are listed as joint tenants with a right of survivorship on the deed. This creates at least three problems.

First, joint tenancy requires equal ownership at the time the tenancy is created. Second, because the contribution was unequal, the partners' share of the equity remains unequal, even as the home appreciates. This may cause an unintended estate tax problem when the wealthier partner dies. Third, one-half of the down payment may be construed as a gift to the other partner.

One way to solve these problems is through a loan made prior to closing. The partner with the down payment loans the other partner an amount that makes the partners' contributions equal. In return, the "lending partner" takes back a promissory note from the "borrowing partner," which is then recorded following closing as a lien against the deed. At this point, the partners have equal ownership in the property, but not equal equity because the "borrowing partner" owes a debt that will be repaid from his or her share of the equity.

The terms of the note are entirely up to the partners, although there may be some gift tax issues depending on the interest rate. Repayment on the note can be deferred until the house is sold, or if the "borrowing partner" can pay more than half of the mortgage payment, the difference could be credited against the note.

It is harder to equalize income differences in a relationship. Where one partner makes a greater financial contribution to the household, the contribution is more likely to be viewed as a taxable gift to the other partner. One way is to contractually recognize the non-financial contributions to the household, such as responsibility for repairs or yard work. If the wealthier partner owns a business, the other partner can be an employee and receive an income that helps pay household expenses. See *Transfer Taxes*, below for more information.

Financial Record Keeping

You and your partner must keep accurate and complete financial records, particularly in regard to joint assets in case you need to prove your individual contribution to ownership. There are several situations in which such proof will be required.

- First, if a judgment is entered against your partner and an attempt is made to collect this judgment from a joint asset, you may be required to prove your contribution in order to protect your share.

- Second, if your partner dies before you, the IRS will take the position that your deceased partner owned 100% of the equity in all jointly owned property and include the entire value in your partner's taxable estate. You must be able to prove your individual contribution in order to exclude your share.

- Third, if you and your partner decide to terminate your domestic partnership, accurate records will be necessary to establish your ownership in joint assets or to prove a particular asset was entirely yours.

- Finally, if your partner dies without a valid will, you may be required to prove the extent of your ownership in certain assets.

If neither you or your partner is good at keeping such records, you should consider working with an accountant who can help you establish the proofs necessary to protect your ownership in your joint assets.

Banks and Other Financial Accounts

If you and your partner maintain any joint financial accounts, the financial institution will require you to decide how you will each access these accounts. There are several options:

Joint Accounts

A joint account should always be set up with a right of survivorship. This ensures that, when one partner dies, the entire contents of the account belong to the surviving partner, who can continue to use the account or close it. The one drawback to a joint account is that both of you have access, and both of you can withdraw the entire balance of the account without the other's permission. If you are concerned about this, you can impose limitations on the account, such as requiring both of you to sign checks over a specific dollar amount and restricting ATM withdrawals.

Totten Trusts (POD Accounts)

A Totten trust, sometimes referred to as a "payable on death (POD)" account is a bank or other financial account that is maintained in your name, with your partner named as beneficiary of the account. Upon proof of your death, the account is closed and your partner (or other beneficiary) will receive the current balance. Your partner otherwise has no right to access the account.

Separate Accounts

If you have individual investment accounts, you must make certain that you name at least one beneficiary for that account, otherwise, the account becomes part of your estate upon your death and will be distributed according to your will.

In some cases, banks will require you to execute their own form of financial power of attorney in order to open or maintain these accounts.

If you and your partner are maintaining joint investment accounts containing securities, you may want to take advantage of the *Uniform Transfers on Death Securities Registration Act*, which acts similarly to a POD account, but which has some specific tax requirements. You should discuss ways to set up these accounts with a financial advisor who is knowledgeable about the financial needs of same-sex couples and the Domestic Partnership Act.

Joint bank accounts, like all jointly owned property, are subject to certain tax issues, particularly in regard to the federal gift tax. See *Transfer Taxes*, below, for more information.

TAXATION

There are many kinds of taxes collected by the state and federal government. For same-sex partners, the three most important taxes are income tax, property tax, and transfer taxes.

- **Income Taxes**. New Jersey residents pay federal and state income tax. There is currently no recognition for same-sex couples in the federal tax code and only limited recognition of domestic partners in the New Jersey income tax code.

- **Transfer Taxes**. These are taxes paid any time property is transferred from one person to another. There are three federal transfer taxes, the gift tax, the estate tax, and the generation-skipping tax. In New Jersey, there are two transfer taxes, an estate tax and the transfer inheritance tax.

- **Property Taxes**. Most real estate is taxed at the local level in New Jersey. In addition, the State collects a tax on the sale of real estate.

Federal Taxes

The two federal taxes that most affect same-sex partners are the federal income tax and the federal transfer tax. Because of the federal Defense of Marriage Act, none of the tax breaks given to married couples are available to same-sex couples, regardless of legal status.

Federal Income Tax

You and your partner must file individual income tax returns, even if you register as domestic partners, or marry in Massachusetts or Canada.

There are certain deductions that are available to you and your partner, however. First, you may deduct mortgage interest and property taxes on your jointly owned home, at least in proportion to your ownership in the home. Second, you may be able to take a deduction for your partner, your partner's children, or your partner's parent, if you meet the following test:

1. The person lived with you during the entire tax year.

2. The person is a U.S. citizen, a resident alien, or a citizen of Canada or Mexico.

3. The person was not required to file a tax return.

4. The person had gross income less than $3,100 for 2004, or the child is under age 19 at the end of the year or is a full-time student under the age of 24.

5. You have provided more than half the support for that child during the entire tax year.

If your partner would otherwise have claimed the children as a deduction on his or her return, you will need to disclaim the deduction by filing IRS Form 8332.

For more information, see *Appendix O: IRS Tax Topic 354 - Dependents*, or download Publication 501 from the IRS web site (http://www.irs.gov/pub/irs-pdf/p501.pdf).

Exemptions, Deductions and Credits

There are three ways taxes can legally be reduced.

1. Exemptions are amounts that are entirely excluded from taxation.

2. Deductions are amounts that are subtracted from gross income or the gross estate before the tax is calculated. Examples of deductions are mortgage interest or burial expenses.

3. Credits are amounts that reduce payable taxes, usually to offset other taxes paid.

Taxation of Benefits

Unlike opposite-sex married couples, if your employer extends any benefits to your domestic partner, they are considered taxable income unless you can show they meet some federal exemption. This income issue arises because federal law does not normally recognize a domestic partner as a dependent.

In general, imputed income is calculated based upon the premium your employer pays for single coverage less any amount paid by you. If your employer pays all or any part of the premium for your partner and your partner's dependents, you will have imputed income. On the other hand, if your employer requires you to pay the entire amount, then you have received no additional income and, therefore, owe no additional tax.

Your employer will be required to withhold federal income tax, social security, and Medicare taxes on the imputed income from this benefit unless you can show that your partner qualifies as your dependent under federal law. See *Appendix O: IRS Tax Topic 354 - Dependents* to determine if your partner qualifies as your dependent.

If your partner does qualify, you will need to demonstrate this to your employer so that they stop withholding for imputed income. State employees can submit an "Employee Tax Certification - Domestic Partner Benefit" form if they qualify for this exemption from withholding. See *Appendix P: Employee Tax Certification* for an example of this form. State retirees must file a "Retiree Tax Certification" so the benefit is not reported and taxed. See *Appendix Q: Retiree Tax Certification* for an example of this form.

Federal Transfer Taxes

In addition to income tax, the federal government taxes certain kinds of transfers of assets to other persons. The federal transfer taxes (sometimes called the "death tax") is made up of three components, the gift tax, the estate tax, and the generation-skipping tax.

The gift tax is a tax on gifts made while the donor is alive (called an "inter vivos" gift or transfer.) The estate tax (sometimes called the "death tax") is a tax on gifts made after the donor dies (called a "testamentary" transfer or gift.) The generation-skipping tax, is an additional tax on testamentary transfers that skip a generation, most commonly from a grandparent to a grandchild.

Many of these taxes will only apply to the wealthiest of individuals and can be minimized by proper estate planning. See *Chapter 13: Estate Planning*.

Federal Gift Tax

The gift tax is another area in which domestic partners are discriminated against as compared to married couples. The federal gift tax is a tax on gifts that is paid by the donor, rather than the recipient. Every person is entitled to give a total of $1,000,000 of assets in their lifetime without having to pay taxes. Each person may give gifts totaling $11,000 per year to as many persons as they choose.

Married couples are entitled to an unlimited exclusion for gifts to spouses. Same-sex partners may only exclude the first $11,000 given to their partner per year. If you give your partner assets totaling in excess of that amount in any one year, you will be required to report the excess by filing a gift tax return when you file your tax return for that year. The excess counts toward your lifetime exclusion of $1,000,000.

Legally, any support you provide your partner constitutes a gift. This includes up to one-half of payments you make on behalf of both of you. For instance, if your partner is not working and you are supporting the entire household, up to half the mortgage or rent payments, utility bills, groceries and other expenditures could be considered to be a gift to your partner.

In practice, the IRS has never gone after any couples for these kinds of payments and it is unlikely that they would do so. However, if you are providing cash payments to your partner, such as a monthly allowance, you may want to be careful about reporting this since it is a gift.

Exempt gifts

Payments for tuition and medical expenses made on behalf of another person are not limited, so long as they are made directly to the school or to the medical provider. Therefore, you can pay these on your partner's behalf (or for you partner's children or other relatives) without gift tax liability and without having to report them.

It is very easy to make unintended gifts to your partner that must be reported. For example, transferring an asset, such as a car, to your partner for less than its fair market value constitutes a gift of the value in excess of what your partner paid you. Adding your partner's name to the title of your home is a gift if your partner pays less than fair market value for the share. Even money you deposit into a joint checking account becomes a taxable gift when your partner withdraws the funds without obligation to repay.

There may be good reasons for giving your partner assets in excess of your annual exclusion, if the assets are rapidly appreciating in value, such as real estate. Gifting can be an important for transferring assets to your domestic partner but you should discuss it first with an estate planning attorney or other professional before actually making any transfers.

Federal Estate Tax

Same-sex couples do not fare any better when it comes to the federal estate tax but many will never feel its bite because the estate tax exemption is currently $1,500,000 and will increase to $2,000,000 in 2005, $3,500,000 in 2009, is repealed in 2010, then returns to $1,000,000. This exemption is the value of the assets you can leave to your heirs (including your domestic partner) tax-free.

Your estate tax is calculated by first determining the value of your taxable estate, which includes the value of life insurance, pensions and certain other death benefits, as well as your home and other valuable assets, less the debts you owe at your death. Often, couples are surprised to discover that their estate is worth far more than they initially thought. The total value of your estate is reduced by the estate tax exemption and the federal government taxes the excess at a maximum rate that is currently 47%. The estate tax exemption works hand-in-hand with the gift tax exclusion; the estate tax exemption is reduced by the value of the taxable gifts you made during your life.

Married couples get an unlimited deduction, which means they can leave their entire estate to their spouse without paying any taxes. However, when the second spouse dies, the federal estate tax is applied to all assets in excess of that spouse's estate tax exemption. As a result, married couples frequently set up an estate plan that sets aside (shelters) an amount equal to the current estate tax exemption when the first spouse dies, with the remainder going to the surviving spouse tax-free using the marital deduction. This allows both spouses to use the estate tax exemption to pass the maximum amount tax-free to their heirs.

Although same-sex couples don't get the unlimited marital deduction, each partner can still leave an estate that is largely exempt from federal estate taxes through judicious tax and estate planning.

Generation-Skipping Tax

The generation-skipping tax is the third component of the federal transfer tax. If you are considerably older than your partner, and quite wealthy, leaving your estate to your partner may trigger this tax. Most same-sex couples will never need to worry about this tax,

State Taxes

In addition to federal taxes, there are several state taxes assessed in New Jersey. The taxes most affecting same-sex couples are the state income tax, property taxes, and several transfer taxes.

State Income Tax

The Domestic Partnership Act now includes registered domestic partners within the definition of "dependent." This means that you may take an additional exemption of $1,000.00 on your New Jersey tax return if your partner would not otherwise be required to file separately. Note, however, that this does not mean that you and your partner can file a joint New Jersey tax return.

You will also not be penalized on your state taxes if you are able to enroll your partner in your employer's health and pension plans. Although considered a taxable benefit for federal taxes, the New Jersey Division of Revenue has taken the position that employer-paid benefits are not taxable in New Jersey. However, if you live outside New Jersey, these benefits may be taxable depending upon your state's laws.

You should keep in mind that the IRS is constrained by federal law from recognizing same-sex relationships. Thus, you and your partner must still file separate federal tax returns, and you must pay federal gift taxes on accumulated transfers to your partner of more than $11,000.00 in any one tax year. Furthermore, you will not be able to declare your domestic partner as a dependent on your federal tax return.

Disabled Veteran's Property Tax Exemption

Based on a recent case, registered domestic partners are eligible for a 100% property tax exemption on any property they jointly own, if either partner is an honorably discharged disabled veteran. In order to apply for the exemption, you must file Form D.V.S.S.E. with the municipal tax assessor where your home is located. You may file the form at any time during the year. You may obtain the form on the New Jersey Taxation web site, at http://www.state.nj.us/treasury/taxation/pdf/other_forms/lpt/dvsse.pdf.

It is likely that the exemption, once granted, will continue after the death of the disabled partner, so long as the property remains owned by the surviving partner.

New Jersey Homestead Property Tax Rebate

The Domestic Partnership Act did not modify the New Jersey Homestead Rebate program, nor did the recent 2004 Homestead Property Tax Rebate Act recently passed and signed into law as part of the Fair and Immediate Relief (FAIR) legislation add domestic partnership as a recognized status. As a result, domestic partners must continue to claim their homestead rebate separately, unlike opposite-sex couples that are entitled to file jointly. Fortunately, in most cases, the result is more favorable for same-sex couples.

Domestic partners who own their home in common are considered joint tenants and are allowed a homestead rebate on a proportionate share of the taxes assessed on the home. By default, each partner is assumed to hold an equal share in the homestead, unless they can demonstrate that title provides for unequal ownership. You may be able to increase your total rebate if you and your partner have considerably different incomes and can reasonably show that your percentages of ownership in your homestead are not equal.

If you and your partner are tenants, rather than homeowners, you will each be required to file separately for your rebate, basing your calculation on your separate incomes.

State Transfer Taxes

New Jersey imposes four kinds of taxes on transfers of assets: a real estate transfer fee, the motor vehicle transfer fee, the transfer inheritance tax, and the estate tax. Of these, domestic partners are currently exempted from the transfer inheritance tax if they have registered.

Real Estate Transfers

If you own separate real property, and you decide to sell half of that property to your partner so that you can become joint owners, the sale will be subject to the realty transfer tax. The tax is imposed on the amount of the transfer, not the full value of the property, and will be collected at the time the new deed is recorded.

Currently, real property transfers between a husband and wife are exempt from the fee and the amount can be significant depending upon the value of the house. If you sell any real property to your registered domestic partner, it would be worth your while to challenge this tax.

Vehicle Sales Tax

Under New Jersey law, vehicles being titled upon the death of the owner by an immediate family member are exempt from sales tax. However, this definition does not include domestic partners. Thus, you will be subject to a 6% sales tax on the value of a vehicle when it is transferred to you upon the death of your partner.

New Jersey Estate Tax

There is no relief for domestic partners under the New Jersey Estate tax because calculation of the tax relies on the Federal Estate tax credit, which does not provide an exemption for domestic partners. This is another discriminatory tax that is probably ripe for a legal challenge.

Practically speaking, your estate will only be subject to the New Jersey estate tax if it is worth more than $675,000, the current state exemption. If you have current assets in excess of this amount (including life insurance death benefits), you should meet with a competent estate planner to discuss ways that the estate tax can be minimized. See *Chapter 13: Estate Planning* for more information.

Transfer Inheritance Tax

One of the most unfair burdens on domestic partners prior to the enactment of the Domestic Partnership Act was the taxation of personal and real property transferred from one partner to the other pursuant to a will or immediately prior to one partner's death. Fortunately, this burden has been alleviated under the Domestic Partnership Act.

Ordinarily, the transfer of real estate or personal property worth more than $500 to your partner, whether by will or within a three-year period prior to your death, is subject to inheritance taxation in New Jersey. Prior to the enactment of the Domestic Partnership Act, transfers between domestic partners were taxed at the maximum rate. Now, the DPA provides registered domestic partners with the same exemption as transfers to husbands or wives. Thus, your partner will incur no New Jersey inheritance tax liability upon your death.

Unfortunately, this applies only to New Jersey's taxation of estates; since there is no federal recognition of domestic partnerships, you must still pay any federal tax on property inherited from your partner. Thus, you should meet with a qualified estate-planning attorney in order to make sure your wills make allowance for any federal death taxes.

In-state transfers

For registered partners who are resident in New Jersey, the new rules apply to transfers by will of all real or tangible property located within the state, and all intangible personal property wherever located. Thus, if you and your partner reside in New Jersey, all property located within the state, as well as any intangible property that you transfer to your partner is exempt from the inheritance tax. However, any real or tangible personal property you own in another state, will be subject to that state's transfer rules.

Out-of-state transfers

For non-resident registered domestic partners, the new rules apply only to the transfer of real or tangible personal property located within the state of New Jersey. Thus, if you and your partner reside in another state, only the property located in New Jersey is exempt from inheritance tax. The remainder of your estate will be subject to the laws of your state of residence.

Transfers before death

Transfers of property to your partner, by deed, grant, bargain, sale or gift, are exempt from the New Jersey inheritance tax if made "in contemplation of death." Under New Jersey law, any such transfer of property made for less than adequate value, will be considered "in contemplation of death" if made within the three years prior to the grantor's death.

For example, if your registered partner transferred ownership of half of his or her house to you, the transfer would be exempt from inheritance tax if it were made within the three-year period prior to your partner's death. Note, however, that this does not exempt you from other applicable state and federal taxes.

Exemption for pension transfers

In addition to exempting other types of transfers between domestic partners, the Domestic Partnership Act now exempts any transfer of benefits from a qualified pension or retirement plan to your domestic partner. Thus, if your pension, annuity, retirement allowance or return of contributions under certain retirement plans is made payable to your domestic partner, the transfer is entirely exempt from New Jersey inheritance transfer tax.

Transfers to surviving joint tenants

If you and your partner hold property as joint tenants, including real estate, personal property, or joint bank accounts, the immediate transfer of such property outside of probate as a result of a right of survivorship is considered an exempt transfer.

Other exemptions

The transfer inheritance tax exemption also applies to the transfer of membership certificates or stock in cooperative housing corporations (co-ops).

INSURANCE

In addition to health insurance, other kinds of insurance are affected by the Domestic Partnership Act primarily as a result of the addition of domestic partners to the Law Against Discrimination. This means that every kind of insurance policy and every kind of discount made available to married couples must be provided to registered domestic partners, with the exception of employer-provided health insurance.

There are several kinds of insurance you and your partner should have:

- **Life insurance**. This can be a great way to ensure that your partner has funds for paying off your mortgage and other debts upon your death. You can name your partner as your beneficiary, and if you do, the proceeds will not be a part of your probate estate but will go directly to your partner or other named beneficiary. Insurance proceeds count as part of your taxable estate, so if you have substantial death benefits, you may want to consider passing insurance through an irrevocable life insurance trust (ILIT). See *Chapter 13* for more information.

- **Long-term care insurance**. This insurance can help pay for in-home and nursing home care, thereby saving more of your assets for your partner, your children, or other heirs. It is better to get this when you are younger because the rates are more favorable.

- **Disability insurance**. This insurance will replace some or all of your income should you become disabled. You have to look carefully at the limitations on this insurance, however. Some disability insurance requires complete or nearly complete disability rather than if you are unable to continue practicing your current job or profession.

- **Homeowner's or tenant's insurance**. If you own a home, you must have adequate insurance to cover the contents, the home, and liability for accidents on your property. Tenant insurance covers only the contents of your rental home or apartment. You should consider adding coverage for computers (especially laptops), and opt for replacement value.

- **Automobile insurance**. Once almost unobtainable in New Jersey, many companies are again providing coverage in the state. Be sure that the company allows both of you on a single plan, if you so desire.

Some insurance companies have been asking for proof of registration from same-sex partners who apply for insurance policies and discounts. This is not discriminatory if the insurance company applies this policy equally to married couples, requiring them to provide a marriage license. However, if the company applies this policy only to domestic partners, and refuses to provide the insurance even if the proof is not required, the policy is in violation of the Law Against Discrimination.

CHAPTER 10
PROPERTY RIGHTS

Traditionally, the law of property ownership for same-sex couples and other unmarried cohabitants was quite clear: property was assumed to be individually owned unless there was a clear indication otherwise, such as holding joint title in a home, or a valid written agreement between the parties. This rule often produced some harsh results when the couple broke up, or when one partner died without leaving a will.

The Domestic Partnership Act, unfortunately, has muddied the waters by addressing property ownership in only two places, both of which have to do with the termination of a domestic partnership. The Act gives the judge in a termination proceeding the jurisdiction to decide the "division and distribution of jointly held property." The Act also gives the judge the option of distributing individually or jointly owned property using equitable distribution, the same rules of distribution used in divorce. See *Distribution of Property* in *Chapter 15: Termination Proceedings*.

Another part of the Domestic Partnership Act that complicates property ownership for domestic partners has to do with the liability for debts and judgments. As previously discussed, the DPA limits your liability for your partner's debts, whether your partner contracted these debts before you registered or during your partnership. (See *Joint Liability for Debts* in *Chapter 3*.) If a creditor attempts to satisfy that debt by seizing your partner's property, it can be difficult to sort out what property belongs to you and is therefore exempt from the debt.

The New Jersey courts or legislature may ultimately resolve these and other questions relating to property ownership in domestic partnerships. Until they are clear, you and your partner should execute some form of agreement regarding property ownership in order to clearly establish who owns what in the partnership.

Whatever decisions you make about who owns what, your property agreement, whether set out in a separate written document or included in a domestic partnership agreement, will need to address three issues.

First, both you and your partner need to be clear on what property each of you brings to the partnership and what property belongs to each of you individually. If you have lived together for some time before you registered, and particularly if you acquired significant property together during that time, you also need to agree on a date when your partnership began. Second, you will need to decide how you will handle titled property, such as real estate and motor vehicles. Third, if you end up terminating your partnership, you will need some basis for dividing up your property.

BASICS OF PROPERTY RIGHTS

You and your partner probably own many kinds of property. For example, you may own a home or other real estate, which is referred to as real property. Your home furnishings are your personal property, and they are also considered movable property because the location of the property can be changed. Even your pets are a form of property. Typically, property is legally classified as follows:

- **Real property**. This kind of property consists of land, and everything built upon it or growing on the land. Even if you live in a high-rise condominium, you have ownership in real property.

- **Personal property**. Generally, all property other than real property is classified as personal property. Personal property can consist of things which you physically possess, such as an automobile or a television, as well as things which evidence debt, such as a promissory note or a bank account.[1] Cash is a common form of property.

- **Tangible property**. Property that has a real existence and a physical form, whether it is personal property or real property is characterized as tangible.

- **Intangible property**. Property that has no physical form, such as copyrights, patents and trademarks (called intellectual property.) Other kinds of intangible property include legal claims against another person, such as a claim for damages as the result of an accident.

- **Titled property**. Certain kinds of property are required to have a written indication of ownership that is recorded somewhere, such as in a county clerk's office. Common forms of titled property are real estate, automobiles and boats.

Property rights are also classified in certain ways depending upon whether it is individually owned or owned by two or more persons.

- **Tenancy in common**. A form of property right where two or more persons hold an undivided interest in the property. The share of a deceased tenant in common is part of his or her estate.

- **Joint tenancy**. A form of property ownership where two or more persons hold an undivided interest in the property. The share of a deceased tenant goes to the surviving joint tenants.

- **Tenants by the entirety**. A tenancy that is created between spouses and which has automatic rights of survivorship. Currently, tenancy by the entirety is limited to husband and wife in New Jersey. Dissolution of the marriage converts the ownership to tenancy in common.

Life estates or terms of years

Two other forms of property right are life estates and term of years.

- A life estate is a right to remain in possession of property (usually a home) until the life tenant dies.

- A term of years is a right to remain in possession of property for a specific period of time.

If you own your home individually, you may grant your partner a life estate in your Will. This allows your partner to remain in your home after your death, until he or she dies or chooses to vacate, after which the ownership of your home goes to another person.

Joint tenants and tenants in common have equal rights to possession and occupancy. The main difference, however, is the right of survivorship, which means that when one tenant dies, his or her rights in the property pass automatically to the surviving cotenant(s), without the need to convey the rights in

---

1.   A bank account is a form of debt owed to you by a bank.

a Will. This can help reduce the possibility of a challenge to a Will in probate court. See *Chapter 11: Estate Planning* for more information.

How Ownership Arises

You become an owner of property when you receive title to the property in some way. Most commonly, you acquire ownership (title) when you purchase property. Other ways you can obtain ownership in property include receiving a gift from someone, by inheritance, or by creating something, such as a book or painting.[2]

There are formal requirements associated with acquiring certain types of property, such as purchasing an automobile or home. For example, when you purchase a home, you acquire ownership at closing by taking possession of the deed, which is subsequently then with the clerk in the county in which the property is located. Similarly, when you buy a car or boat, the prior title holder transfers ownership by signing the title and delivering the title to you. The transfer of the signed title is what gives you the right to take possession of the car.

REAL ESTATE

Although you and your partner are required to have a common residence in order to be eligible to register under the Domestic Partnership Act, you are not required to jointly own or lease your common residence in order to register; the common residence can be owned or leased in one partner's name only. Neither are you required to live full time in New Jersey and, in some cases, you may not be required to live in New Jersey at all. For more information on the common residency requirement, see *Chapter 5: Eligibility*.

Regardless of whether you live together in a rented home or in a home that one or both of you own, you will need to have one or more real property agreements. If you and your partner are renting your home, you should read the following. If, on the other hand, you and your partner are, or plan to be homeowners, then you should read *Owning a Home*, below.

Renting a Home

If you and your partner intend to rent a home or apartment, you need to determine whether you will lease your home in both names or only one. This may not be up to you, but may be a requirement imposed by your landlord.

If you lease a home or apartment in both of your names, you and your partner need to be aware that this makes you each equally responsible for the entire rent. If your partner refuses or is unable to pay his or her share of the rent, you are still legally responsible for the entire rent payment, and the landlord can sue both of you or either of you for back rent as well as any expenses.

To counteract this, you and your partner should execute a written agreement. This agreement could be in a separate document, or it could be a clause added to your written domestic partnership agreement. This is particularly important if you and your partner have agreed to unequal contributions to your rent or if the lease is in one partner's name only.

Even without this agreement, you and your partner agree to be jointly responsible for your basic living

---

2.   You cannot obtain ownership of something by theft. Even though a stolen item may be in your possession, you can never acquire title.

expenses as part of your Affidavit of Domestic Partnership. Therefore, unless you have an agreement to the contrary, it is possible that one partner could sue the other for failure to pay his or her share of this and other household expenses.

Rental Discrimination

Some landlords may attempt to restrict your right to rent a residence together, or to live together in a home or apartment that is rented in only one partner's name. If these restrictions do not apply equally to opposite-sex married couples, the landlord is probably violating the New Jersey Law Against Discrimination, as amended by the Domestic Partnership Act.

For example, if a landlord allows a married couple to lease an apartment in only one spouse's name, but requires you and your registered partner to both sign the lease, the landlord is in violation of the Law Against Discrimination (NJ LAD). A similar violation would occur if a landlord refused to rent to you because you were "unrelated."

Whether you may move into your partner's rented home or apartment may also be a problem if your partner's lease requires him or her to obtain permission prior to adding a roommate. Such a restriction would have to apply equally to an opposite sex couple, however, or it would be in violation of the New Jersey Law Against Discrimination.

As an example of this, assume that the lease restricts you from allowing another person to move in with you without the landlord's permission. Your landlord would be required to allow your registered partner to move in with you if a newlywed would be allowed to live with his or her spouse. See *Chapter 7: Discrimination* for more information.

OWNING YOUR HOME

If you and/or your partner are or intend to become homeowners, you will need to determine how you will hold title to your home and how each of you will contribute to the upkeep of that home. Because the Domestic Partnership Act fails to address some important issues related to estate planning and taxation, you will need to use some careful planning in order to minimize the inequities imposed on same-sex couples.

There are several ways you and your partner can handle home ownership. First, one partner can own the home and the other pay a monthly cost - a form of rent. Second, both partners could purchase the home jointly at the same time, with each paying approximately the same costs. Third, one partner owns the home but transfers equity in some way to the other.

Individual Ownership

If one of you owns the home, the other is essentially a tenant, paying some agreed-upon amount (or nothing at all) to the other toward the monthly expenses. This has the drawback that the partner who owns the home has all of the equity in the home and the other partner has no ownership rights and no opportunity to build up ownership rights. This may be ideal if the non-owner partner has substantial debts, since a creditor could not attach a lien to the property.

If you choose this form or home ownership, the property-owning partner needs to make arrangements in his or her will to ensure that the surviving partner either inherits the house or has some right to remain in the house after the owner dies.

Joint ownership

There are two forms of joint ownership for unmarried couples in New Jersey, joint tenancy and tenancy in common. The main difference between the two is that joint tenants hold ownership with a right of survivorship. This means that when one joint tenant dies, his or her title to the property automatically transfers to the surviving tenant, completely independent of the deceased tenant's Will. Tenants in common, however, do not have rights of survivorship, as a result of which a deceased owner's share passes according to his or her Will. See *Chapter 13: Estate Planning* for more information.

By default in New Jersey, any transfer of property to two or more persons creates a tenancy in common, rather than a joint tenancy. In order to create a joint tenancy, there are four conditions that must exist at the time title transfers to you and your partner. These four conditions, called "unities," require that you must have equal interest in the property, at the same time, with equal right to possession, and in the same conveyance. In addition to these four unities of interest, time, possession and conveyance, the deed must expressly state that the ownership is intended to be as joint tenants. It is important that all four unities are present at the time the deed is transferred because otherwise, the joint tenancy is not created and you and your partner will hold the property as tenants in common.

As a result, when you and your partner take ownership of property as joint owners, at closing you must have equal interest, at the same time, with undivided rights to possession, and take ownership in the same conveyance. In order to ensure you have equal interest, you should each contribute an equal amount to the down payment and closing costs. See *Chapter 9: Money, Taxes and Insurance* for suggestions on ways to equalize your ownership.

Your deed should also have words that express the intention to hold the property jointly, such as "joint tenants with rights of survivorship and not as tenants in common," in order to make ownership clear.

If you own your home and want to create a joint tenancy with your partner, you no longer have to convey your ownership to another person (called a "straw man") in order to unity of ownership at closing. Instead, you can now grant your sole ownership to you and your partner directly at closing.

Terminating Joint Ownership

Just as you must have the four unities at the time you take ownership of the property, the four unities of time, title, interest and possession must remain in place in order for the joint tenancy to continue. If any of these unities are destroyed, the ownership becomes that of tenants in common and the rights of survivorship cease. These unities can be destroyed by, for example, conveying part ownership to another person, or forcing one partner to leave the joint property. In order to avoid possible destruction of your joint tenancy, you and your partner should require all decisions regarding jointly owned property to be agreed to by both partners in writing. See *Modifying Rights and Obligations* in *Chapter 3* for more on domestic partnership and other agreement.

Joint tenancies can also be terminated through a proceeding called a partition. This is accomplished by filing a complaint in Superior Court asking for the property to be divided. If you have filed for termination of a registered domestic partnership, your complaint should include a request that joint property be partitioned after termination is granted. See *Chapter 15: Termination Proceedings*.

Changing Title

If one of you owns your home and you decide to convert from single ownership to joint ownership, or if you both own your home as tenants in common, you need to change the title. This will entail several fees, such as a title search fee, attorney fees, and recording fees, and may trigger some additional costs depending upon whether you are adding your partner to the deed or changing the percentage of ownership.

When it comes to real estate, married couples get several financial breaks that are not provided to same-sex couples. First, they are exempt from any gift taxes on property they give to their spouses, regardless of the value. Second, they are exempt from the real estate transfer fee that New Jersey imposes on sellers of real property. Third, if one spouse is eligible for a property tax exemption or reduction, both partners get the benefit of any reduction in taxes.

Domestic partners, on the other hand, get none of these advantages. Thus, if one partner transfers all or part of his or her interest in real estate to the other, the transfer is a taxable gift, if it is not for value, or a sale on which the real estate transfer fee will be imposed. In addition, any property tax reduction or exemption would only be applicable to a percentage of the house and not the entire property.

There isn't much you can do to eliminate these inequities, other than taking legal action as one couple has done recently, or by lobbying for modifications to the law. You should be aware, however, that there are extra costs associated with home ownership by same-sex couples.

Mortgages

You are not required to jointly obtain a mortgage on your jointly-owned home. In some cases, one partner's credit may prevent you from obtaining a better interest rate or even from obtaining a mortgage at all. However, you need to determine how to equalize your payments on the mortgage so you do not inadvertently create unequal ownership and, perhaps, cause your ownership to change from joint tenancy to tenants in common. See *Terminating Joint Ownership*, above.

You also need to decide how you will handle the mortgage interest deduction. If you are both making equal payments, you both are entitled to split the deduction on your income tax return. On the other hand, it may be that only one of you needs the deduction. If that is the case, you should have an agreement to that effect.

Other Costs and Duties of Home Ownership

There are many other costs and responsibilities associated with home ownership. You and your partner need to determine who will handle these duties and who will pay these costs. If you and your partner have significant differences in your incomes, you should take into consideration work that is done when determining your contributions to your home. If you need to do this, you should specify the value of this work in an agreement between you.

Condo and Other Fees

If you and your partner are living in a condominium or a residential community with a homeowners' association, there will be fees that are separate from mortgage, taxes and insurance payments. You must decide who is responsible for making these payments as well as who will respond to homeowner or condo association complaints.

Improvements, Maintenance and Repairs

You and your partner should also decide who will take responsibility for improvements and maintenance of your home, particularly if there are significant costs involved. If one partner is particularly handy and is making these repairs around the house, you may want to consider the value of this work as a contribution to equity in your home.

Proof of Ownership

One problem that joint ownership of assets causes is proving your percentage of ownership. When one joint tenant dies, the IRS and the New Jersey Department of Taxation take the position that the deceased tenant owns 100% of the equity in the joint property, and will include this in the decedent's taxable estate. It is up to the surviving tenant to prove his or her equity ownership in the property.

For that reason, it is important that one of you keeps good records as to each partner's initial contribution, maintenance, payments, etc.

AUTOMOBILES AND OTHER TITLED PROPERTY

Other titled property you may own includes automobiles, boats and recreational vehicles. Wherever possible, you should jointly own these items with a right of survivorship, and you may need to indicate this on your title.

There are three problems with separate ownership of this type of property. First, if you leave your automobile or other motor vehicle to your partner in your Will, or if you transfer ownership to your partner during your lifetime, the transfer of title will be subject to a transfer fee and sales tax. Second, if you leave your automobile or other motor vehicle to your partner in your Will, he or she will take ownership subject to any loan noted on the title. Third, if you die, your partner does not have an automatic right to possession of your motor vehicle and, unlike a married spouse, you do not have a legal right to drive your deceased partner's car prior to probate.

The first problem is one that represents one of many discrepancies between the rights afforded domestic partners under the Domestic Partnership Act and those afforded to married couples. There is, unfortunately, no way to contractually avoid these taxes without modifying the law.

To alleviate the second problem, you may make arrangements in your will to either pay the balance of the automobile or other loan out of your estate, or allow him or her to take ownership subject to the loan but take out a separate insurance policy sufficient to cover the outstanding amount of any loan and name your partner as beneficiary.

To alleviate the third problem, you should include the right to use your automobile and other motor vehicles in an appropriate document. See *Rights of Entry and Possession*, below.

As a side note, you should be aware that it is discriminatory under the Law Against Discrimination for an insurance company to treat you and your registered partner as unrelated when it comes to insuring your automobile or other vehicle, if they treat married couples differently.

OTHER PROPERTY

Like any other couple, you and your partner will acquire lots of other property over the years. Some property will be purchased together and some will be purchased individually. Unlike married couples, property acquired by domestic partners is assumed to be individually owned except where you demonstrate an intent to own property jointly.

Personal Property Agreements

Unless you and your partner keep very accurate records about everything you purchase, you need to have some form of personal property agreement. Such an agreement can be structured in many ways. For example, you and your partner can agree that all items purchased by either of you or both of you together constitute joint property. Alternatively, you can agree that only property explicitly purchased from joint funds constitutes joint property and individually purchased items belong to the person who bought them.

Three things that you should address in a personal property agreement are how property purchased individually or jointly prior to registering your partnership should be owned, how items which you jointly purchase on credit are paid for, and how certain items are disposed of upon termination of your partnership.

In the first case, you may have acquired substantial property prior to registration, particularly if you and your partner have been together for any length of time. It may often be hard to separate out ownership of individual items from those that were intended to be jointly owned. The easiest thing to do is to separate out only those items that have particular personal meaning to you and list them as individually owned in the property agreement. All other property can be lumped together in a single statement declaring them to be jointly owned.

In the second case, you will most likely have to decide who will have responsibility for paying for the item. You can then give that partner the right to seek contribution for half of the cost of the item.

Finally, you need to decide how personal property will be divided if your partnership is terminated. As in the first case, you should first list particular items that belong to individual partners. You may then agree on one of several ways of dividing these items. For example, you may declare that all items will be distributed on a 50-50 basis, with the judge making the determination. Alternatively, you may declare that all items are to be valued and sold, with each partner having a right to bid the items, and with the proceeds from the sale of the remaining items split between you on an equal basis. A third alternative is to agree to submit any disputes on property disposition to a mediator. See *Chapter 15: Termination Proceedings* for more on distribution of property and property settlement agreements.

The personal property agreement can be set out as a separate contract, or it can be included as a clause in your domestic partnership agreement. See *Modifying Rights and Obligations* in *Chapter 3* for more on domestic partnership agreements.

RIGHTS OF ENTRY AND POSSESSION

Unlike opposite-sex married couples, you and your partner do not have an automatic right to use property that belongs to your partner if he or she should die. For example, if your partner holds separate title to his or her automobile, you have no right to drive it, store it, or even remove anything from it, should your partner die. If your home is leased or owned in your partner's name only, you may not have the right to enter or stay in your home, or even to remove your own possessions, if your partner dies.

If you or your partner own separate property, such as an automobile or a house, you need to execute documents that grant each other rights of possession and entry. These documents should be notarized and should specifically state that you have the right to remain in possession of your partner's home, and to drive your partner's car, during the period between your partner's death or incapacity and probate or adjudication of your partner's estate.

PETS

For many of us, our pets are like children - so why treat them with any less love because you are unable to care for them. However, in the eyes of the law, animals are simply another form of property.

In order to ensure that your pets are taken care of if you become disabled or die, you and your partner should execute a pet directive. You may also want to consider adding language regarding the care, feeding, financial responsibility, and ownership of your pets to your domestic partnership agreement, particularly if you own financially valuable pets, such as show dogs or horses.

A pet directive simply appoints someone to take possession of and care for your pets should you and your partner be unable to do so. The pet directive should be a separate document from a Will because it should come into effect as soon as you become incapacitated or die, thereby making sure someone is looking after your pets immediately. The directive should simply state that, in the event that you die or are incapable of taking care of your pets, possession passes to your partner or to another designated caretaker.

You should also name a backup caretaker for your pets in case your partner is also unable to care for them. If you name a friend or relative, be sure to check with them to see if they are willing to take your pet. As a backup, you can also name one of New Jersey's many "no kill" animal shelters or one of the many rescue organizations for purebred dogs or cats. You may also want to consider including some form of bequest in your Will to help with the costs of caring for your pets.

Be sure to put information about your preferred veterinarian in the directive, if you have one, along with any special instructions. This document should also give permission to enter your home and remove your pets along with their bedding, cages, food, toys and medicines. If you board your pets, you should also include permission for the kennel or other facility to release your pets to your care-taker, and should include a directive that your agent under a power of attorney, or your executor either directly pay or reimburse any bills for their keep and care. Keep the original directive with your original powers of attorney for financial matters and give copies to the same people who have copies of that document.

CHAPTER 11
PARENTING

Another important area of the law that the Domestic Partnership Act completely ignores is the issue of parenting. There are no provisions in the DPA that provide registered domestic partners with any automatic rights or responsibilities. Thus, if you and your partner have or intend to have children, you will need to rely on some combination of legal agreements and/or adoption proceedings in order to build your family.

If you and your partner have children, you need to have some form of parenting agreement, particularly if only one of you is the legal parent. This agreement should address several important issues, including:

- **Decision-making**. You and your partner need to decide who will make the medical and legal decisions about your children. If you are both the legal parents, then you both have an equal right to make these decisions. You should also decide who will be called in an emergency and make sure that person has all the legal permissions required to make medical decisions on behalf of the children.

- **Day-to-day Care**. If you and your partner both work outside the home, you should decide who will make arrangements for getting the children to and from school, day care, and after-school activities. You should also decide who will take the children to doctor and other appointments and who will be called in non-emergency situations.

- **Financial Support**. You need to decide if both of you will contribute to the support of all your children or simply for your own children. The financial support agreement should address the smaller questions, such as who will pay a child's allowance, as well as the larger questions, such as who will contribute toward a child's education. You should be aware that, if you contribute substantially to the support of your partner's children, you might be required to pay child support if your partnership is terminated, even if you have not legally adopted any of his or her children.

- **Dispute Resolution**. Your agreement should consider how you would resolve any disputes between you and your partner when it comes to parenting.

- **Termination Issues**. You and your partner should address the questions of custody, visitation rights and child support after termination. Although these decisions would not be considered binding by a family court judge, who must act in the best interests of the child, they might be considered by the judge and, if reasonable, could be particularly persuasive.

Another important area you need to address is that of estate planning. In addition to providing for your partner in your will, you will need to provide for your own children, if any, and/or your partner's children, if you so desire. If the children are minors, you will want to set up some form of trust, in which case you will also need to designate one or more trustees.

In your will, you should also designate a primary and a secondary guardian over your children.

Finally, unless you and your partner are both legal parents of your children, you will need to execute health care proxies in order to ensure that the non-parent has the right to make medical decisions if the child's legal parent is unavailable or unable to do so.

Even if you and your partner do not have any children, and you do not intend to have any children, you may still need to address parenting issues in your domestic partnership agreement. For example, you may initially decide against children but one or the other of you may change your mind at a later time. If you think this is at all likely, you should probably include some form of general parenting language in your agreement addressing questions such as who will support the child and whether both will adopt the child.

CREATING A FAMILY

If you and your partner already have children, or intend to have a family in the future, you have four options available to you: (1) adoption, (2) giving birth using artificial insemination or surrogacy, (3) foster parenting, or (4) co-parenting. Each of these options has its strengths and weaknesses. None of these options, unfortunately, is found in the Domestic Partnership Act, which currently does not address parenting issues.

The first two options, adoption and giving birth, establish a legal relationship between parent and child that creates a set of enforceable rights and obligations, such as the child's right to support from the parent and the parent's right to control the child. This relationship extends equally to every child and to every parent and is independent of the parents' marital status. Once established, the parent and child relationship is recognized by all states and can only be terminated by a court.

The foster parent relationship comes about when a state agency or court places a child into the care of a single adult or couple. The obligations of the foster parent are similar to those of a natural or adoptive parent, but the rights are significantly less, and the agency or court may easily remove the foster child from the foster parent's care.

The last option, co-parenting, is similar to the stepparent-stepchild relationship. It carries with it few, if any, legally recognized rights or obligations, nearly all of which terminate when the co-parent's relationship with the natural parent ends.

The Parent-Child Relationship

In the 1970s, a standardized set of laws relating to parent-child relationship was developed, called the Uniform Parentage Act. Since that time, the UPA has been enacted in some form by all states, including New Jersey. As a result, a parent-child relationship established in one state is recognized in all others — at least, with regard to heterosexuals. For same-sex couples in legally recognized relationships, however, parenting has become a complex problem.

In New Jersey, as in most other states, a mother establishes her parent-child relationship by giving birth or by adoption. A father, on the other hand, establishes his parent-child relationship order of a court in this state or another, by signing a certificate of parentage and filing it with the State, or by adoption.

In addition, a man is the presumed biological parent of a child under several circumstances, including:

- If he was married to the child's mother and the child was born during the marriage or within nine months after the marriage was ended by divorce, annulment or his death; or

- If the child was born during an apparently legal marriage to the mother that is or could be declared invalid.

These presumptions can be overcome only by "clear and convincing evidence" to the contrary or by establishing that another man is the child's biological or adoptive father.

Adoption

In New Jersey, the requirements to adopt a child are fairly liberal. Any person who is at least 18 years of age and at least 10 years older than the prospective adoptee may adopt any other person. New Jersey has afforded single homosexuals and same-sex couples the same rights as any other adult.

One important consideration with adoption is that adoption is forever, creating a parent-child relationship that cannot be legally terminated. Adoption brings with it all the parental responsibilities that natural parents have, including health and welfare obligations, and continuing support obligations if your domestic partnership ends. Adoption, as with any life-altering relationship, should not be entered into without considerable forethought.

Adoption proceedings are initiated by filing a petition in the Family Part of the Superior Court-Chancery Division in your county. Costs will vary depending upon the cost of the home and background investigation. If the judge finds the adoption to be in the child's best interests, the court will grant the adoption.

Normally, the judgment of adoption terminates the natural parents' rights and obligations, except where a stepparent is adopting his or her spouse's natural child. This stepparent exception has been applied to same-sex couples so that both partners are the legal parents. Following the adoption, the child's birth certificate will be changed to list both partners.

Individual Stranger Adoption

As in many other states, a single GLBT adult may adopt a child in New Jersey. Unlike married couples, you and your domestic partner are not required to jointly adopt, nor are you required to obtain your partner's consent to the adoption.

For domestic partners, however, the court may question why only one partner is adopting the child. Neither your domestic partnership nor the unwillingness of one partner to join in the adoption is currently a barrier to this kind of adoption, but you should be aware that the decision to allow the adoption to proceed is one in which the judge has broad discretion. You should therefore be prepared to show that the individual adoption is in the child's best interests.

If you are in a domestic partnership and you choose to adopt a child individually, your partner can still take on the role of co-parent. Furthermore, he or she can later adopt your child through a second-parent adoption.

Joint Adoption

New Jersey is one of only a handful of states that permit unmarried couples, including same-sex couples, to jointly adopt a child. This can save you considerable time and cost over separate proceedings, since both of you would be listed as the prospective parents. Once the adoption is finalized, both of you have equal rights and responsibilities toward your child.

Second-Parent Adoption

If you or your partner, or both, have biological or adopted children of your own that precede your partnership, you may want to consider second-parent adoption. You will also need to undertake second-parent adoption if one of you has become a parent via insemination, surrogacy or egg donation but both of you want to be the legal parents. See the discussion below for more information.

Normally, these kinds of adoptions can often proceed smoothly, since the partner with the child is clearly not objecting to the adoption. There can be significant problem if the child has two legal parents and the other parent objects to the adoption. These objections are usually on the basis that a same-sex relationship is not a healthy environment in which to raise a child.

The other parent's objections are not fatal, however, and a judge can allow the adoption to proceed if he or she believes it is in the best interest of the child. If the other parent's objections continue to cause problems, you and your attorney should discuss terminating their parental rights.

For married couples, the court is entitled to waive the home investigation when it involves a stepparent adoption. If you and your partner have registered as domestic partners, you should consider asking the court for such a waiver, since it can save you a considerable cost.

Giving Birth

As an alternative to adoption, some same-sex couples are resorting to having their own child through insemination or surrogacy, in some cases using assisted reproductive technologies such as egg or embryo implantation. For example, a lesbian couple may choose to have one partner inseminated by an anonymous semen donor, or a gay male couple may find a woman willing to bear a child for them. In some cases, a lesbian partner has been implanted with her partner's fertilized egg as a way of sharing the parenting roles.

Regardless of the medical method used, all of these have important legal implications, most notably, that only one partner is currently considered the legal parent of the child in New Jersey. If you and your partner choose one of these methods of parenting, the other partner will still have to undergo a second-parent adoption.

If you and your partner choose one of these methods to create your family, you absolutely must consult with an attorney to ensure that only you and your partner have legal rights in regard to your children.

Artificial Insemination

In some states, including New Jersey, the use of artificial insemination by a married couple creates a special exception in the Parentage Act. When a married woman is artificially inseminated with semen from another man, her husband is treated as the legal father of the resulting child if the insemination is carried out under the supervision of a licensed doctor and the husband consents in writing. The donor in that situation has no legal relationship to the child conceived by the married woman even though genetically related.

In New Jersey, when an unmarried woman is artificially inseminated the semen donor is not the legal father **unless** he agrees in writing. The child born under these circumstances has only one legal parent, which has enormous implications for lesbian couples, since there is no need to provide notice to the father prior to adoption.

Vermont does not have a law regarding the use of artificial insemination by married or unmarried couples. However, in a recent case involving civil unions, the court held that a child born to a lesbian couple as a result of artificial insemination of one of them was a child of the civil union.

Surrogate Parenting

There are two kinds of surrogacy: the traditional form involves the insemination of a woman who contributes the egg, and gestational surrogacy, in which the surrogate is implanted with another woman's fertilized egg. In the first case, the surrogate is the genetic mother and birth mother. In the second case, she is the birth mother but not the genetic mother.

New Jersey does not permit traditional surrogacy but does allow uncompensated gestational surrogacy so long as any contract does not provide compensation and does not require the surrogate to surrender the child. Furthermore, the surrogate must not surrender the child to the intended parents for 72 hours, although she may surrender the child to an agency immediately.

For lesbian or male couples, surrogacy in New Jersey will invariably result in one partner being the natural parent and the other having to undergo second-parent adoption. For lesbian couples an extra level of intricacy is involved if one partner's fertilized egg is implanted in the other. In that case, there should be a clearly written contract as to which partner is the legal parent.

In a few states, including California, Connecticut, Massachusetts and Vermont, surrogacy agreements are permitted.

Foster Parenting

Another option you may wish to consider is foster parenting. New Jersey allows same-sex couples to provide foster homes and holds them to the same standards as heterosexual couples. The New Jersey Department of Youth and Family Services regularly places foster children in qualified same-sex households. For more information, see their web site at *http://www.njfostercare.org*.

Co-parenting

A co-parent, like a stepparent, is a partner who takes on the role of a parent without legally adopting the child. You and your partner are not required to formally adopt each other's children in order to live as a family. In fact, many couples, same-sex or heterosexual, have raised each other's children together without formal adoption.

In the past, co-parenting has been the only option for same-sex couples who were legally prohibited from second-parent adoption. Now that New Jersey no longer prohibits joint adoption or second-parent adoption, co-parenting may simply become an option as opposed to the norm among same-sex couples.

Co-parenting does have some significant disadvantages. First, it becomes harder to prove that a child is your dependent if you have no legal relationship. This is particularly true in regard to matters such as federal tax deductions and federal entitlement programs like Aid to Families with Dependent Children or Medicaid, which are prohibited by the federal Defense of Marriage Act from recognizing same-sex couples.

Second, you may find it difficult as a co-parent to participate in child-care issues such as medical care, visitation, schooling, and other matters that may require you to prove that you are either a child's parent or legal guardian. A co-parent simply has few, if any, legal rights in regard to his or her partner's children.

PARENTAL RIGHTS AND RESPONSIBILITIES

Because the Domestic Partnership Act does not currently address parenting, parental rights and responsibilities are found elsewhere in New Jersey law. For biological and adoptive parents, the rights and responsibilities are established when the parent-child relationship is formed. For non-adoptive partners, however, there is no legal parent-child relationship, although there are some currently recognized rights and responsibilities equivalent to those of a stepparent.

CUSTODY AND VISITATION

New Jersey has recently recognized that former partners may have custody and visitation rights after their partnership has ended, even if they have not legally adopted a child. The relationship is created based upon a finding that the partner has become a "psychological parent" as a result of bonding with the child. The courts have held that these "psychological parent" relationships, once formed, should be protected where possible. For more on child custody and support issues after termination of a domestic partnership, see *Parenting Issues* in *Chapter 15: Termination Proceedings.*

Although there have been no cases involving same-sex couples, New Jersey courts have sometimes imposed support obligations on stepparents after a marriage has terminated. The basis for this support obligation is that the stepparent had taken on a financial role during the marriage that would considerably harm the child if the support were withdrawn once the marriage terminated. A similar ruling involving domestic partners could emerge once the New Jersey courts begin holding termination proceedings.

Psychological Parent

Some states, including New Jersey, recognize that a kind of parent-child relationship can arise where a child has bonded with another adult and has come to look to that adult as a parent.

FAMILY MEDICAL LEAVE

Under federal and state law, your employer may be required to provide you with up to 12 weeks of family leave for any of the following reasons:

- The birth of your child and to care for your child;

- The placement with you of a child for adoption or foster care and to care for the newly placed child; or

- To care for a family member, including your child, parent or spouse, during a serious illness.

Family medical leave is generally unpaid but you may apply any paid leave you may have accrued, and your employer must continue your medical insurance, including payment of premiums. Upon your return from leave, you are entitled to be returned to your prior position or a position with equivalent benefits, pay, and other terms of employment, even if you were replaced or your position was eliminated during your absence.

The federal Family and Medical Leave Act (FMLA) provides up to 12 workweeks of leave during any 12 month period whereas the New Jersey law limits you to 12 workweeks during any 24 month period.

Federal Rights

Because of the federal Defense of Marriage Act, the federal FMLA would not apply to you if your partner was giving birth or adopting your child, nor would your partner, your partner's parents, or your partner's children be considered family members. On the other hand, it does apply if a child is being placed with both of you for adoption or foster care, or if you are adopting your partner's child. Furthermore, unlike married couples working for the same employer, you and your partner are not limited to a total of 12 workweeks but may each take up to 12 workweeks of FMLA leave.

State Protection

Unlike the federal FMLA, the New Jersey Family Leave Act probably does allow you to take unpaid leave following the birth of your partner's child. Under the New Jersey act, "child" includes a biological, adopted, or resource family child, or a stepchild. Although this right has yet not been tested, state courts have treated same-sex partners equivalent to a stepparent for purposes of adoption and it is reasonable to believe that they would do so here, if it could be shown that it was "in the best interests of the child."

Furthermore, although "family member" is defined in the New Jersey act to mean a child, parent, or spouse, it may also be reasonably found that the term now includes registered domestic partners. If so, you may be able to take leave to care for your seriously ill partner, as well as your partner's parents.

RECOGNITION OF SAME-SEX PARENTS

Recognition of parental rights involving same-sex partners or ex-partners vary from state to state, and you should be aware of how other states will view your family before visiting or relocating to such states. In general, New Jersey couples will find the highest level of protection comes from parental rights that are recognized independent of your partnership.

For New Jersey couples, parent-child relationships are not currently created as a result of registration in a domestic partnership but instead arise from an order or a judgment of a court. In most states, these judgments or orders will be respected under the Full Faith and Credit Clause of the United States Constitution. Some states, however, have taken a harder position on GLBT rights involving children and, as a parent you must make yourself aware of and avoid these states.

Most often, these problems arise out of custody or support disputes between former same-sex partners. In other cases, they have arisen in the context of adoptions, when an attempt is made to change the birth certificate of a child born in another state that prohibits adoptions by homosexuals or same-sex couples.

Parentage Determinations

For same-sex couples, parentage determinations that arise out of the couple's legal status are the most likely to be ignored in other states. The states of Vermont, California, Connecticut and Massachusetts have provided all rights of marriage under their laws to same-sex couples who register (or marry) in those states. Among the rights of marriage are those involving parentage determinations that arise out of the legally recognized relationship. For example, a child born to a married lesbian couple in Massachusetts, or the partners in a Vermont civil union, is legally presumed to be the child of both spouses.

For states that have adopted Defense of Marriage laws, such as Virginia or Ohio, these laws frequently forbid recognition of these legal relationships and any rights and benefits that arise from these relationships. Since same-sex couples cannot be expected to avoid these states, legal collisions will occur.

One such dispute, currently being heard in the Supreme Court of Vermont and in the Court of Appeals of Virginia, involves a custody dispute arising out of a Vermont civil union. The Virginia court has refused to recognize a former same-sex partner as the parent of a child born during the civil union, claiming that it is forbidden to do so under Virginia's Defense of Marriage laws. The Vermont court, which had original jurisdiction, has declared the birth mother in contempt of court for failing to allow court-ordered visitation by the former partner.

On the other hand, states that have legal protections for same-sex couples are more likely to recognize parental rights created as a result of these legal relationships. It is not yet clear whether these parental determinations would be recognized in New Jersey.

Adoptions

Although New Jersey does not prohibit adoption by gays or lesbians, there are several states that currently do have such prohibitions, including Florida and Mississippi. Many more are considering enacting such a prohibition. It isn't clear at this time whether these states will recognize your adoption or parental rights derived from such adoptions.

For example, Oklahoma passed a law prohibiting the recognition of same-sex adoptions from other states or countries. As a result, an Oklahoma gay couple had to sue to force the state to list both as parents on the child's birth certificate. In another case, the Nebraska Supreme Court upheld a Pennsylvania second-parent adoption, reversing a lower court's rejection of that adoption.

Among neighboring states, Pennsylvania and New York allow both joint adoption and second-parent adoptions by same-sex couples. Some courts in Delaware have allowed second-parent adoptions, but not joint adoptions. It is likely that these states would recognize a second-parent adoption decree from New Jersey.

The questionable status of adoptions by New Jersey GLBT persons and couples in other states should not be your only consideration. There is also danger that certain states may be so hostile toward such adoptions that they may consider them a danger to the child and remove the child from the home. You may also find that only one partner is allowed to make medical and other decisions on behalf of your children or to visit them in a hospital or school.

Custody and Support Enforcement

All states are supposed to abide by the custody decrees made in another state under a federal law called the Parental Kidnapping Act. The law is designed to prevent a parent from fleeing to another state or country with their child in order to prevent the other parent from having custody or visitation with the child. All states recognize a final decree from another state but some will attempt to use a "public policy" exception and refuse to give full faith and credit to the decree. The case involving the lesbian couple from Vermont may help to clarify this situation.

Where a dispute involves a co-parent, however, another state may find it easier to ignore the Parental Kidnapping Act and refuse to enforce a custody or visitation order, since the co-parent is without substantial recognition in most states.

Even the most hostile states, however, are unlikely to refuse to enforce a child support order, since it would often result in the parent needing some form of state financial assistance. Even if the support order arose out of a legal same-sex relationship, states like Virginia can be expected to ignore public policy and require enforcement of the order.

Just passing through?

When traveling with your children, you should be certain to carry with you advance directives or other documents that you have legal rights regarding any children that are not your biological or legally adopted children. Your advance directives should also specifically state that your children, and your partner's children if they are with you, should be placed in the custody of your partner or another trusted adult if you are incapacitated or killed.

You should also carry medical authorizations for any child that is not your biological or legally adopted child. In many states, you will not be able to authorize medical treatment in an emergency.

CHAPTER 12

HEALTH, DISABILITY AND END OF LIFE ISSUES

As part of the findings and declarations included in the Domestic Partnership Act, the Legislature clearly stated its recognition that the lack of any right to make emergency medical decisions for a partner was among the greatest indignities suffered by couples that were unable to legally marry.

Although that sentiment is debatable, it is a fact that same-sex couples have often been prevented from making the same kind of life-and-death health care decisions that married couples take for granted.

Even though more and more hospitals and health care facilities have independently implemented policies allowing domestic partners to visit each other and to participate in health care decisions, these policies have not been backed by law. Furthermore, since these are policies and not laws, they can be rescinded by unsympathetic staff.

HEALTH CARE RIGHTS

With the enactment of the Domestic Partnership Act, many of the health care directives that domestic partners had to contractually provide are now, in part, embodied in the law. The fact that these rights are now provided under the Act does not mean you do not need these directives.

Last year, the New Jersey Department of Health and Senior Services released an advisory letter to all hospitals and other health care facilities advising them on the health care and visitation rights of registered and unregistered domestic partners. A copy of this letter is provided in *Appendix R: Hospital Compliance Guide*. Thus, health care providers are now on notice of your rights.

Visitation Rights

Registered domestic partners are now entitled to the same visitation rights in hospitals and other health facilities as married spouses. The right to visit extends to the children of a domestic partner as well as to the domestic partner of a patient's parent or child.

You must be allowed to visit your hospitalized domestic partner, even if other family members object, unless one or more of the following conditions apply:

- The hospital or other facility does not allow any other visitors;

- The staff has reasonably determined that your presence would endanger the health or safety of a patient, a staff member, another visitor, or would cause significant disruption; or

- Your partner has indicated that he or she does not want you to visit.

You do not have free reign, however. The hospital or other facility is entitled to establish reasonable visitation rules and restrictions, including the right to limit hours and number of visitors, so long as these are equally applied to all family members.

Immediate Family

For many health-care related purposes, the DPA has expanded the definition of "immediate family" to include a domestic partner, and the domestic partner's parents and adult children. Although the Act does not include a domestic partner's minor children, this is most likely an oversight, and minor children should be considered immediate family.

If either you or your partner has a family member and you do not want them to visit you in a hospital or other health care facility, you should execute a hospital visitation directive. This document can help you exclude family members who you believe will be disruptive or who you simply do not want to have visit when you are not well. For more information on this document, see *Hospital Visitation Agreements*, below.

Designating Your Health Care Representative

You and your partner may designate each other as your health care representative in an advance directive, such as a living will or medical proxy directive (also called a ***medical power of attorney***.) Once appointed in a valid advance directive, you and your partner has the legal authority to participate in each other's health care decision making process and to make health care decision's on each other's behalf.

If you have not specifically designated a particular person as your health care representative in an advance directive, or if the person you have designated is unavailable, unwilling or unable to serve, your domestic partner or other family member is automatically designated. See *Appendix R: Hospital Compliance Letter*.

Do I need a written directive?

Strictly speaking, if you are registered, you do not need a written directive naming you as your partner's designated agent for health care and financial purposes. Section 2 (d) of the Domestic Partnership Act makes it clear that registered domestic partners have the "right to make medical or legal decisions" for an incapacitated partner.

Unfortunately, hospitals, banks and others are not clear on this concept and the matter has not been decided by the courts, so it is a good idea to execute written directives. Furthermore, your rights as domestic partners are not recognized in most states outside New Jersey, so you need to have written directives to back you up.

Your designation of your registered domestic partner as your health care representative automatically ends if your partnership is legally terminated, unless the directive specifically states that the designation continues after termination. For more information, see *Advance Directives* later in this chapter.

Miscellaneous Consents

The Domestic Partnership Act allows you to give consent on behalf of a deceased or legally incompetent partner, if required to disclose medical records if your partner is known or suspected to have AIDS or HIV infection. You may also consent to an autopsy on a deceased domestic partner.

Tissue and Organ Donation and Disposition of Remains

As a registered domestic partner, the Domestic Partnership Act gives a registered domestic partner priority over all other family members when it comes to providing consent to organ or tissue donation. Consent may only be provided in the absence of actual notice (usually written) of a contrary intent by the deceased. After removal of the part or parts, the deceased's body will be returned to his or her domestic partner for disposition of the remains.

In another of the many oversights in the Domestic Partnership Act, you otherwise have no automatic right to claim your deceased partner's remains, or to make arrangements for his or her funeral, unless you acquire this right to consent to tissue or organ donation.

Under the New Jersey Cemetery Act, even the most sympathetic funeral director would be legally required to follow the directives of the deceased partner's relatives. Only if the deceased had no living relatives would his or her domestic partner have any right, and this right would be equal to that of any other interested stranger.

There are only two ways to alter this unfortunate oversight. First, you may go to court seeking an order from a court, something that is far from your mind during such a trying time. Alternatively, you and your partner may execute a disposition of remains directive in advance, as recommended in *End of Life Issues*, below.

ADVANCE DIRECTIVES

Although the Domestic Partnership Act provides you with rights equal to those of a married couple in regard to making health care decisions for each other, it is not a substitute for proper health care and end of life planning. After you register, you and your partner should make sure that you have executed advanced directives for health care, such as a health care proxy or a living will. Other types of advanced directives include financial powers of attorney, pet directives, and rights to use or occupy property.

These documents are particularly important if you travel to other states or countries, where your domestic partnership may not have any legal recognition. When you travel, you should carry copies of these documents with you in case you or your partner need emergency medical care.

Under New Jersey law, hospitals and other health care facilities must make a routine inquiry as to whether you have an advance directive. If you do have one, the attending physician must keep a copy of your advance directive in your file.

An advance directive is not operative until it is given to your physician or other responsible person at the health care facility and it is determined that you lack capacity.

Living Will or Health Care Directive

This document, known in New Jersey as a Health Care Instruction Directive, is a directive to your physician that states whether or not the physician should take extraordinary measures to keep you alive (such as maintaining you on life support or intravenous feeding) or whether you should be kept comfortable and allowed to die peacefully, should you have a terminal condition. Be sure to discuss this with your doctor and give a copy to your primary care physician.

For women, there should always be a clause included that determines how your instructions should be interpreted if you are found to be pregnant at the time the directive comes into effect. In New Jersey, there are three alternatives for pregnancy directives. At one extreme, you may direct the health care provider to follow your instructions regardless of whether you are pregnant, even though it will result in the death of the fetus. At the other extreme, you may direct the health care provider that your instructions are to be suspended until either you give birth or the pregnancy naturally terminates. Alternatively, you may direct your provider to suspend your instructions, but only if it can be determined that the fetus, if carried to term, will be born physically and/or mentally able.

In all cases, you should also include an instruction that requires your care to be transferred to another health care facility, physician or other medical personnel if that facility or person is unable, for moral reasons, to abide by your directives. For example, if the nearest hospital in an emergency is owned by a religious organization, and you have included a directive that would violate the policies of that hospital, such as aborting an unborn child, you can require the hospital to transfer your care as soon as possible to another hospital that is able to follow your instructions.

Proxy Directive or Medical Power of Attorney

Known as a Proxy Directive for Health Care in New Jersey, this may also be referred to as a Medical Power of Attorney in other states. This document lets you assign your health care decision-making process to someone you trust, such as your partner or a friend, rather than to someone who may not make decisions about your medical care that are in accordance with your wishes. This document does not come into effect until you are legally incompetent and, even then, if you are able to express your wishes, they must be followed. You can revoke this at any time, by writing "revoked" or something similar on the original, destroying the original, or orally tell another person. When a new proxy directive is created, it should always include a specific statement revoking any prior medical power.

You should provide a copy of this to your primary care physician as well as give copies to your designated agent and all alternatives. You may also want to list in the document where the original and all copies are located. As in the physician's directive, this document must also be witnessed.

HIPAA designation

Your proxy should also be designated as your "personal representative" as required by the Health Insurance Portability and Accountability Act (HIPAA). This allows your proxy to have the same access to your health care and treatment information as you have. If you do not do this, your proxy may be prevented from obtaining necessary information for making a decision.

Do Not Resuscitate Agreements

If you don't want to be resuscitated, you should execute a Do Not Resuscitate document. Otherwise, emergency medical technicians will try to bring you back to life. Although you may include this in a Living Will, it is sometime s useful to have a separately executed document, which you may keep in your wallet. You should be aware that if a person has signed an organ donation card or document, their body may be kept artificially alive until the organs are removed. This does not mean the person has been resuscitated.

Hospital visitation agreements

Even though the Domestic Partnership Act protects your right to visit your partner in a hospital or other health care facility, you and your partner should each execute a hospital visitation agreement.

This is a fairly straightforward document that simply states who should be allowed to visit you and should also list anyone who should be excluded, including friends and family members. The document should be signed by you and notarized. It is unnecessary for it to be witnessed.

The advantages of having this agreement are three-fold. First, if you are incapable of communicating your wishes, it can help enforce your desire to have your partner visit you in the face of opposition from family members who may be hostile to your domestic partner. Without this, you are relying on the hospital having to sort out competing interests in what may be a very tense environment.

Second, it will help the hospital exclude particular visitors if you have provided a signed directive listing people who you do not want to visit.

Third, it can help enforce these rights if you are traveling in states or countries that do not provide the same or similar rights as New Jersey. Thus, if you suddenly find yourself in a hospital in Philadelphia, you can ensure that your partner will be entitled to visit you.

Financial Powers of Attorney

This document lets you designate someone who will manage some or all of your financial affairs if you should become unable to do so yourself. It does not allow this person—your "agent"—to manage your medical affairs, which is why you need both a financial power of attorney and a medical power of attorney, called a Proxy Designation in New Jersey. For more information on the latter, see *Proxy Directive or Medical Power of Attorney*, above.

There are two kinds of financial powers of attorney: general powers that cover all non-medical powers and specific, or "special" powers of attorney, which cover only those things that are designated in the document. Most people will want to use the general powers.

Powers of attorney can come into effect when they are signed, or they can be "springing" powers, which mean they lie dormant until some specific event described in the document occurs, such as incapacity. They remain in effect until you say they are revoked, either in language in the document, such as a specific date or when capacity is regained, or by a specific revocation, as in the medical powers. They also expire when you expire. Many people use a standard power, called a durable power, which remains in effect indefinitely.

This document can be misused - after all, you're giving your agent permission to do things like sell your property, write checks, etc., - so you don't want to give them to someone you wouldn't trust with your affairs and you may want to use springing powers if you don't completely trust the person you designate as your agent.

This document must be signed when you are competent to do so and you should provide copies to the person you designate as your agent, as well as anyone named as an alternate. This document must be notarized or signed by an attorney in New Jersey.

GUARDIANSHIP

Guardianship and the lesser-used conservatorship are court-supervised surrogate decision-making tools used to protect individuals who are unable to manage their own affairs.

Conservatorship is a voluntary legal process in which a person who is unable to manage his or her estate, or to care for his or her dependents (the "conservatee"), voluntarily allows a court to appoint a person to manage the estate on his or her behalf (the "conservator.") Guardianship, on the other hand, is an involuntary process that allows a court to determine the mental competency of a alleged incompetent person (the "ward") and to appoint a guardian over the person, a guardian over the estate, or a guardian over the person and estate.

Guardianship in particular becomes an important procedure when the alleged incompetent person lacks valid alternative surrogate decision-making documents, such as a durable power of attorney. Even where valid powers of attorney exist, guardianship can be used to limit or override the proposed ward's choice of attorney-in-fact. Under New Jersey law, a guardian can even initiate a termination proceeding on behalf of a legally incompetent domestic partner.

New Jersey guardianship laws give preference to family when it comes to deciding who is entitled to be named as someone's guardian. These priorities are, in descending order:

- The incapacitated person's spouse, if they are living together as man and wife at the time incapacity arose. Notably, the term spouse does not include domestic partner.

- The incapacitated person's children, if any.

- Parents, siblings, and other blood relatives.

As in the rules regarding inheritance, domestic partners have less right to be named guardian over their partner than their partner's next of kin.

Because the Probate Code currently fails to give domestic partners priority over all other family, guardianship can be particularly problematic for same-sex couples. It can be even more of a problem if you and your partner have had to conceal the nature of your relationship from family members, or if family members are hostile toward your relationship, as in the case of Sharon Kowalski and her partner (see *Chapter 1: Introduction.*)

In order to help ensure that you and your partner are each other's preferred guardian, you should include guardianship directives in both your medical proxy directive and your financial powers of attorney. Such a directive should state that in the event you are legally found to be incapacitated and need a guardian, your attorney-in-fact or successor attorney-in-fact shall be appointed as your guardian. Although this is not binding on the courts of New Jersey, it is quite persuasive.

RETIREMENT AND ELDER LAW PLANNING

As you and your partner age, your estate planning needs will change, sometimes drastically. Many senior citizens have come to rely on federal entitlements, such as Social Security, Medicare and/or Medicaid, in order to supplement their private pension plans. For same-sex couples, the planning process is complicated by different state and federal income and qualification requirements.

As a result of the federal Defense of Marriage Act, all federal entitlements for couples, such as Social Security death benefits, are limited to legally married heterosexual couples. Any federal program that uses the term "spouse" must use a definition that excludes same-sex partners, even if legally married in Massachusetts or some other jurisdiction.

On the other hand, state-administered assistance programs are not necessarily bound by this definition and may interpret registration in a domestic partner as equal to marriage for purposes of placing Medicaid and related liens on jointly-owned property. You may also find that health care facilities may seek to have you agree to joint responsibility for medical expenses in order to ensure that they may recover one partner's expenses from the other. Thus, if you and your partner are retired, disabled, or facing a medical crisis, you may want to avoid joint ownership of assets.

If you and/or your partner were members of a New Jersey state-funded pension system, you may have been allowed to sign up for domestic partnership pension and health care benefits. These benefits have particular tax and other implications for you and your partner that should be discussed with a competent estate planning or elder law attorney.

END OF LIFE ISSUES

If you are like most couples, you and your partner have had little or no discussion regarding end of life issues, such as how you would like to be buried, or whether or not your organs should be donated after your death. For same-sex couples, such discussions are vitally important, because in many cases, domestic partners, whether registered or not, have little or no right to make these decisions on behalf of each other.

Registered domestic partners have the right to consent to the following on behalf of a deceased partner:

- Disclosure of the deceased partner's medical records if AIDS or HIV infection is suspected;

- Post-mortem and necroscopic examination of the deceased partner; and

- Donation of the deceased partner's entire body, organs or tissue;

If you and your partner have registered, the Domestic Partnership Act grants you a right of consent in these areas is superior to all other next-of-kin. However, in the absence of a written authorization by your deceased partner, you do not have a currently recognized right to take custody of your beloveds remains and make final arrangements, even if your partner told you what arrangements he or she wanted. Outside of New Jersey and those states that recognize a New Jersey domestic partnership, you have none of these rights unless your partner granted these to you in a valid written authorization.

In particular, you and your partner should prepare written authorizations that address each of the following items:

- **Disposition of Remains**.

- **Autopsy and Necropsy Permissions**.

- **Tissue and Organ Donation**.

- **Funeral, Cremation and Burial Arrangements**.

If you and your partner do not make written arrangements for all these matters before you die, you are very likely to be the subject of a posthumous "tug of war," particularly if your family becomes aware of your sexual orientation and your partnership upon your death.

Appointment of Person to Control Remains

The easiest way to avoid problems after your death is put your instructions in writing and appoint your partner, or some other trusted person, as your agent to carry out your directions and to make any decisions that you may have overlooked.

By law in New Jersey, a person appointed by you in your Will is entitled to control the funeral and disposition of your remains, even before your Will has been admitted to probate. If your executor is not that person, he or she is required to notify the person you have named in your Will of their appointment and to advise that person of what financial resources are available for that purpose. If you have named your partner as your executor and your agent to control remains, your partner has full rights to claim your remains and make funeral arrangements, subject to any instructions you have left, either in your Will or in a separate written directive. If you have not appointed anyone for this purpose in your Will, but you have left written instructions, your executor may carry out your written instructions, even before probate of the Will.

However, in the absence of an appointment in either a Will or a written directive, the right to control your funeral and dispose of your remains is given in the following order:

1. The surviving spouse.

2. A majority of the surviving adult children.

3. The surviving parent or parents.

4. A majority of the brothers and sisters.

5. Other next of kin of the decedent according to the degree of consanguinity.

6. The written authorization of any other person, if there are no known living relatives.

Without appointment, your partner has no more right to claim your remains and make funeral and other end-of-life decisions than a complete stranger.

The easiest way for you and your partner to avoid having someone else make these decisions is to provide written appointment and instructions on all end-of-life issues. Done properly, these instructions legally take precedence over any other contrary wishes and can ensure that your final wishes are followed.

These instructions may be as simple as designating your partner as your appointed representative for making all decisions relating to the disposition of your remains and the control of funeral arrangements. On the other hand, they may be as elaborate as designating your partner but specifying in detail how each matter should be handled.

Regardless of how simple or elaborate these instructions are, you should do the following:

First, include a disposition of remains clause in your Will and appointing your partner as your agent for this purpose. This clause will be the fall-back in case other arrangements you make are not found at the time of your death. If you intend to have a separate written directive, you should state this in your Will but allow for your appointed agent to make all arrangements if a separate written directive is not found within a reasonable time after your death.

Second, you should draft a written directive that appoints your partner as your agent for purposes of receiving and controlling your remains. The directive should contain your wishes regarding your funeral arrangements, burial location, and any organ donation or other instructions you prefer.

Third, each partner should sign these instructions in front of at least two witnesses other than the other partner, who must also sign the document. Signing and witnessing the documents in this way makes them self-proving, which means the witnesses do not need to be produced in court in order for a judge to uphold the validity of the instructions.

Finally, you should make sure that these written instructions are located where they can easily be obtained upon your death. Often times, a will is not available when you need to make critical after-death decisions and plan funeral arrangement. Having these instructions in a separate document that can be presented to a funeral director or crematorium will relieve you of one less problem during an otherwise stressful time.

Your written directive should address the following items, as appropriate:

Autopsy Agreement

You do not need to include any instructions regarding autopsies or necropsies unless you are specifically opposed to having an autopsy performed.

Body and Organ Donation Agreements

If you intend to allow your organs and tissues to be donated, you should provide instructions in regard to this and should also carry an organ donation card. If you want to donate your entire body to research or for some other purpose, you may want to provide specific instructions on the return or other disposition of remains, particularly if you want your partner to bury you after the remains have been used for their intended purpose.

Cremation, Funeral and Burial Arrangements

If you intend to be cremated, it is particularly important to include instructions to that effect in your disposition instructions. Sometimes relatives will attempt to prevent cremation, which is usually done soon after death, in favor of a burial. Since cremation is considered irreversible, some judges may be inclined to prevent cremation from occurring.

Although you may include funeral instructions in your will, it is really more useful to include them in the Disposition of Remains documents where they are readily available. If you have made prior arrangements with a particular funeral director, or if you have prepaid your funeral, you should include the name and contact information in the instructions.

Under New Jersey law, a funeral director is not liable for cremation or internment if he or she receives written authorization for disposition of remains. Thus, you can ensure that the funeral director will follow your partner's instructions and not those of some other family member if you provide authorization in the disposition of remains.

Financial arrangements for the funeral, such as the limits on amounts and payment instructions may be included if you include instructions in your will about any repayment. You may also include in the Disposition document instructions that the executor of your estate should be contacted for any financial arrangements

CHAPTER 13
ESTATE PLANNING

By some estimates, more than three-quarters of all couples - both same-sex couples and opposite sex couples - do not have even a simple Will. Of those who do, most have never done more than the most rudimentary estate planning, and many of them fail to update their estate plan on a regular basis.

Unfortunately for same-sex couples, the New Jersey Domestic Partnership Act fails to address most of the estate planning needs of same-sex couples. First, it did not change the rules of intestacy, which determine who inherits your estate in the absence of a valid Will. Second, it did not provide that same-sex couples would be treated as equivalent to married couples in regard to all gifts and property transfers.

Therefore, it is particularly important for you and your partner to take the time to meet with a knowledgeable estate planning attorney and, perhaps, financial advisor, in order to make sure that upon your death, your property will pass to your heirs, including your domestic partner, in accordance with your wishes and with the minimum allowable tax burden on your estate and your surviving partner.

ESTATE PLANNING BASICS

Estate planning is a form of financial planning that helps to ensure that your estate, that is, the net of all assets you own at the time of your death, is distributed in a way that meets your personal goals. These goals may include maximizing the amount of your assets that pass to your partner and other beneficiaries, minimizing estate and other death taxes, creating a legacy by benefiting a charity, designating guardians for any minor children you may have, and preparing for your incapacity.

Estate planning involves the use of certain kinds of legal and financial tools, including a Will, various forms of trusts, choosing and appointing fiduciaries such as trustees and executors, gifting, setting up appropriate forms of property ownership, obtaining certain kinds of insurance, setting up beneficiary designations, and creating advance directives.

Reasons for Planning Your Estate

There are many reasons for planning your estate, including:

- **Avoiding or limiting taxes**. If you have an estate in excess of the current state and federal estate tax exemptions, estate planning may help you reduce or even eliminate these taxes, thereby preserving more of your estate for your partner and other heirs. See *Taxation* in *Chapter 9* for more on this topic.

- **Avoiding intestacy and will challenges**. As discussed above, intestacy can usually be avoided and potential will challenges can be minimized if you have implemented an appropriate estate plan.

- **Avoiding probate**. With proper planning, you can transform many assets into non-probate forms that remove significant portions of your estate from the inconvenience of probate.

- **Avoiding fights with family**. A good estate plan can help avoid problems with hostile family members, by reducing probate assets, and putting in place appropriate advanced directives.

- **Minimizing public scrutiny of asset transfers**. Your Will, and the assets that are transferred pursuant to your Will are subject to public scrutiny.

- **Ensuring children and pets are cared for**. In your plan, you can make arrangements for the appointment of a guardian for your children and make sure your pets have a home as well.

Achieving any one of these goals can fully justify the time, effort and expense associated with estate planning. However, for same-sex couples, good estate planning is critical in that they do not currently have the benefit of state and federal laws that favor married couples.

After you have determined you estate planning goals, you need to establish the strategy by which you will achieve your goals. This strategy is best developed after you evaluate the kinds of assets you have in your estate and the manner in which those assets can be transferred.

Kinds of Assets

Most people own one or more of the following assets:

- **Cash**. Usually in a checking or savings account.

- **Real property**. Including your home as well as any other real estate you may own.

- **Personal property**. For example, automobiles or boats, clothing and other personal effects, household furnishings, jewelry, antiques, etc.

- **Securities and other financial instruments**. This includes stocks and bonds, as well as mutual funds, investment accounts, or government securities.

- **Business interests**. Including business partnerships, license agreements, family-owned companies, or business assets.

- **Insurance and annuities**. Including proceeds of life insurance or a right to receive an annuity.

- **Pensions, IRAs and 401(k) plans**. For example, pension distribution rights as well as a right to receive ongoing payments.

- **Notes payable**. The value of promissory notes and other notes securing loans made to others.

- **Intangible assets**. For example, intellectual property such as a copyright, patent or trademark, or the right to sue someone for malpractice or wrongful death.

Any of these assets that are still owned by you at the time of your death will need to be transferred in some way or another to your heirs. The way in which they are transferred varies depending upon the kind of asset and the way it is owned.

How Assets Are Transferred

All estate planning ultimately involves the transfer of assets in one of three ways: by gift, by operation of law, or through probate.

- **Gifting**. At any time during your life, you may give any of your assets to anyone you choose, including your partner, your children, or even some organization. Gifting can be an important way to remove assets from your estate before you die.

- **Non-probate transfers**. Certain assets, such as life insurance proceeds, individual bank accounts, investment accounts, and certain pension benefits, can be transferred by making a beneficiary designation. These assets are transferred directly to those beneficiaries when your death certificate is provided. Title to property you own jointly with another person, such as your partner, also transfers automatically if there is a right to survivorship. These assets are commonly called non-probate assets. See *Chapter 10: Property Rights*.

- **Probate transfers**. Most other property is distributed according to your written Will, if you have one, or by laws of intestacy, through a court-supervised process called probate. These kinds of assets are commonly referred to as probate assets.

There are disadvantages and advantages to each method of asset transfer that may affect your choices.

Gifting

Giving a gift to your partner is a reliable way to transfer assets out of your estate. When the gift is complete, the asset is no longer a part of your estate and it is nearly impossible for a relative to take that gift away. On the other hand, a gift to your partner is irrevocable and there is nothing to prevent your partner from keeping the asset if your partnership is terminated, or leaving the gift to someone else in his or her will.

Inter vivos gifts also have significant tax implications. If the value of an individual gift to another person exceeds the gift tax exemption of $11,000 in any one year, you must file a gift tax return, and the excess counts against the total amount you can gift in your lifetime.

Nevertheless, inter vivos gifts of rapidly appreciating assets, such as real estate and stocks, can make very good sense from a estate planning point of view. If the asset were to remain in your estate until you died, it would be taxed at its appreciated value at the time of your death. Although you will pay gift tax at the time of the transfer, the tax will be less because it will be calculated on the current value of the asset.

Non-probate transfers

Any asset that transfers immediately upon your death is considered a non-probate asset, since the transfer takes place outside the probate process. As a result, the asset transfer takes place without regard to your Will, and even if you die intestate, your designated beneficiary will receive the asset.

There are three common forms of non-probate transfers:

- **Beneficiary designations**. Individually owned assets, such as life insurance policies, pensions, bank accounts, brokerage and other financial accounts, can be left to one or more named beneficiaries by changing the beneficiary designation. This is normally done using a form that the insurance company, your employer, your bank or other institution can provide, and the designation is easily revoked if necessary. If you do not make a designation, however, the asset becomes payable to your estate and thus becomes subject to probate. You can also designate a trust as the beneficiary, if you do not want to leave the proceeds outright to your partner or other designated beneficiary.

- **Joint property.** Another common way to transfer assets outside probate is through the use of jointly-owned assets with a right of survivorship. Joint bank or brokerage accounts should be designated this way to ensure that jointly-held funds are not tied up during probate. If you and your partner own your home or other real estate as joint tenants, title passes automatically to your partner at your death, but only if the deed correctly specifies that the property is held with a right of survivorship. If you own the property as tenants in common, however, transfer of your partner's share of the property is subject to probate. You and your partner should review the deeds to all property in which your intent is to hold the property as joint tenants to make sure it reflects the ownership you intended. See Chapter 10: Property Rights for more on joint property ownership.

- **Inter vivos trusts.** There are several kinds of trusts that you can set up during your lifetime that can transfer your assets outside the probate process. These trusts can be revocable trusts, such as a living trust, or irrevocable trusts, such as a grantor retained income trust. See *Trusts*, later in this chapter for more information.

Non-probate assets do not escape taxation, however, since they are counted as part of your taxable estate. However, with proper planning, you can minimize and sometimes completely eliminate estate taxes on transfers.

Probate transfers

Any assets that remain in your estate at your death and do not automatically transfer to a beneficiary at that time are considered probate assets. These assets are transferred either according to your Will, if you have one, or according the rules of intestacy, if you die without a valid will.

For same-sex couples, probate transfers are the least desirable kind of asset transfer because of the chance that your intended transfer to your partner could be defeated by a challenge to your will. Furthermore, once your executor has filed your will with the probate court, it becomes a public document that anyone can obtain and examine.

Transfers and look-back periods

There are certain timing issues related to asset transfers that are important in estate planning:

1.   If you die within three years of a transfer of an asset, the IRS considers the transfer to be in "contemplation of death" and will include the value of the asset in your gross estate.

2.   Transfers made for less than fair market value within three years of applying for Medicaid are counted when determining eligibility.

Outright or in Trust

Regardless of whether your choose to transfer assets by gifting, by non-probate transfers or through the probate process, you will also need to determine what, if any, controls you will place on the use of your assets once they are transferred.

Outright transfers are those that come without strings attached. For example, if you give your partner a car, he or she may drive it, sell it, borrow money against it, or even give it to someone else. If, on the other hand, you want to prevent your partner from taking some or all of these actions, then you need to limit your partner's ownership rights. The only way you can do this effectively is to transfer the asset in trust for the benefit of your partner. In that way, your partner can get the use and benefit of an asset, but not the actual title.

There are several common situations in which transferring an asset in trust makes sense.

- **Special needs trusts**. If your partner became severely disabled, he or she might need to qualify for Medicaid in order to pay for treatment and related needs. Because Medicaid is a needs-based program, your partner could only qualify if he or she had limited resources. If you gave your partner a car as an outright gift, it would count toward the resource threshold and your partner could be disqualified from Medicaid assistance. If, however, you gave the car in trust to your partner, your partner would have the use and benefit of the care but not ownership.

- **Spendthrift trusts**. If your partner were incapable of handling money, or was inclined to gamble or otherwise waste money, giving a substantial gift of money or other property in trust would help prevent the assets from being swiftly depleted.

- **Keeping assets in the family**. Any assets you give to your partner outright will be distributed at your partner's death according to his will or by intestacy. Leaving your assets in trust to your partner ensure that, after your partner dies, your remaining assets will go to whomever you choose as the remaindermen.

- **Gifts to minors**. Any testamentary gifts you make to minors must be left in trust. If you do not create the trust in your will, the probate court will impose a trust under the Uniform Gifts to Minors Act.

- **Obtaining substantial tax savings**. If you have a sizeable estate, you may be subject to federal and state estate taxes. There are a number of situations where you can avoid some or all such taxes by making a transfer in trust. For example, naming your partner as the outright beneficiary of a substantial life insurance policy would most likely result in a hefty estate tax, whereas using an irrevocable life insurance trust, the entire amount of the insurance could pass to your partner without tax.

On the other hand, if you do not care what happens to your assets after your death, you do not expect to leave a taxable estate, or you do not want to restrict your partner from using those assets after your death, then leaving your assets outright may be an entirely reasonable choice.

Choosing a Strategy

After you have reviewed the kinds of assets in your current estate you can develop a strategy for transferring those assets. This strategy will usually involve some combination of gifting, non-probate transfers, and probate transfers. There are advantages and disadvantages to each form of asset transfer that will influence your choices and you should discuss your particular situation with an estate planning professional before embarking on a particular strategy.

Estate Planning Documents

Your estate planning process typically results in the creation of a set of documents that determine what will happen to your assets when you die, who will take care of your children or other dependents, and who will make financial and medical decisions on your behalf if you become legally incompetent. At a minimum, theses documents include a Will and a set of advance directives. Other documents that may comprise your estate plan include various forms of insurance, usually life insurance and long-term care insurance, and one or more revocable or irrevocable trusts. For more about the use of advance directives, see *Chapter 12: Health, Disability and End of Life Issues.*

Wills and Trusts

A Will is a written document, that is signed by the maker (called the "testator") and two or more witnesses and which contains the testator's instructions for the disposition of his or her estate. A Will takes effect at the testator's death. A person who dies without a valid Will is said to be *intestate.* Simple modifications and updates to a Will can be made through the use a supplemental document called a *codicil,*; more extensive modifications usually require a Will to be redrafted. A person can only have one valid Will; the latest valid will revokes all prior wills by the same person.

A trust is a legal entity created by a person, called the grantor or settlor, into which assets are transferred for the benefit of specific beneficiaries. Trusts are created by a trust document, called an instrument, under the laws of a particular state and are subject to tax regulations. Certain kinds of trusts can be modified or amended with a supplemental document. Unlike a Will, a person may create more than one trust.

Probate Process

Probate is a court-supervised procedure in which your Will is confirmed as the valid expression of the way you want your property distributed. Probate also confirms the appointment of the individual or individuals, called your executor, you named in your Will to carry out your estate distribution. The probate process also involves the gathering together of all of your assets, the payment of any debts, taxes and expenses associated with your estate, and the distribution of your remaining assets to those persons you named as your beneficiaries.

In New Jersey, probate is initiated by filing a request for the issuance of letters testamentary, along with an original death certificate and the original Will. For most estates, probate can take anywhere from six months to over a year before all the probate assets are distributed.

At any time during the probate process, almost anyone can file a Will challenge by filing a complaint called a "caveat." The usual basis for filing a caveat is that the Will is invalid as a result of undue influence by another heir, or that the person has been left out of the Will. Although Will challenges often fail, they can significantly slow down the process of distributing the estate, and they can be quite expensive to defend.

Some of the costs and complexity of the probate process can be avoided by the use of non-probate asset transfers, including the use of living trusts, life insurance, "payable on death" accounts, and joint ownership with rights of survivorship. However, non-probate transfers are still subject to state and federal estate taxes.

Many of the challenges associated with the probate process, as well as some of the tax burden associated with the estate tax can be minimized or even eliminated through proper estate planning. However, minimizing challenges and taxation are not the only reasons for estate planning.

Intestacy

If, at the time of your death, you have not created a valid Will or if a valid Will cannot be located, you are said to have died intestate, and distribution of your estate is subject to a set of rules in the probate code that govern intestate distribution. The rules of intestacy also apply to any part of your estate that is not accounted for by a distribution in your otherwise-valid will.

Intestate distribution for married couples generally results in the kind of distribution that most spouses intend by leaving most of the deceased spouse's estate to the surviving spouse, although without the tax savings that a good estate plan might have produced. For same-sex partners, however, intestate distribution is a disaster.

Under current interpretations of the New Jersey Domestic Partnership Act and the probate code, registered domestic partners are not included in the intestacy rules. Thus, if you die without a valid Will, your partner will receive nothing of your estate that passes through probate; all of your probate assets will go to your legal next-of-kin. Even if you have no living relatives, or if your relatives all disclaim their rights to your estate, your entire intestate estate will go ("escheat") to the State of New Jersey.[1]

Intestate distribution only applies to assets that are part of your probate estate; non-probate assets are entirely unaffected. Thus, estate planning can prevent intestate distribution, by making sure you have a valid will and by eliminating many of your assets from your probate estate.

Executors and Trustees

As part of your estate plan, you designate certain individuals or institutions, called "fiduciaries," to distribute your estate and manage any trusts that you may create.

An executor (or executrix) is the person who will file your Will with the probate court, gather together all of your assets, pay all of your creditors out of your estate, and distribute the remaining assets to your heirs. Once your estate has been fully distributed and closed out, your executor's role is ended. You should name at least one individual, usually your partner, as your executor in your Will; it is usually better to name several successor executors in case your first choice is unwilling or unable to accept appointment.

If part of your estate plan entails the use of trusts, you will also appoint one or more individuals or corporate entities to act as trustee. Trustees take title to the property that is placed into trust and manage the operation of the trust, including investment of the property in the trust, maintaining the financial accounts, filing of tax returns, payment of taxes, and distribution of the income and principal of the trust. Just as in an executor, you must name one or more trustee in the trust instrument. You should also name several successor trustees as back-up.

If your partner is a beneficiary of the trust you have created, he or she can serve as a trustee. However, to avoid problems with the Internal Revenue Service regulations, your partner should not serve as the sole trustee if he or she has complete control over distributions from the trust. For more on choosing an executor or trustee, see *Choosing a Fiduciary* in *Chapter 16*.

---

[1]   The author recently filed a challenge to the current probate code on behalf of a registered domestic partner whose partner died intestate. The suit, which was filed against the State of New Jersey may help establish that registered domestic partners are entitled to the same treatment as married spouses under the rules of intestacy.

Fees and Bonds

When you designate your executors and your trustees, you may specify that they serve without receiving a fee. In New Jersey, if your will is silent on this, your executor may be paid a fee from the estate that is set by law. This fee is a deduction for the estate but taxable income for the executor, and can be waived by the executor. Similarly, a trustee can serve without fee, however, it is more common to allow trustees to take fees and commercial trustees will always take a fee.

An executor will normally be required to post a bond, unless your will specifies that a bond is not required. The amount of the bond will vary depending on the value of your estate. A trustee should always be required to post a bond.

Intestate Administration

If you die intestate, the probate court will name one of your next-of-kin as the administrator of your estate. Currently in New Jersey, the probate code does not recognize your registered domestic partner as your heir. Thus, if you die without a will, your partner will not be appointed as your administrator unless all of yours heirs defer to your partner. Furthermore, even if your next-of-kin waive their right to administer your estate, you will be required to post a bond in an amount determined by the surrogate.

PREPARING OR UPDATING YOUR WILL

Your Will is one of the most important documents in your estate plan because it determines who will get your property at your death. Among the many reasons for having a Will are:

- You get to choose who gets your property, and who doesn't.

- You get to name your partner or some other person as your children's guardian.

- You get to decide who will oversee the distribution of your assets.

- You decide who plans your funeral and what arrangements should be made.

A Will can be quite simple if you don't have a lot of assets, or it can be quite complex, creating various trusts and the rules governing those trusts. At a minimum, you and your partner should have reciprocal Wills, which should be drafted by an attorney according to your specific needs, printed, and signed by you in the presence of at least two witnesses who will then each sign your Will.

Technical Requirements

There are certain technical requirements necessary for preparing a Will, and your Will should have at least the following provisions:

- **Identification of the Testator.** This clause identifies the person making the Will (the testator), and his or her domicile.

- **Revocation of Prior Will.** This clause revokes all previous Wills and Codicils (Will amendments), and establishes that this is the testator's last Will and Testament.

- **Naming of Executors and Fiduciaries.** This clause names the Executor of the estate - the person who will oversee the distribution of the estate.

- **Powers of Executors.** This clause establishes any powers the executor may have in addition to those conferred by law.

- **Payment of Debts and Taxes.** This clause specifies how debts of the estate are to be paid and how taxes will be paid.

- **Disposition of Personal Property.** This clause is used to distribute tangible personal property, such as clothing, jewelry, books, and other personal effects. The clause can be general or it can be used to distribute specific items of special or sentimental value to particular individuals. In New Jersey, you may reference a written memorandum as an alternative to specific dispositions within the Will. The advantage is the memorandum can be changed without affecting the validity of the Will.

- **Bequests.** This clause is used to make special distributions of cash or other assets. The bequests can be made to specific individuals or institutions, including charitable institutions.

- **Distribution of Real Property.** This clause identifies any real property to be distributed and any limitations on that property. It can also indicate whether the real property passes to your partner or other heir subject to any mortgages.

- **Disposition of Residuary.** The residuary clause is used to distribute any remaining portion of the estate, including any lapsed (failed) bequests or other distributions. It is essentially a catch-all that ensures that no part of the estate passes via intestacy rules. For domestic partners, who are not covered by the intestacy rules, it is particularly important to ensure that your partner receives the remainder of the estate.

- **Testimonium.** In this clause, the testator testifies that he or she signed the Will, with full knowledge of its contents and import, and establishes the date, time and place it was executed. It also contains the signatures of the witnesses to the Will.

Once you have executed your Will, the original should be kept in a safe location, such as a safe-deposit box at your bank. Regardless of where you keep the original, you should ensure that it is readily available to your executor, in the even it is needed. If you use a safe deposit box, you should make sure that your primary and secondary executor will be granted access after your death by, for example, giving written instructions to the bank.

Can I use a handwritten Will?

A handwritten Will, called a "holographic will" is valid in New Jersey as long as it is entirely written in your own handwriting, and otherwise meets the requirements for a valid Will However, a pre-printed Will in which you fill in the blanks is not a valid Will.

Other Provisions

Some other provisions that you may want to include in your Will, depending upon your particular situation, include the following:

Testamentary guardian for children

If you have children, you should name a guardian for your children. If your partner is not a legal parent, then you will need to name your partner as your first choice. If your partner has legally adopted your children, he or she will have legal custody upon your death. However, you should each name a back-up guardian for your children in case both of your die at the same time, or one of you dies first and the other neglects to name a testamentary guardian.

Disposition of remains and funeral arrangements

As discussed in Chapter 12: Health, Disability and End of Life Issues, you should appoint someone to take control of your remains and carry out your funeral arrangements. You may also have a separate written directive, which should be referenced in this provision.

Definition of domestic partner

For many years, same-sex couples would refer to their partner in their Will as "their friend" or some other designation that would avoid any hint of a sexual relationship, so as to avoid anything that might trigger a Will challenge. However, many couples resented this deliberate denial of their true relationship..

For same-sex couples in New Jersey, it is perfectly appropriate now to use the term "domestic partner" when referring to your partner in your Will. However, you should define the term in the Will itself, so there is no question about its meaning in this and other states where your Will may be probated. For example, the following language would provide a definition that would encompass both registered and unregistered domestic partners.

> "The term 'domestic partner' means the person who is my domestic partner, if this person and I meet the requirements for registration as defined in N.J.S.A. 26:8A-4(b) or N.J.S.A. 26:8A-6(c), even if we have not filed an Affidavit of Domestic Partnership."

You should avoid referring to your partner in your Will as your "spouse" since, in most states, the word has a legal meaning of "husband" or "wife."

Termination of partnership

Your Will should also include a provision that invalidates any provisions referring to your domestic partner if you and your partner terminate your partnership after your Will is signed. Ideally, following termination you should revise your Will and other legal documents to exclude your former partner. However, it is easy to forget to revise all such documents following a break up, and this clause would prevent your former partner from taking under your Will.

Survival presumptions

Reciprocal Wills should always contain matching survival presumptions. These presumptions are made if you and your partner die simultaneously, or under circumstances that make it impossible to determine who died first. In such a case, one partner's survival presumption will specify that he or she "predeceases" the other partner. The other partner's presumption specifies that he or she "survived" the other partner. This causes the predeceased partner's Will to be probated first and allows the two Wills to work together to fulfill a joint estate plan.

Creation of one or more testamentary trusts

For any trusts you will create upon your death ("testamentary trusts,") you need to include the trust creation and operation language within the Will.

Memorandum disposition

As an alternative to including specific gifts of person property in your Will, New Jersey allows you to use a separate document called a "memorandum disposition" which is then referenced in your Will. The advantage of this document is that you can easily change gifts of particular personal property by creating a new memorandum rather than having to change the Will or execute a codicil. The memorandum should refer to your Will by the date your Will was executed and must be signed and notarized.

Changing Your Will

Unless your Will needs significant revisions, you may make deletions, modifications and additions to your Will by means of a document called a codicil. The codicil should specify the Will it is amending, and must be signed, witnessed and notarized. You should keep the codicil with your original Will.

You should review your will and revise it if necessary, any time you make a significant change in your life, such as entering into or terminating a domestic partnership, the birth of a child, the death of your partner, or a move to another city or state.

USING TRUSTS IN YOUR ESTATE PLAN

For many same-sex couples, trusts are often a great estate-planning vehicle. A trust can be used to protect assets from creditors, provide support over many years, keep assets out of probate, and reduce estate and gift taxes.

Although trusts and wills are both used to distribute property to beneficiaries, they differ in that a Will controls who receives property but does not generally limit the use of that property except while the Will is being probated. As such, property that you leave to your partner outright in your Will can be freely used by your partner after your death and can even be transferred to another person, such as your partner's family or a new domestic partner.

A trust, on the other hand, can be used to limit the use and transfer of the assets in the trust throughout its duration. For example, if you wanted your partner to have the use and enjoyment of all of your assets during his or her life and then have the remaining assets distributed to your immediate family, you would set up a trust that names your partner as the beneficiary during his or her life and names your family members as remainder beneficiaries.

Kinds of Trusts

There are many kinds of trusts and they can be categorized as either testamentary (established under your Will) or inter vivos (established while you are alive). Another way trusts are classified is revocable and irrevocable.

An irrevocable trust is one in which the grantor gives up all rights to the assets in the trust and cannot make any changes to the trust terms, including beneficiary designations. A revocable trust can be modified at any time by the grantor, including changing the trust terms, changing the beneficiary designation, and reserving the right to control of the assets in the trust.

Trust principal, income and distributions

The assets that are transferred into a trust are commonly referred to as the *trust principal, trust property* or *corpus* of the trust. In many kinds of trust, the principal will generate income as a result of investments of the trust property.

Throughout the trust's existence, periodic distributions may be made to the beneficiaries. The distributions can be limited to income only, or to income and principal. In general, distribution to beneficiaries should come first from the income and then from the principal. Undistributed income is usually added to the principal. Distributions of the principal and any undistributed income will also be made as part of the process of terminating a trust.

Creating a Trust

Trusts are generally created in one of two ways. Inter vivos trusts are created during your lifetime using a written document (the "trust instrument") that is signed by the settlor, who may also be a beneficiary, and the trustee. Testamentary trusts are created in your Will. Neither kind of trust actually comes into being until the trust instrument (or Will) is signed and some assets, such as money or real estate are transferred from the settlor to the trustee.

Funding the trust

Testamentary trusts are not funded until the settlor dies, after which the trust is funded with the assets of the probate estate. Because of this, testamentary trusts are public records, and creditors and other claimants can easily obtain information about the assets that have been placed into trust at your death.

On the other hand, an inter vivos trust can be created by transferring one dollar from the settlor to the trustee when the trust instrument is signed. This allows you to set up a trust that remains unfunded until you have some reason to fund the trust, such as after your receive the proceeds of life insurance or a settlement of a case. Because such a standby trust is created prior to your death, it is not a public record and is therefore kept private. After your death, certain kinds of non-probate assets can be transferred into the trust.

Naming beneficiaries and trustees

When you set up a trust, you will name one or more individuals as the beneficiaries of the trust, and one or more trustees. The beneficiary has equitable or beneficial title to the assets in the trust but does not hold legal title. The trustee holds the legal title to the trust assets.

Equitable title? Legal title?

Equitable (beneficial) title means the right to receive a benefit from an asset, such as income from investments or the right to use a vacation home. Legal title means the right to own and possess, but not the right to receive benefits from the asset.

Generally, you hold both equitable and legal title in most property you own.

When you name a beneficiary, you decide whether he or she is entitled to receive the income from the trust, and to what extent and under what circumstances he or she can dip into the principal. You will also determine the person or organization (called the "remainderman") who will receive the assets remaining in the trust when it is terminated.

If you name your partner as a beneficiary he or she should not be the sole beneficiary. Since your partner would then hold both beneficial AND legal title, the two titles merge and your partner becomes the sole owner of the trust property. This causes the trust to fail and can have significant tax implications.

Successor trustees

It is not sufficient to name one or more trustees for the trust. You must be certain to name one or more successor trustees, that is, a person who will become a trustee if one of the existing trustees dies or is removed as a trustee. You may want to include a clause that allows each trustee to name a successor .

Corporate trustees

It is not uncommon to name a bank or other corporate trustee as a trustee or co-trustee. The benefit of having a corporate trustee is that there is usually no need to name a successor, since corporations tend to remain in existence for many years. Another benefit is that a corporate trustee will be less likely to allow the beneficiaries to take unnecessary distributions from the trust. The main disadvantage of a corporate trustee is that they always charge a fee, usually a small percentage of the income of the trust, for managing the trust. Another disadvantage, at least from a beneficiary's point of view, is that a corporate trustee will be less likely to allow the beneficiaries to take unnecessary distributions from the trust.

Terminating a trust

Although trusts can remain in existence for a very long time, they may not have indefinite duration.. Thus, when you create a trust, the trust instrument will state the conditions for terminating the trust. The reason or reasons for terminating the trust can include:

- When it is uneconomical to continue to operate the trust, such as when the principal remaining in the trust is less than $50,000;

- Termination upon the occurrence of a specific event, such as the death of a beneficiary; or

- Termination when the purpose of the trust fails.

At the time the trust terminates, the trustee will distribute the remaining assets of the trust to the remaindermen in accordance with the terms of the trust instrument.

For example, a trust for the benefit of minor children may provide that the trust will terminate when all of the children have reached a specific age., such as 25 years of age, at which time the children will receive all of the remaining funds in the trust in equal shares. Another trust could provide income and principal distributions to your partner for life, after which the corpus of the trust would be distributed to a favorite niece or nephew.

Use of Trusts in Estate Planning

Trusts can play an important part in your estate plan if you and your partner have a medium to large estate, have relatives who are hostile to your relationship and may challenge your will, need to impose financial controls on one another, or wish to provide for minor children

One of the more common trusts used by same-sex couples is a revocable or irrevocable living trust. This trust can be a useful way to handle assets that cannot, for some reason, be converted to a non-probate asset. For example, if one partner has significant liabilities, it would be risky for both partners to own their assets jointly without some additional protection.

Other kinds of trusts can play an important part in your estate planning strategy. For example, an irrevocable life insurance trust ("ILIT") provides an excellent way to leave a substantial amount of money to your partner upon your death. Another type of trust, called a credit shelter or bypass trust, can be used to shelter assets in your estate worth up to the current federal estate tax exemption (set to increase to $2 million in 2005).

Although you and your partner are currently unable to obtain all of the estate planning benefits currently provided to opposite-sex married couple under federal law, certain kinds of trusts can help reduce the unfair burden on same-sex couples in the United States.

There is even one kind of trust that is more beneficial to same-sex couples than it is to opposite-sex married couples. Under current tax law, domestic partners are not considered "family members," thereby allowing them to use a grantor retained interest trust ("GRIT") as a way to gift assets at a discounted value.

Trusts are not will substitutes

A living trust is never a substitute for a will in an estate plan. If there are assets that you have not transferred into the living trust before your death, they can be transferred into trust at your death by adding a "pour-over" clause to your will. If you don't have a will, however, these assets will be distributed as part of your intestate estate and not to your partner or other beneficiary under your living will.

Trusts and look-back periods

Transferring an asset into a trust is a "transfer in contemplation of death" if it is within three years prior to your death. Transfers into trust are subject to a five-year look-back for purposes of Medicaid eligibility. See *Transfers and Look-back Periods* earlier in this chapter.

Types of Trusts

Some of the more common forms of trust used in estate planning for same-sex couples are:

Living Trust

A revocable living trust (and less commonly, an irrevocable living trust) is an inter vivos trust set up by both partners into which most or all individual assets are transferred. Both of you are named as beneficiaries and both are trustees, so if one partner dies or becomes disabled, the other partner still has control and use of the assets.

A living will can be set up as a revocable trust, in which case you and your partner, as the grantors, retain control over the administration and can revoke (that is, terminate) the trust at any time. If you set the trust up as an irrevocable trust, you lose the ability to terminate the trust. When one partner dies, a revocable trust becomes irrevocable.

Unlike a will, a living trust is less likely t be challenged by family members, particularly the longer it is in existence and the more it has been used for all assets of the partnership. However, a living trust is not secure from creditors unless it is set up as an irrevocable living trust.

Many estate planners believe that revocable living trusts are one of the best planning tools for same-sex couples.. The benefits of living trusts have been oversold, particularly by financial planners who have earned substantial fees by marketing these as a way to avoid probate. In New Jersey, where the fees associated with probate are not all that high, the costs saved are minimal especially compared to the costs associated with establishing and maintaining a living trust. Furthermore, if most of your assets consist of property that can be held jointly with a right of survivorship, or that can be transferred on death by means of a beneficiary designation, then a living trust is probably unnecessary.

Credit Shelter (Bypass) Trust

Although this trust is most commonly used in estate planning for opposite-sex married couples, where it is coupled with a marital trust, this trust can also be used by anyone who wants to shelter all or part of the amount that can be passed free of estate tax. This is usually set up in your will, as a testamentary trust, and funded with probate assets. Anything left to your partner in excess of the federal estate tax exemption (currently $1.5 million) would be taxed at the current estate tax rate, however, there would be no further taxes on the assets in this trust when your partner dies. Furthermore, your partner could shelter a similar amount at his death, leaving the entire remainder to your children.

The main advantage of this for same-sex couples is that the surviving partner has the use of the interest and principle during his or her life, but the remainder can go to other heirs.

For large estates, the credit shelter trust can be coupled with life-time transfers, such as a grantor-retained annuity trust or qualified personal residence trust in order to significantly reduce or even eliminate any federal estate tax.

Irrevocable Life Insurance Trust (ILIT)

Normally, proceeds from your life insurance policy (the "death benefit"), is counted as part of your taxable estate regardless of whether the proceeds are paid directly to your partner, another named beneficiary, or to your estate. Using this kind of trust, however, you can leave the entire proceeds to your partner without it being included in your taxable estate, thereby allowing you to shelter other assets with your estate tax exemption.

This trust is set up in your lifetime as an irrevocable trust with your partner named as the beneficiary. After the trust is created, you give the insurance policy to the trust, naming the trust as the beneficiary of the insurance proceeds (not your partner). Because the policy has little or no present value, the gift is generally less than your annual gift tax exclusion of $11,000. Each year, you give the trust an amount equal to the annual premium for the policy and instruct your partner, as trustee, to make the premium payment.

Upon your death, the trust is funded with the insurance proceeds, but because you do not own the policy at the time of your death, the proceeds are not included in your estate. Depending on the size of the death benefit, you will be able to leave your partner a sizeable gift.

The main disadvantage of the ILIT is that it is irrevocable. Once you have funded the trust by giving the policy to the trust, you may not change the beneficiary designation or anything else about the trust. The only recourse is to stop paying the premiums, thereby causing the policy to lapse and the trust to fail.

Charitable Remainder Trust (CRT)

This is a form of irrevocable trusts that takes advantage of charitable deductions in order to give your partner a stream of income over his or her lifetime, with the remainder going to a charity.

If you create the charitable remainder trust in your will (a testamentary trust), your estate will receive a deduction in the amount of principal placed in the trust. If you create the CRT during your lifetime (an inter vivos trust), you receive a gift tax deduction and, perhaps, an income tax deduction. Because the CRT is tax-exempt, it can buy and sell appreciated assets and take advantage of diversification strategies in order to ensure that your partner and other heirs get higher after-tax income than they might otherwise.

Grantor Retained Annuity Trust (GRAT)

A GRAT is an irrevocable trust into which you transfer individual assets and take back a fixed annuity, paid at least once a year, for a specific number of years, naming your partner or some other entity as the remainderman.

If at the end of the term, you are still alive, the trust principal passes to your partner and/or other beneficiaries completely free of federal gift or estate taxes. If, on the other hand, you die before the end of the term, some portion of the trust assets will be included in your probate estate and subject to taxation.

Qualified Personal Residence Trust (QPRT)

This is a special form of GRAT that allows you to transfer your home to another person or entity but retain the right to live in your home for a specific period of time. Your transfer is treated as a gift to the beneficiaries, such as your partner, equal to the present value of your home minus the present value of your retained interest. At the end of the term, called the "QPRT term", the trust terminates and ownership of the home passes to your partner or other beneficiary free of federal gift and estate taxes.

There are two main disadvantages to the QPRT. First, at the end of the QPRT term, your ownership and, therefore, your right to remain in your home ceases. However, you can remain in your home after the term if you pay fair market rent.

Second, if you die before the end of the QPRT term, your home will be included in your probate estate, where it may be subject to federal and state estate taxes.

To get the best advantage of a QPRT, you should be young enough that you can set a QPRT term of 10 to 15 years in order to get maximize the discount on the value of the home. If you are over the age of 55, it is harder to set a QPRT term that you will outlive. However, since the beneficiary of a QPRT can be another trust, older persons can set up a series of "rolling" GRATs with shorter terms to get some of the advantages of a longer term.

Grantor Retained Interest Trust (GRIT)

A GRIT is similar to a GRAT except that you take back a whatever interest the trust assets generate for a fixed number of years, naming your partner or some other entity as the remainderman.

If at the end of the term, you are still alive, the trust principal passes to your partner and/or other beneficiaries completely free of federal gift or estate taxes. If, on the other hand, you die before the end of the term, some portion of the trust assets will be included in your probate estate and subject to taxation.

SUMMARY

Estate planning for most couples is a complex discipline, involving tax planning, financial planning, and legal issues. For same-sex couples, who have few of the protections provided to married couples under state and federal law, estate planning can be even more complex. Hopefully, this chapter has provided you and your partner with enough background that you can intelligently discuss your planning needs with a qualified estate planning professional.

Because drafting documents like wills, advance directives or disposition of remains, involves planning for your eventual disability and death, it is often an uncomfortable topic to address. However, it is vitally important that you and your partner take the time to discuss these subjects and plan accordingly in order to ensure that you have taken care of each other to the fullest extent possible under the current law.

CHAPTER 14
SEPARATION, TERMINATION AND NULLIFICATION

As remote as it may seem to you and your partner now, same-sex relationships are just as likely to go sour as their opposite-sex counterparts. Even long-term partners may find the need to end their relationship, too often with a nasty, angry breakup that makes it hard to remain friends afterward.

If you are considering ending your registered domestic partnership, you should review this part of the guide. You should also review this part if you are a resident of New Jersey and considering ending a civil union or domestic partnership you entered in another state.

Finally, you and your partner should review this part of the guide prior to registering your domestic partnership so that you set up the necessary protection for yourself even if you know in your heart that your partnership is rock-solid. There is no way to predict the vagaries of the human heart, but a clear understanding of what may happen if you and your partner decide to part ways may help strengthen your relationship in unexpected ways.

THE RULES OF DISENGAGEMENT

In the past, breaking up may have been messy for a same-sex couple but it rarely involved the courts. More recently, this changed with palimony being granted in some cases but, by and large, same-sex couples found it relatively easy for one or the other partner to end the partnership by simply walking out the door.

The Domestic Partnership Act changes this by requiring registered domestic partners to undergo a formal termination proceeding, similar to a divorce, presided over by a judge who will ultimately issue a termination decree. Unlike opposite-sex divorce proceedings, domestic partners are not obliged to support each other after termination has been granted nor is the court to make an equitable distribution of the partners' joint and individual assets. During the termination proceeding, the court can also address parenting issues, such as custody, visitation, and child support.

Registered domestic partners can also apply to the court for relief such as support, separate maintenance, child support, custody, or partition of property without filing for termination. Thus, domestic partners who have separated now can be sure that important rights and obligations are protected even while the partners are separated.

SEPARATION

There may be times when you and your partner decide to or are required to live separately. Although the Domestic Partnership Act requires you and your partner to have a common residence, you are not required to live together at all times during your partnership. For example, if you and your partner have separate residences, you may choose to live apart some or even much of the time, so long as you intend to return to your shared residence.

There may be any number of reasons for your separation, such as one partner attending school, going on sabbatical, or working in another city or state. Although the period of separation is normally expected to be finite, it can involve a long-term or even permanent, such as confinement to a nursing home, or even incarceration. The key to separation is that both of you intend to return to a shared residence at some point, even if this is unrealistic or ultimately impossible.

Your separation may be deemed a "trial separation" in which you or your partner live separately in order to determine whether you want to continue your partnership. This kind of separation can lead to termination of your partnership if you or your partner ultimately decide that you cannot reconcile your differences and you live separately for at least 18 months. See *Permanent Separation*, below.

Plaintiff and Defendant

Throughout this chapter and the next, the terms "plaintiff partner" or "plaintiff" are used to refer to the domestic partner who initiates the termination proceeding. The terms "defendant partner" or "defendant" refer to the domestic partner against whom the complaint is filed.

Support During Separation

When domestic partners register, they agree to be "jointly responsible for each other's common welfare."[1] This obligation means that each partner "agrees to provide for the other partner's basic living expenses if the other partner is unable to provide for himself."[2] Although your obligation ends when your partnership is terminated, it continues during any period of separation unless you contractually agree otherwise.

If you depend upon your partner's support and are unable to provide for your basic living expenses, and if your partner is able but unwilling to provide you with support during the separation, you may ask the court to order such support by filing an application ***pendente lite*** for support.

In order to bring a claim for support, the plaintiff partner must show both partners were in a valid domestic partnership, that the defendant partner has actually abandoned the plaintiff, that the separation was not justifiable, and that the defendant has either neglected to or refused to provide support. The plaintiff partner should also make a written demand for support from the defendant by regular and certified mail with a return receipt requested.

The defendant partner can defend himself or herself by showing that the plaintiff is able to provide for himself, or that the partners had signed a valid agreement that altered or removed the obligation to provide support during the partnership. The defendant can also bring a counterclaim for termination

---

1.   N.J.S.A. 26:8A-4(b)(1).

2.   N.J.S.A. 26:8A-3.

of the domestic partnership.

Separation Agreements

As an alternative to filing for interim support during a period of separation, you and your partner can create a separation agreement, which is a written agreement that defines your rights and obligations to each other, and towards any children you may have, during the separation.

A separation agreement differs from a property settlement agreement in that you are defining rights and obligations during a period when you live apart but are not contemplating termination of your domestic partnership. If the purpose of living separately is to fulfill the waiting period required for termination based on separation, and you do not have any "reasonable possibility of reconciliation," you and your partner should negotiate a property settlement agreement. See *Property Settlement Agreements* in *Chapter 15: Termination Proceedings*, for more information.

The contents of your separation agreement are entirely up to you and your partner, and it may be as detailed or as general as you wish. If you have children, you should address issues such as shared duties, visits, and child support. You should also address personal issues such as fidelity during the separation and sharing time together.

Some common clauses include:

- **Financial Obligations**
    - Household and personal expenses
    - Partner maintenance and support
    - Payment and maintenance of life, health, auto and other insurance

- **Property Use and Distribution**
    - Use of residences and other real estate
    - Use of automobiles, boats, etc.
    - Personal and household items
    - Custody and care of pets
    - Management of rental and other investment properties
    - Banks and other financial accounts and instruments

- **Debts**
    - Payment of mortgages on property
    - Acknowledgement of joint debts
    - Apportionment of joint debts
    - Prohibitions on use of credit cards or other liability accounts
    - Agreement as to new debts

- **Taxes**
    - Liability for property taxes
    - Apportionment of exemptions for dependents
    - Apportionment of mortgage interest and other deductions
    - Homestead rebates

- **Children**
    - Custody and visitation

- Individual and shared responsibilities
- School and religion
- Alienation of affection
- Relocation and out-of-state trips
- Payment for schools, camps, vacation
- Amount of support
- Escalation, reduction and cessation of support
- Payment of health-related expenses
- Insurance

- **Litigation costs and expenses**
  - Court costs
  - Attorney's fees
  - Accountant's fees
  - Experts' and litigation fees

If your separation is a trial separation, you should also include a clause that restores your status as cohabiting domestic partners and voids your separation agreement upon reconciliation.

When you negotiate and draft your agreement, you and your partner have a legal obligation to deal fairly with each other. You must provide each other with a complete financial disclosure regarding your assets, liabilities and income, as well as disclose other relevant information. Your obligations of fairness to each other and full disclosure continue during the separation. If one of you is represented by an attorney, the other should have independent counsel to negotiate and/or review the agreement. See *Chapter 16: Legal Matters* for additional information on contracts and agreements.

Enforcement of a Separation Agreement

If you and your partner have entered into a settlement agreement, and one of you refuses to abide by the agreement, the other can ask the family court to enforce the agreement, at least in New Jersey. To enforce the agreement, you would file a complaint in the Family Part of the Superior Court - Chancery Division in either the country where you live or where your partner lives.

If your partner has relocated to another state, however, enforcement may be more difficult and in some states, impossible. First, you must seek enforcement of the agreement in New Jersey and obtain a judgment against your partner. This judgment will be enforceable against any property your partner has in New Jersey. Then, you must attempt to enforce the judgment in your partner's state of residence. In order to facilitate this, your order should omit references to your status as domestic partners. Even this will probably be useless in states such as Virginia, which prohibit recognition of any same-sex relationships or any rights or obligations arising from such relationships. See *Recognition of Your Rights* in *Chapter 2: The Domestic Partnership Act*, for more information.

TERMINATION IN A NUTSHELL

Termination of a domestic partnership is initiated when the plaintiff partner files a Complaint in the Superior Court, Chancery Division — Family Part, which states the essential facts of the case, the relief sought, the law on which the complaint is based, and the addresses of the parties involved. The plaintiff will also need to prepare a Summons to be served on the defendant partner, along with a copy of the Complaint, within ten days after the Complaint is filed.

The defendant partner has 35 days to answer the Complaint and to file any counterclaims or cross-claims against the plaintiff partner. If a defendant fails to answer, the termination may be granted by default, with the appropriate relief determined by the judge based on the evidence presented by the plaintiff partner.

As in marriage dissolution cases, neither party has a right to a jury trial to decide termination-related matters, such as the actual termination, distribution of assets, custody, and other termination matters. However, either or both parties have a right to request a jury trial if the Complaint includes causes of action such as personal injury, domestic torts, or related matters.

Once filed, the case will be assigned to one of four case management categories, either priority, complex, expedited, or standard, depending upon information provided in a Case Information Statement that each party must file. The case management category determines the speed with which the case proceeds. The court may also assign the case to a mediator to see if the termination can be resolved without the necessity of a trial.

After initial filings and assignment to a case track, the discovery phase of the case begins. The New Jersey Courts follow a broad discovery rule, allowing depositions of any person except a family member under age 18, written interrogatories, production of documents, and requests for admissions. The discovery process can feel quite intrusive and is designed to prevent the parties from hiding information and assets from each other during the termination process. It also allows the judge to make an educated decision regarding the division of assets between the parties.

Once the discovery process has completed, the judge will conduct a trial to determine the merits of the case. In most cases, the judge will grant the termination, if all the requirements have been met. However, the judge can dismiss the termination complaint if the plaintiff and defendant have not met all the requirements for termination. For example, if the reason for termination requires a specific waiting period, and the plaintiff filed prior to the expiration of that waiting period, the case will be dismissed. The plaintiff partner must also actively prosecute his or her case or the case will be dismissed by the judge.

After the judge grants the termination, the judge will have to determine how the jointly owned assets of the partnership will be distributed. Although under the Domestic Partnership Act, the judge is not required to resort to equitable distribution in a termination proceeding, the judge is allowed to do so and, since most family law judges are accustomed to its use in marriage dissolutions, equitable distribution will most likely be the norm rather than the exception.

Finally, after the termination is granted and the assets are distributed, the judge will notify the State registrar that the domestic partnership has been terminated, and the domestic partnership will be officially dissolved. However, the parties have a responsibility to notify any persons who may have received a copy of the Certificate of Domestic Partnership that the partnership has been terminated.

Should You Be Represented Or Do It Yourself?

One of the first decisions you will need to make is whether you should be represented by an attorney or whether you can handle the termination proceedings yourself. The answer to this will depend upon three factors: (1) how intertwined you are; (2) the degree of hostility between you and your partner; and (3) whether your partner is represented by an attorney.

If you and your partner have few or no jointly owned assets, are not financially dependent, and do not have any custody issues, you may not have great need for an attorney to help you with your termination. However, you and your partner may want to hire an attorney to prepare the termination complaint and related filings and to assist you with any filing questions you may have.

If there is a great deal of hostility between you, if you have substantial assets or one of you is greatly dependent upon the other, or if you have children, you will need representation by an attorney. Each partner should have his or her own attorney, and both of you should work closely with your attorneys and not attempt to circumvent the process.

If your partner has retained an attorney to handle the termination, then you should not attempt to represent yourself. Your partner's attorney, no matter how friendly he or she may seem, represents your partner's interests, not yours, and would be negligent if he or she did not fully advocate on behalf of your partner. You need someone equally zealous to represent your interests and, unless you are fully trained in the intricacies of marriage and partnership dissolution, you will be no match for your partner's attorney.

Alternatives To Court

Although your termination agreement must be finalized by a judge, this does not mean that you are required to conduct the entire termination process in the courts. There are several alternatives that can help you reduce the financial and emotional traumas that result from termination of your partnership.

You and your partner may want to consider working with attorneys who are part of the collaborative divorce movement. This movement consists of lawyers who help you and your partner terminate your partnership amicably without resorting to lengthy court battles. Not only can this process save you time and money, it can also help you and your ex-lover part as friends and not life-long mortal enemies. Collaborative divorce is particularly useful if you and your partner will need to remain actively involved in raising children.

You and your partner may also want to consider using a mediator or arbitrator to help you resolve your termination. Mediation is a process during which a trained facilitator helps you and your partner work out a termination agreement that is reviewed by your attorneys and then accepted by the judge. Mediation is a non-binding process, that is, you may revoke any agreement reached during the mediation process prior to it being approved by the judge. Arbitration is similar to mediation, except that you and your partner are legally bound by the agreement you work out with the assistance of the arbitrator.

Residency

Unlike the New Jersey divorce statutes, termination of a domestic partnership does not require that either party be a New Jersey resident for any particular length of time prior to filing. The only requirement is that one or both partners be domiciled at the time.

Residence vs. Domicile

Residence means any address at which you live more than temporarily. Domicile means having a bona fide connection with some fixed home. You may have several residences, but you have only one domicile.

Terminating Out-Of-State Partnerships And Civil Unions

Because the Domestic Partnership Act explicitly recognizes civil unions, reciprocal beneficiaries and domestic partnerships entered into in other jurisdictions, New Jersey courts have jurisdiction to terminate these in the same way they terminate domestic partnerships, if one or both partners establish a domicile in New Jersey. However, this raises certain issues related to such terminations.

First, because there is no length of residency requirement for termination, a New Jersey court may dismiss your termination action if the judge believes you have no present intent to make your New Jersey residence your domicile.

Second, upon termination, the court is required to notify the state registrar of your termination. However, they are not required to notify the state where you actually registered and may require you to do this yourself.

Third, the state in which you and your partner actually registered may or may not recognize the termination as equivalent to termination in that state. For example, New Jersey does not require you to be a resident for any specific period of time before you file. Vermont, however, requires one partner to reside in Vermont for at least six months prior to filing, and be a resident of that state for at least one year before the termination is granted.

Finally, courts in Vermont and Maine have yet to rule on whether they recognize a New Jersey domestic partnership as equivalent to a civil union or domestic partnership entered into in those states. If they do not recognize New Jersey domestic partnerships, then they would probably not recognize a termination decree from New Jersey.

Alternate Dispute Resolution

Courts today favor alternatives to trials, such as mediation or arbitration, as ways to resolve all kinds of disputes, including domestic disputes. Often, alternative dispute resolution ("ADR"), can be an effective way to minimize the financial and emotional cost of terminating a marriage or domestic partnership. At the very least, alternative dispute resolution will help you and your partner identify which issues you agree on and which issues remain to be resolved at trial. The most commonly used form of ADR in domestic disputes is mediation.

Mediation

You and your partner may want to consider mediation, particularly if you hold most of your assets in common, or have children. Divorce mediation has been quite successful and frequently result in couples that part as friends rather than sworn enemies. A good mediator can help you achieve a fair and equitable termination that minimizes the anger and hurt you may both be experiencing.

Mediation can be a highly beneficial process of resolving your differences and terminating your partnership. The mediator guides you through the process of developing your own, mutually acceptable termination agreement. The mediation process can also save you and your partner a considerable amount of time and expense. All mediation proceedings are confidential and, should the mediation fail, the discussions held during mediation may not be introduced in any further court proceedings.

Mediation is strictly a non-binding dispute resolution process. You may terminate the mediation at any time during the process and you are not bound by any proposed agreement. Even if the mediation is unsuccessful, it may at least help you and your partner reduce the number of disagreements you may have, thereby helping to simplify the termination process.

Even if you choose to use a mediator, you and your partner will still need separate representation by an attorney. In this case, however, your attorney will only advise you on the selection of a mediator, review any proposed settlement, and, if mediation is successful, file the termination agreement with the Superior Court. Although your attorney may be available by telephone during the mediation session, your attorney will generally not attend.

The process of mediation is fairly simple. You and your partner jointly select a mediator, who should be knowledgeable and experienced in divorce and termination proceedings, and should be trained and experienced as a mediator. Mediators may be attorneys, or they may be experienced professionals in fields such as finance or psychology. All mediators contribute the first three hours, including preparation, at no cost to you.

Once you have selected a mediator, you will first meet together with the mediator, who will explain the process of mediation to you. Some mediators will then want to meet with each of you separately, whereas others will try to get you to discuss your differences with each other. If feelings get a little raw, the mediator may place each of you in separate rooms and meet separately with each party, frequently going back and forth with proposals in a process known as "caucusing." If the mediator feels that the mediation is at an impasse and will not result in any form of agreement, he or she will usually suggest that the mediation be terminated. If, on the other hand, agreement is reached, the mediator will usually bring both of you back together to reduce the agreement to proposed settlement.

Once you and your partner have settled on an agreement, you should each have your attorney review the proposed settlement. The attorneys will then reduce the agreement to a formal termination agreement, which you and your partner will then sign.

Finding a Mediator

If you live in Atlantic, Bergen, Burlington, Morris, Ocean, Somerset, or Union Counties, there is a pilot program for mediation. For more information, check with the Family Court in these counties, or go to the New Jersey Courts Online web site at http://www.judiciary.state.nj.us/family/rosters/ for a list of mediators. In other counties, you should call the local Family Court to see if they maintain a list of mediators.

Binding Arbitration

Although it is similar to mediation, in that you voluntarily submit your entire dispute or some portion of it to a neutral third party, arbitration differs in that you and your partner agree that the arbitrator's decision is final and binding. This means that you cannot back out of the process once you have begun arbitration, and you cannot renege on the final decision.

Unlike mediation, arbitration is best used when you and your partner have been able to narrow down your dispute to a clearly defined issue or set of issues on which you are unable to agree to a decision. The arbitrator conducts a mini-trial on that issue or set of issues, during which he or she will listen to both parties, ask questions, establish the facts of the case, determine the applicable law, and render a final decision. The decision has the force of law, will almost always be confirmed by the judge in your case, and will rarely be disturbed on appeal.

REASONS FOR TERMINATION

The Domestic Partnership Act provides a list of seven causes of action for termination. These are:

- Voluntary sexual intercourse between a domestic partner and someone other than his or her domestic partner.

- Willful and continuous desertion for 12 or more consecutive months.

- Extreme mental and/or physical cruelty at least 3 months prior to filing.

- Separation for at least 18 or more consecutive months, with no reasonable prospect of reconciliation.

- Drug addiction or habituation, or habitual drunkenness for 12 or more continuous months.

- Institutionalization for mental illness for 24 or more consecutive months.

- Imprisonment for 18 or more consecutive months.

In addition, in the case of an opposite sex couple 62 years of age or older who have established a domestic partnership, their registered partnership is automatically terminated if they marry each other.

The above reasons for termination are nearly word-for-word counterparts to the reasons listed in the New Jersey divorce laws. Because of this, it is reasonable to assume that New Jersey courts will use the same reasoning when deciding to grant a petition for termination as they would use for granting a divorce.

The reasons for termination are divided into two forms: fault and no fault. Fault-based terminations are those where the partner filing the termination petition (the plaintiff) alleges that the other partner (the defendant) is at fault in the matter. No-fault terminations, on the other hand, simply allege that the two partners mutually wish to terminate their domestic partnership, or the partnership cannot be maintained due to one partner's mental or substance abuse problem. As in divorce, some termination proceedings will be filed as "no fault" terminations, which require at least 18 months of separation. However, because the fault-based reasons have shorter, or even no waiting periods, the majority of termination proceedings will be brought for one or more of these reasons.

Notably absent is one cause of action found in the divorce statute, "deviant sexual conduct." This may be because there have been few, if any, divorces granted on this basis, and that this cause is, therefore, an anachronism. More likely, however, this was omitted because of the U.S. Supreme Court decision in the *Lawrence v. Texas* case, which struck down laws that would regulate sodomy and other forms of private sexual conduct within the partnership.

Voluntary Sex Outside The Partnership

This cause of action for termination is similar to the provision of the New Jersey statute granting a divorce on the basis of adultery, although it uses broader language. Specifically, you must allege that your partner engaged in "voluntary sexual intercourse" with someone other than you after the domestic partnership was registered.

The sex of the other person does not matter; both heterosexual and homosexual intercourse is sufficient. Nor does it matter what particular sexual act or acts took place, so long as they took place with the consent of another person. Finally, it is sufficient cause if your partner engaged in voluntary sexual intercourse on only one occasion. The DPA does not set a minimum number of occurrences.

Unlike all other reasons for termination, this does not require you to wait any period of time prior to filing for termination. You may file for termination immediately upon finding out that your partner has had sex outside your partnership. Nor does it appear to matter if, for some reason, you chose not to act as soon as you learned about the outside sex.

You will be required to provide some form of proof that your partner is engaged in sex outside your domestic partnership. It does not really matter what form of proof you provide, so long as it meets legal standards for evidence and is more than mere suspicion on your part. You need to be careful, however, that you do not overstep legal bounds when attempting to corroborate your partner's infidelities; doing so could subject you to civil and/or criminal liability.

> ### Co-respondent
>
> The person your partner is having sex with is referred to at the "co-respondent." He or she must be named in the complaint for termination, if known, or must be described in as much detail as possible, if unknown. If the co-respondent's name is unknown, you will be required to show that it was not known at the time you filed your complaint. The co-respondent must be notified, if possible, and be given an opportunity to respond to the complaint. See *Chapter 15: Termination Proceedings*.

If you and your partner are both having sex outside your partnership, either of you (or both) may still use this as a basis for termination. The fact that you both have "unclean hands" is not supposed to affect the judge's determination on distribution of the partnership's assets. See *Distribution of Property* in *Chapter 16* for more information.

Desertion

Desertion is defined as "willful and continued desertion for a period of 12 or more consecutive months." The definition focuses on the intent of the defendant partner alone, even if the plaintiff partner ultimately agrees to the separation. Desertion is considered a fault-based cause of termination.

In a nutshell, you could claim desertion if your partner has intentionally and voluntarily acted upon his or her determination to end your domestic partnership, regardless of your wishes or intentions. Even if you ultimately acquiesce or even expressly agree, you are not prevented from bringing a desertion cause of action.

The courts in New Jersey have long recognized a form of desertion called constructive desertion. This form of desertion occurs when the defendant partner's behavior causes the other partner to initiate a separation. Your partner's misbehavior must be such that it causes you to abandon your shared residence. In this case, your partner is viewed as the deserter, even though you are the one who ultimately chose to leave.

Although less common, it is possible to claim constructive desertion based upon one partner's persistent refusal to sleep in the same room, or to engage in sexual relations, even if both partners continue to reside together.

If you file a petition for termination based upon desertion, you will need to prove the form of desertion, that it was against your wishes even if you ultimately agreed, and that it was for at least 12 consecutive months prior to filing for termination. The most common way to establish this is by proof that you and your partner have ceased living together as domestic partners for 12 or more consecutive months.

Extreme Cruelty

Extreme cruelty is a fault-based cause that includes "any physical or mental cruelty that endangers the safety or health of the plaintiff or makes it improper or unreasonable to expect the plaintiff to continue to cohabit with the defendant." The acts must be sufficiently extreme as to offend an ordinary person.

Physical acts can range from the obvious, such as assaults resulting in broken limbs or bruises, to more subtle acts, such as continuing to tickle someone even when asked to quit. It may even include physical violence directed at others or at physical objects in the vicinity. Mental cruelty can include hostility, persistent criticism, uncommunicative attitude, constant belittlement, abusive language and threats, and the like.

Extreme cruelty would normally be brought by a plaintiff in a termination proceeding. However, it can also be brought by a defendant as a counterclaim. Although only one act of extreme cruelty is required, it is more likely demonstrated by multiple acts over a period of time.

If you intend to terminate your partnership on the basis of extreme cruelty, you must wait at least three months from the date of the last act of cruelty complained of before filing, unless you are bringing this as a counterclaim. This last requirement does not mean you need to continue subjecting yourself to your partner's cruelty. Instead, you should first focus on getting yourself away from the abuse and cruel behavior and into a safe environment. Once three months have elapsed, you can then file your termination complaint.

Drug Addiction And Habitual Drunkenness

Any form of substance abuse can be the cause of termination, if it is voluntary and continued over at least a year. Habitual drunkenness has been defined as a fixed, frequent, irresistible or regular habit of drinking alcoholic beverages in such excessive quantities as to produce drunkenness. Substance abuse is now considered a medical problem rather than a behavioral choice. Thus, it is no longer considered to be a fault-based cause of termination.

This cause of action requires you to show evidence that your partner has been habitually using drugs or alcohol for at least 12 contiguous months following registration of your domestic partnership. Your partner's behavior prior to establishing your domestic partnership is not measured, although evidence of prior behavior could probably be presented in order to reinforce a claim that your partner's behavior is unlikely to change. You must also wait to file for termination until you can demonstrate at least 12 months of habituation.

The habitual substance abuse must also have taken place during a contiguous 12 month period immediately preceding the filing of the complaint. If your partner was a habitual drinker but stopped two months before you filed, the 12 month test has not been met. The courts will not grant termination based on this cause where someone has rehabilitated him or herself and is currently substance-free. However, if your partner relapses, the period of sobriety is viewed differently.

New Jersey courts have held that periods of sobriety during the 12 or more months, particularly during stays at rehabilitation facilities, do not automatically restart the 12 month waiting period. For example, if your partner is addicted to drugs, and during the 12 months prior to filing for termination, he or she goes into a rehab unit for 30 days, it does not start a new waiting period. The court will look at the defendant's behavior over the entire course of the prior 12 or more months to determine if there has been contiguous habituation.

Institutionalization Or Imprisonment

Institutionalization for mental illness is a no-fault cause for termination that requires you to show that your partner has been institutionalized, either voluntarily or involuntarily, for at least 24 consecutive months. Imprisonment, on the other hand, is considered a fault-based cause, for which you are required to wait the full 18 consecutive months before filing for termination, even if your partner has received a sentence that requires him or her to serve at least 18 months.

Although the institutionalization or imprisonment may have begun prior to registration of the domestic partnership, the waiting period does not begin until the domestic partnership is legally established. Thus, if you entered a domestic partnership with a prison inmate, assuming you met the common residence requirement, you would be required to wait 18 months before filing for termination, regardless of when your partner had originally been imprisoned.

Both causes require you to show proof that your partner was institutionalized or imprisoned for the full period of time. It isn't sufficient to allege that your partner was imprisoned and thereafter separated from you for the required period of time, if your partner was released in less than the required number of months.

For example, if your partner were arrested, removed from your common residence, imprisoned, released after 6 months, and took up residence apart from you for the next 12 months, you would be unable to file for termination based upon imprisonment. Instead you would have to file for termination based upon desertion.

If you resume living together after your partner's release from imprisonment for 18 or more months, you may not use imprisonment as a cause for termination. What has yet to be determined is what happens if, after serving a sentence of less than 18 months, your partner is released to a residential facility, such as a halfway house, to serve the remaining sentence. Since the residency at the halfway house is mandatory, it could be considered a form of imprisonment. Thus, you may be able to terminate the domestic partnership after the required 18 month wait.

If your partner had been institutionalized for mental illness, you may only file for termination based on this cause if, at the time of filing, your partner is still institutionalized and has been so during the last 24 months. If, on the other hand, your partner had been institutionalized for 24 months and was released prior to your filing for termination, you will have to find some other reason for termination. However, occasional or even regular leave from a mental hospital does not interrupt the period of consecutive institutionalization, particularly if it is part of a regular rehabilitation program.

Permanent Separation

A permanent separation is one of the most common no-fault reasons for termination of a domestic partnership. However, it can sometimes be the costliest, because it requires the partners to live "separate and apart" for at least 18 consecutive months before they can file for termination. At the end of that time, you and your partner must show that there is "no reasonable possibility of reconciliation."

This so-called "no fault" termination is begun when you and your partner mutually agree to separate.

During the 18 month "cooling off" period, you and your partner must maintain separate residences, and may not cohabit. You should also avoid having sexual relations during this period, lest the court decide there was "reasonable possibility of reconciliation."

For a variety of reasons, you and your partner may want the termination process to be as short as possible. In that case, you and your partner may want to consult with an attorney to explore whether any of the fault-based causes would shorten the termination process. Unlike the "no fault" separation, you and your partner may continue to live together after filing for termination on a fault ground.

NULLIFICATION

In order to register as domestic partners, the Domestic Partnership Act sets out nine requirements that must be met at the time of registration[3] (see *Chapter 5, Eligibility*.) If all of these requirements are not met at the time of registration, then the domestic partnership is not established, even though an affidavit of domestic partnership has been sworn to and filed and a certificate has been issued. Although such a domestic partnership is invalid, the fact remains that the local registrar and the State registrar will have recorded the partnership.

Void or Voidable?

A *void* domestic partnership is one that is completely invalid for any purpose from its inception. A void domestic partnership does not need to be terminated or nullified by the courts; the partners can simply separate, although they may have equitable rights in property.

A *voidable* domestic partnership would be one that is legally binding until either partner obtains a court order declaring the domestic partnership a nullity. The nullification can only be obtained while both partners are alive.

Neither the Act nor the Regulations specifically set out a procedure for removing an invalid domestic partnership registration from the local and state registry. However, New Jersey law does provide a proceeding called nullification (annulment) that is used to end marriages that are invalid. Since the requirements for entering a marriage are similar to those in the DPA, it is reasonable to believe that courts will adopt a similar procedure with domestic partnerships.

If either partner, at the time of registration, was in a marriage recognized by New Jersey law, or was a member of another registered domestic partnership, civil union, or reciprocal beneficiary relationship with another person, the new domestic partnership would be void. Since a valid domestic partnership had not been formed, neither termination nor nullification would be required. Instead, one or the other partner would need to file a notice of correction with the state registrar.

On the other hand, failure of any of the following would render the domestic partnership voidable:

- The partners did not share a common residence as defined in the Act, at the time of registration;

- The partners are related to each other up to and including the fourth degree of consanguinity;

- The partners are of opposite sex and at least one is under the age of 62;
- One or both partners is under the age of 18; or

---

3. N.J.S.A. 26:8A-4(b) Establishment of domestic partnership; requirements; affidavit.

- Failing to wait the required 180 days after termination of a prior domestic partnership, civil union or reciprocal beneficiary relationship.

In this situation, nullification would be appropriate unless the partners chose to ratify the partnership after the defect had been cured. How this ratification would be accomplished is not yet clear but it may require some public act such as providing some form of notice to the registrar.

Nullification Procedure

If you and your partner registered even though you did not meet all the requirements, you could have the domestic partnership declared null by seeking a judgment of nullity in the Family Part of the Superior Court of your county of residence.

You should be aware of one possible complication of filing for nullification of your partnership. If a proceeding is brought a judge could impose a fine of $1,000.00 on the partner who made the misrepresentation in the affidavit of domestic partnership.

Effect Of Nullification

The effect of nullification of a domestic partnership would be similar to annulment of a marriage—the domestic partnership would be as if it never were registered. The court would also be expected to send notification of the nullification to the local and State registrar so that they may revise the records of domestic partnership they maintain. As far as any property you may have jointly acquired during the period, the court would probably use its powers to effect an equitable distribution. See *Equitable Distribution* in *Chapter 15: Termination Proceedings*.

CHAPTER 15
TERMINATION PROCEEDINGS

Like dissolution of marriage, termination of a domestic partnership is initiated when you file a pleading called a Complaint for Termination in the Family Part of the Superior Court, Chancery Division in the appropriate New Jersey county, after which your partner is served with a copy of your Complaint and a Summons. If you have hired an attorney to represent you, he or she will prepare and file the necessary documents for you.

In your Complaint, you will allege either one or more fault-based reasons (called "grounds") for termination or no fault. You will also need to provide the facts of your case, your partner's name and address, the statute you are relying on for relief, and information about any prior family actions between you and your partner.

If the basis for your complaint is voluntary sexual relations outside your partnership, you will need to provide the name and address of the person or persons with whom your partner was having sex. If you are unable to identify this person (called the co-respondent), you must be able to provide at least a description of the co-respondent, as well as all information you have regarding the time, place and details of the outside sex. If you know the name of the co-respondent, you will need to serve a Notice to Co-respondent on that person.

In New Jersey, you do not have a right to have a jury decide whether your domestic partnership should be terminated, and what relief should be granted. However, if you have included claims for personal injury, domestic torts, or some other causes of action related to your termination complaint, or if your partner has done so in his or her counterclaim, either of you can ask for a jury trial on the non-termination issues.

> **Caution**
>
> Nearly every aspect of termination discussed here is subject to change, by legislative modification of the DPA, by adoption of new Rules of Court, or by interpretation of the Courts. Thus, you should periodically check this book's associated web site for updates and new information.

WHERE TO FILE

Before determining where to file, you need to determine two things: (1) jurisdiction and (2) venue. Jurisdiction refers to the legal authority of a particular court to hear your case and decide whether a domestic partnership should be terminated. Venue refers to the county in which your termination proceeding should be filed.

Determining jurisdiction

Jurisdiction is determined by two statutory questions: what kind of court can hear your case and how soon can it be heard. By law, termination cases are filed in the Family Part of the Superior Court, Chancery Division, a special court found in every county that hears all family-related matters, including divorce, domestic violence, child custody and support. However, you cannot file your case until it is "ripe" for determination, that is, a statutory time limit has passed.

The date on which your reason for termination arose determines when and where a termination proceeding may be filed. The basic rules are:

- **Voluntary Sexual Intercourse Outside the Partnership**. Termination cases based on this cause of action can be filed immediately.

- **Willful Desertion**. This cause of action has a 12 month waiting period from the time of desertion.

- **Extreme Mental / Physical Cruelty**. This cause requires you to wait 3 months after the last act of cruelty complained of.

- **Drug Addiction / Habitual Drunkenness**. This cause of action has a 12 month waiting period. Note that even if there are periods of sobriety, it does not necessarily mean that you must wait 12 months again.

- **Institutionalization**. The cause can be filed after 24 months of continuous institutionalization. It does not matter if the person gets weekend or other short-term passes so long as they are not fully discharged.

- **Imprisonment**. The cause requires a wait of 18 months of continuous imprisonment, including time spent in a halfway house.

- **Separation (No Fault)**. This cause arises when the partners have maintained separate residences for at least 18 months without prospects for reconciliation.

Unlike divorce, the Domestic Partnership Act does not require a person to be a bona fide resident of New Jersey in order to file for termination of a domestic partnership. Thus, the only requirement is that the county court in which you file have venue, a legal term that means that the court is the proper and most convenient location for trial of a case. However, the venue rules are based on your domicile, that is, the place where you have your permanent home making it likely that the residence requirement will be interpreted to mean your primary residence in New Jersey.

Plaintiff and Defendant

Throughout this chapter, the terms "plaintiff partner" or "plaintiff" are used to refer to the domestic partner who initiates the termination proceeding. The terms "defendant partner" or "defendant" refer to the domestic partner against whom the complaint is filed.

Determining Venue

The proper venue, meaning the county in which your termination action should be filed, is a little more difficult to determine than jurisdiction. Venue is determined by one of three things: (1) where the cause of action arose, that is, in what state and county did the events surrounding termination occur; (2) where the parties are domiciled, which generally means where they make their homes; or (3) where the non-resident defendant partner was served with legal process.

Venue for termination, divorce, nullity and separate maintenance actions is determined as follows:

- If the plaintiff partner was a New Jersey domiciliary at the time the cause of action arose, that plaintiff may file the complaint in the county in which he or she was domiciled at that time. If the plaintiff was not a New Jersey domiciliary at the time the cause arose, then the complaint can be filed in the county where the defendant partner was domiciled at that time.

- If neither the plaintiff nor the defendant partner was domiciled in New Jersey when the cause of action arose, then the plaintiff must file the complaint in the county where he or she is currently domiciled in New Jersey. If the plaintiff lives outside New Jersey, however, then the complaint must be filed in the county in which the defendant partner is domiciled in New Jersey when served with process.

- If neither the plaintiff partner nor the defendant partner was domiciled at the time the cause of action arose or are not currently domiciled in New Jersey, one or the other partner must establish a domicile in New Jersey in order to file for termination. As previously discussed, there is no length of residency requirement, nor is your New Jersey domicile required to be your sole residence.

WHAT TO FILE

In order to initiate a termination proceeding, the plaintiff partner must file a complaint and serve a summons on the defendant partner. The plaintiff partner must also state whether they will be asking for equitable distribution of the assets of the partnership. If there are children of the relationship, the complaint must also deal with any issues related to custody and/or support of the children. Finally, if there are any additional claims, such as torts related to physical violence, they should be included with the complaint.

The Complaint

There is currently no specific form for domestic partnership termination. Thus, the basic format used for dissolution of a marriage should be used. The basic elements that each complaint must contain are:

- A statement of the essential facts that make up the basis for the relief sought.

- The statute or statutes that the complaint relies on. In this case, the statutory sections that should be cited are N.J.S.A. 26:8A-10a(1), for the jurisdiction, and the specific provision relating to the reason for the termination, N.J.S.A. 26:8A-10a(2)(a)-(e). Couples who are filing for termination of a civil union or another state's domestic partnership should also reference N.J.S.A. 26:8A-6c, granting recognition of their relationship as a domestic partnership.

- The street addresses of all of the parties to the complaint, if known at the time. If defendant partner's address is unknown, the complaint should so state this.

- A statement as to whether there have been any prior family court actions between the parties.

- A recitation of the facts upon which venue is based.

You should also consider any additional claims that may need to be filed with this complaint, including domestic violence claims, or other torts.

The complaint must be captioned "Superior Court, Chancery Division — Family Part".

Co-respondent in Voluntary Sexual Intercourse Complaints

If the basis for the termination is voluntary sexual intercourse outside the partnership, the complaint must name the individual or individuals with whom the defendant had sex (called the co-respondent). In many cases, the plaintiff partner does not know the name of the co-respondent. If he or she is unknown, the complaint must still provide enough information tending to describe the person, the time, place and circumstances of the acts complained of in a way that is sufficient for the defendant and the court to determine the validity of the complaint. A plaintiff partner cannot simply make vague accusations about infidelity as the basis for termination of the partnership.

If the co-respondent is still unknown at the time of the hearing, the plaintiff will be required to show that the person or persons were unknown at the time of filing and are still unknown. If the co-respondent is known, the plaintiff partner must serve him or her with a copy of the complaint within 30 days of filing and the plaintiff partner must file an affidavit that this notice has been provided. The co-respondent is entitled to intervene in the termination proceedings.

Other requirements

The following items must accompany your complaint:

- **Affidavit of verification and non-collusion**. An oath or affirmation made by you that your allegations in the complaint are true to the best of your knowledge, and that your complaint is made without collusion, must by you and attached to your complaint.

- **Affidavit or certification of insurance coverage**. This is a list of all insurance coverage you have and must include any insurance coverage that was cancelled in the 90 day period prior to the complaint. If the only relief sought is termination without equitable distribution, or if both parties have a property settlement agreement, they may file an affidavit stating this in lieu of the insurance coverage.

- **Filing fee**. The filing fee for termination is $250.00. If you are unable to pay this fee at the time you file, you may apply for a waiver of the filing fee.

The Summons

Once the complaint is filed, it must be served within 10 days along with a summons on the defendant partner, using the standard form found in Appendix XII-A of the New Jersey Rules of Court.

If the defendant partner is a resident of New Jersey, the summons should be personally served by having an uninterested person, such as a process server, deliver it personally to him or her, or by leaving a copy at the defendant partner's home or usual abode with a household member who is at least 14 years of age. If you and your partner are cooperatively seeking a termination, the summons may be delivered to any person the defendant partner appoints, including his or her attorney.

If the defendant partner is no longer resident in New Jersey, you may still have the summons served on him or her by someone who is legally qualified to serve process in that state or country. You may also serve them by sending a copy by registered or certified mail, return receipt requested, and simultaneously by regular U.S. mail to his or her last known residence.

Finally, if you are simply unable, after diligently trying, to serve the defendant with process, you may petition the court for permission to serve them in some other way, such as publication of a notice in a newspaper.

The Answer

The defendant partner is required to respond to the complaint by filing an Answer, which may include a counterclaim, or by making an appearance. Most commonly, the defendant will file an Answer, which states the defenses to the original complaint and which admits or denies each of the allegations made by the plaintiff partner. If an allegation is not denied, it is considered admitted. The Answer must be filed within 35 days after service of the original Complaint.

An Answer is served on the plaintiff by mail or hand-delivery. It is unnecessary to have a process server deliver the Answer. If an attorney represents the plaintiff partner, the Answer should be sent to his or her attorney, as should all other correspondence.

Default Judgment

If the defendant does not respond to the termination complaint by filing either an answer and pursuing the case, or by making an appearance, the plaintiff may ask the court to enter a default judgment. This is particularly helpful if the defendant is uncooperative or cannot, in good faith, be located. However, the defendant can later petition the court to have the default judgment set aside, if the defendant can provide a good reason for the failure to respond.

Counterclaims

In the Answer, the defendant partner can state one or more related causes of action, including non-family law causes, as counterclaims. If the defendant partner makes any counterclaims, the plaintiff must file an Answer to the counterclaims within 20 days after having been served with the counterclaim.

CASE MANAGEMENT

In the New Jersey courts, cases are placed into one of four categories, depending upon their priority. Case management determines the speed with which the case proceeds through the courts. The Family Part assignment judge will assign the case as follows:

- **Priority Track.** A case is assigned to this track if it involves child custody or parenting time issues.

- **Complex Track.** A case will be assigned to this track if it appears to be particularly time consuming or difficult.

- **Expedited Track.** A case will be assigned to this track if it appears that there will be a minimum of pretrial proceedings, including discovery.

- **Standard Track.** The "catch-all" for case management.

According to the New Jersey Rules of Court, you can expect that a termination case will be assigned to the expedited track if there is no dispute as to the assets to be divided and no custody or parenting issues, if the parties have been together less than five years and have no children, the parties have a settlement agreement, or the termination is uncontested. However, given the unique nature of termination proceedings, an assignment judge could assign a case to the complex track.

Case Information Statement

Within 20 days after the defendant partner has filed his or her Answer to the complaint, both sides must file a Case Information Statement. This is a mandatory requirement and, if you fail to file one, the judge will dismiss your case. The Case Information Statement is particularly important if you are asking for equitable distribution. An example Case Information Statement is found in *Appendix U: Family Part Case Information Statement.*

Discovery

Once the defendant partner has answered the Complaint, the pretrial period begins. The pretrial process primarily involves the use of discovery.

In termination cases, as in marriage dissolution, discovery is limited in ways that are designed to minimize the hurt feelings that normally accompany the end of a relationship. As such, discovery may be had through the use of written interrogatories (lists of questions that must be answered in writing) and depositions (a question and answer session held, under oath, in a formal setting). All other forms of discovery are permitted only with leave of the court.

Interrogatories can be far-reaching and often seek financial information. Questions regarding such financial information may be answered by reference to the Case Information Statement. Depositions may be taken of any person except minor family members and may include experts who are hired to value property for purposes of equitable distribution.

Discovery must be completed within 90 days from the date of service, if the case has been assigned to the expedited track. If assigned to the standard track, discovery must be completed in 120 days.

The Hearing

If you and your partner are able to arrive at a settlement agreement, your case will be scheduled for an uncontested hearing. If you are the plaintiff, you are required to be in attendance at the hearing. If you are the defendant, you will not need to make a personal appearance at the hearing unless you have filed a counterclaim.

During the hearing, you will be asked to answer a series of questions that are designed to establish that the termination complaint is unopposed, and that you and your partner have reached a settlement that is fair to all parties. If there are children, you will also be asked if you both understand and agree to the custody and support arrangements.

At the conclusion of the uncontested hearing, the plaintiff partner's attorney will submit an agreed Form of Judgment along with a copy of a Settlement Agreement, if one has been prepared.

If the termination proceeding is opposed, then the matter will proceed to trial as a contested matter. At the conclusion of the trial, the judge will render a decision as to the termination.

JUDGMENT

Unless the case is dismissed, either because the plaintiff partner did not pursue the case, or the partners reconcile and the Complaint is withdrawn, a termination proceeding will result in a termination decree that declares that the domestic partnership is now ended. This decree, however, is not the last step.

First, the court must notify the State registrar that the domestic partnership has been terminated. Second, the judge will decide whether or not attorney fees will be awarded to either party. Finally, the court must decide how the property of the partnership will be distributed.

Notification of Termination

After judgment is entered, the court will notify the State Registrar of the termination by faxing it a Notice of Termination. In addition to this notification, however, each partner must notify anyone to whom they have given a copy of the Certificate of Domestic Partnership that the partnership has been legally terminated. See *Post-termination Issues* later in this chapter.

Attorney's Fees and Costs

In most cases, each partner will be responsible for their own attorneys' fees. However, in some circumstances the court may require one partner to shift part or all of the cost of the termination proceeding to the other partner. The most likely circumstance under which fee shifting would take place is when a termination proceeding is coupled with a determination of child custody and/or support.

Another way to shift or share the cost of the termination case is by a court order to sell, mortgage, or otherwise encumber assets of the partnership in order to finance the case. This is particularly helpful if one or both of you have insufficient income or individual assets to pay attorneys' fees. In that case, the financially disadvantaged partner would ask the court to enter an order directing both partners to agree to use the joint assets to finance the case.

Recognition of Termination

Your termination decree and any accompanying order are enforceable throughout New Jersey. However, its validity outside the state is less certain.

The states of Vermont, Connecticut, and California will most likely grant it full faith and credit and enforce any associated order. In states like Maine or Hawaii, where the legal protection for same-sex couples is limited, recognition is less certain. In states without a Defense of Marriage statute or amendment (including Massachusetts), the termination decree would probably not be recognized but the courts may enforce any accompanying order, so long as it was not against public policy. Of the states with Defense of Marriage statutes or amendments, neither the termination decree nor the order would be recognized and enforced. For further discussion, see *Recognition of Your Rights* in *Chapter 2*.

DISTRIBUTION OF PROPERTY

Once the court has entered its judgment of termination, it will turn its attention to the distribution of property. There are two issues that must be dealt with in this regard to distribution. First, what property should be subject to distribution and, second, how should that property be divided.

Jointly-Owned versus Separate Property

The Domestic Partnership Act defines the "division and distribution of jointly held property" as one of the powers of the Superior Court during termination proceedings. This means, however, that you and your partner must be able to show what property is jointly owned and what is individually owned. Furthermore, unless each partner can demonstrate otherwise, each partner will be assumed to have an undivided equal share of each joint asset.

If there are disputes as to percentage of ownership of joint assets, you may be required to demonstrate that you contributed more than an equal amount to the purchase of the asset. There are a variety of ways you can establish this, such as producing receipts, cancelled checks, or other forms of payment. If your basis for joint ownership is "sweat equity," you may have more difficulty proving your ownership without outside corroboration.

You and your partner may also have signed some form of agreement, such as a domestic partnership agreement, that specifically identifies joint and individual assets. Because the DPA affirmatively supports contractual agreements between partners, you may find the court considers this binding and will not look further into the issue of joint versus individual ownership of assets.

Lastly, if you and your partner executed a property settlement agreement either with or without the help of a mediator, the court will consider this when making the distribution.

Beginning and Ending Dates

When determining what assets were acquired during the domestic partnership, the court will need to establish the beginning and ending dates of the partnership. This presents a difficulty if you and your partner have been living together for some time before the Domestic Partnership Act went into effect. Some judges may decide that the only property that can be divided in a termination proceeding is that which was acquired after you and your partner registered. For couples who have been together for much longer periods of time prior to the enactment of the Domestic Partnership Act, you may need to convince the court that an earlier date should be used in determining which property should be divided.

Establishing the ending date becomes the harder problem. In some cases, the court will hold that the partnership terminates on the date of filing the Complaint for Termination. For separation ("no fault") terminations, however, the ending date may be set earlier if you and your partner have somehow agreed to an earlier date.

The most common way to establish an ending date is through a separation agreement, either written or oral. If you and your partner executed a written separation agreement at or around the time you first separated, the date of the agreement is set as the ending date.

Look-Back Periods

When the Domestic Partnership Agreement went into effect on July 10, 2004, many same-sex couples who initially registered had been living together for many years. Prior to registration, these couples acquired substantial property that, had they been registered, would be considered a joint asset of the partnership.

Thus, it would seem particularly unjust if distribution of the joint property of the partnership only took into consideration the property acquired after registration. For many same-sex couples, a significant amount of property would have been acquired by the partners during the years they lived together without the ability to marry or otherwise achieve legal recognition of their partnership. Unless those partners had protected themselves through contractual agreements, such as partnership agreements, living together agreements, and separation agreements, the Domestic Partnership Act as well as the normal rules regarding equitable distribution seem to limit the court to distribution of property acquired after registration.

New Jersey courts have, however, used a limited form of "look-back" when the property was acquired in anticipation of the marriage, in order to include property acquired before marriage within the bounds of equitable distribution. For example, the courts have included in the property subject to equitable distribution a house that was acquired by an opposite-sex couple prior to their marriage. The court reasoned that, since the house was purchased in anticipation of the marriage, it should be considered a part of the assets of the marriage.

Individual partners in a same-sex domestic partnership have a powerful argument to use in favor of distribution of assets acquired before registration, particularly if the couple had been together for quite some time. That argument is based on the concept of "ratification."

As discussed in *Nullification* (in *Chapter 15,*) when an opposite-gender couple discovers after some time that their marriage was defective, the defect results in a voidable marriage. However, the couple can undergo a legal marriage ceremony, which ratifies their defective marriage. The ratification dates back to the date of the defective marriage and results in the marriage being considered valid ab initio, that is, from the initial date.

Using the concept of ratification, a same-sex couple that had been together for many years prior to the enactment of the Domestic Partnership Act could be said to have ratified their partnership if they registered within a reasonable time after July 10, 2004. This ratification may be sufficient to convince a judge that the date of formation of the domestic partnership was some time earlier than the date of registration and, therefore, consider assets acquired during that period to be part of the assets subject to distribution.[1]

Basics of Property Division

Following the entry of judgment in your termination case, the court will use one of two ways to distribute the assets of the partnership. On the one hand, it may use a simple division of jointly-held assets, based on percentage of ownership. Alternatively, it may apply the rules of equitable distribution, as it does for the division of marital property during a divorce. In either case, the court will take into consideration property ownership determinations that you and your partner made in any other contracts between you, such as a domestic partnership agreement or settlement agreement.

Simple Property Division

The simplest method for property distribution under the Domestic Partnership Act is a strict distribution of the jointly owned property that was acquired during the partnership. This may be a particularly unfair way to distribute the partners' assets, since it may be difficult to prove percentage of ownership or that something is separately or jointly owned. It may also be unfair if one partner has acquired substantially more individually-owned assets during the partnership to which the other partner has contributed significantly in non-financial ways. For example, if two partners lived in the house that was owned by one partner, and both had contributed to the upkeep and equity, it would be unfair to treat such an asset as an individual asset not subject to distribution.

---

1.   In many situations, the benefits and obligations of domestic partners will only accrue from the date of registration. For example, in a recently-decided case, a suit for loss of consortium by a domestic partner was allowed to proceed but only for the acts that occurred after the couple had registered. In another case, a disabled veteran's property tax exemption was applied to domestic partners but only from the date of registration.

If a simple distribution of joint property would not result in a fair distribution to you, then you or your attorney should urge the court to effect an equitable distribution of property.

Equitable Distribution

The Domestic Partnership Act specifies that the court "shall in no event be required to effect an equitable distribution of property, real or personal, legally and beneficially acquired by both partners or either partner during the domestic partnership." However, this language does not direct the court that it is forbidden to do such a distribution, and since judges in family court use equitable distribution in divorce cases, you should argue for equitable distribution if it makes sense to do so in your situation.

Equitable distribution means that the court uses its equity powers to bring about a distribution of property in a way that is fair ("equitable") to both partners. Currently, equitable distribution is based on the following set of factors, which are based on those enumerated in the divorce statutes. These are:

- The duration of the partnership (including any period prior to the actual registration);

- The age, physical and emotional health of each partner;

- The income or property each partner brought to the partnership;

- The standard of living during the partnership;

- Any written agreement made by the partners before or during the partnership concerning property division;

- The economic circumstances of each partner at the time the property division becomes effective;

- The income and earning capacity of each partner at the time of property division;

- The contribution of each partner to the other partner's education, training or earning power;

- The contribution of each partner to the acquisition, dissipation, preservation, depreciation or appreciation in the amount or value of the property;

- The contribution of a partner as a homemaker;

- The tax consequences to each partner of the distribution;

- The present value of the property;

- The needs of a custodial parent in regard to the partners' home or household assets;

- The debts and liabilities of each partner;

- The need for any trust funds to secure foreseeable medical or educational needs of a partner or any children.

The court may also take into consideration any other factors it deems relevant to your particular situation. After consideration of all factors, the court will publish its findings of fact in regard to asset eligibility or ineligibility, asset valuation, and its determination of equitable distribution.

The court will also base its determination on a presumption that each partner made a substantial financial or nonfinancial contribution to the acquisition of income and property during your partnership. Either or both of you may produce evidence refuting this determination. For example, you may have contributed substantially more to the mortgage payments on your home.

Liabilities

As part of the property division process, the court will require you and your partner to settle joint debts. In many cases, it will be clear which debts are joint debts of the partnership and which are individual debts. The Domestic Partnership Act provides that debts that are contracted by one partner before the domestic partnership, and debts that are taken on by one partner during the domestic partnership are individual debts for which the individual partner has no liability.

However, there are a number of exceptions that have arisen out of marriage cases that may be applied to domestic partners when it comes to determining liability for debts. When deciding if a husband or wife is responsible for a spouse's individual debts contracted during the marriage, the New Jersey courts have looked at the purpose of the debt and the expectations of the spouses. Where they have determined that the liability came about as a result of payment for a necessity of the marriage, such as food or medicine, the debt can be considered a joint debt.

When same-sex couples register as domestic partners, they agree in the affidavit to joint responsibility for each other's common welfare. Therefore, if one partner takes on debt for this purpose, the debt could be construed as a joint debt. Certainly, the partner who took on the debt would have a right to seek repayment of some portion of that debt from his or her partner.

Other situations where individual debts could be construed as joint debts would be if the debt was taken on in anticipation of the domestic partnership being registered, or where two partners have lived together for some time prior to the enactment of the domestic partnership act.

Property Settlement Agreements

If you and your partner have executed a settlement agreement, either as a result of your own efforts, or as a result of mediation or arbitration, the court will base its division of property on this agreement, unless it finds the agreement is invalid. See *Separation Agreements* and *Property Settlement Agreements* in *Chapter 14: Separation, Termination and Nullification.*

Domestic Partnership Agreements

If you and your partner executed a domestic partnership agreement setting out your property rights, you or your partner may ask the court to enforce the terms of this agreement. So long as it finds the agreement valid, the court will usually abide by its terms.

If you have signed such an agreement, and you believe it is now being unfairly asserted against you, you or your attorney should urge the court to effect an equitable distribution and to consider the agreement in that context, rather than simply basing the distribution on this agreement. However, you will have the burden of proof to show the court that the agreement should not be enforced against you.

Property Held in Other States

Where you and your partner jointly own property in another state, you may encounter some difficulty trying to enforce a court order tied to a termination decree, particularly in states where there is a Defense of Marriage Act. In order to avoid possible problems, you may want to ask the court to execute any orders partitioning out-of-state property separately from the termination judgment, and avoid referencing the termination in the order.

MAINTENANCE AND SUPPORT

The Domestic Partnership Act specifically states that any obligation to support your partner ends with termination. However, the Act lets you contractually add obligations, such as a promise to support the partner, and these support obligations may form the basis for a suit for continued maintenance (commonly known as *alimony*.)

The DPA does not require agreements between partners be written and so it is possible for an oral agreement to provide support after termination of the domestic partnership to be enforceable. However, neither you nor your partner should rely on an oral agreement and any agreements between you should be in a writing signed by both of you.

Before the rules for domestic partnership termination were released by the Administrative Office of the Courts, it seemed clear that the Act specifically discouraged the awarding of support following termination of a domestic partnership. Now, however, the courts appear to be allowing all other relief under dissolution to be used in termination of domestic partnership.

Furthermore, where individuals with registered partnerships wish to apply for relief without terminating the partnership, such as support, separate maintenance or partition of property, they may do so by filing on the dissolution docket.

Since this area of the law is currently unsettled, you should retain a knowledgeable marital law attorney if you are planning on seeking any form of post-termination maintenance or interim support.

Parenting Issues

According to the 2000 Census, nearly one in three New Jersey same-sex couples have children living with them. In many cases, the children are those of one partner from a prior marriage or relationship, and the other partner has occupied the role of co-parent. In other cases, the couple has jointly adopted or undergone a second-parent adoption.

As a result, a termination proceeding may involve the determination of child custody, visitation rights, and child support. These actions should normally be joined as part of the termination complaint by either the plaintiff partner or the defendant partner.

Although the Domestic Partnership Act does not address the issues of child custody and support, the New Jersey courts have been particularly progressive in their support for parental rights among same-sex couples. For example, a New Jersey court awarded visitation rights to a lesbian after she and her partner had terminated their partnership.

You should be aware, however, that some states will not recognize your custodial and/or support arrangements, even if finalized by a New Jersey court. For example, a Virginia court has refused to recognize the jurisdiction of a Vermont court in a disputed child custody matter on the basis that Virginia law forbids the recognition of civil unions, domestic partnerships and similar legal arrangements. Although eventually disputes like these will have to be decided by the United States Supreme Court, the outcome in such a situation is currently legally uncertain. Therefore, if you and your partner have children, it is particularly important that you work together cooperatively, if possible, toward resolving any custody arrangements.

POST-TERMINATION ISSUES

After the court has granted your termination, there are certain things you and your former partner must do in order to notify others of the termination.

If you and your former partner gave copies of the Certificate of Domestic Partnership to any third parties, such as your employers, in order to receive any benefits that are not automatically granted, you must notify these third parties that your partnership has been terminated.

The Domestic Partnership Act requires this notice of termination to be in writing, and given or sent to the last known address of the third party. To protect yourself, you should send all termination notices by certified mail with a return receipt requested. You do not need to send any court documents substantiating the termination notice, nor do both of you need to send notice to the same third party.

Although the Act specifies that ex-partners no longer incur further obligation to each other after the termination has been granted, you should notify any creditors or financial institutions with which you and your partner jointly dealt. As above, at least one of you should notify these third parties in writing, and you should send these notices by certified mail with a return receipt requested.

If you or your former partner fails to notify third parties that your domestic partnership has been terminated, it will not in any way delay or prevent termination. Furthermore, the DPA allows any third party who suffers any loss as a result of a failure to provide notice of termination to sue the former partner who had the obligation to provide the notice for any resulting losses.

You are personally obliged, under the Domestic Partnership Act, to give notice of termination only to those third parties to which you, yourself, gave a copy of the Certificate of Domestic Partnership. However, unless you and your former partner agree in a writing signed by both of you that one of you will take on the obligation to provide termination notices, you should take it upon yourself to provide written notice to all third parties in order to protect yourself from future liability.

Revocation

You should review and update all documents and contracts you and your former partner had executed in order to make sure they reflect your new legal status. At a minimum, you should update your will to disinherit your ex-partner (if you so desire), remove your ex-partner's name from any powers of attorney and declaration of guardianship, and remove your ex-partner as a beneficiary of your life and other insurance. Under New Jersey law, termination causes an automatic revocation of your designation of your ex-partner as your medical proxy, unless you specify otherwise. In other states, no such automatic revocation takes place and your partner would still be viewed as your fiduciary in all documents.

Joint Property

Although the termination decree will divide the ownership of all joint property, you will be required to file appropriate change of title. If your division of property involves one partner buy out the other's share of real property, the seller may be assessed a realty transfer fee in New Jersey. You should also meet with a tax advisor to discuss and (hopefully) minimize any taxes you may be assessed.

If you and your partner will continue to hold joint ownership of any real estate, you should decide how you and your ex-partner will divide the rights and responsibilities, such as whether one of you will occupy the premises, and how financial liabilities, such as taxes and insurance, will be handled. You should also decide whether you want to continue any rights of survivorship and, if not, you will need to modify any deeds that contain this right. You also need to review and update the rights in any other jointly held assets, such as bank accounts, automobiles, and the like.

SUMMARY

It may be some years before we see the full development of the rules and the law regarding termination of domestic partnerships. The only thing that we can be sure of is that, just as some marriages end up being dissolved, so some domestic partnerships will end up being terminated. Until the New Jersey courts become more experienced with handling terminations, the results in many cases will vary.

As time goes on, however, and the judges in the Family Part become more comfortable with the domestic partnership termination proceedings, we can expect to see more consistent and predictable results.

At this time, for example, it is unclear whether equitable distribution will be the norm for termination or an exception. Even if equitable distribution becomes as common in domestic partnership terminations as it is in divorce, judges will be faced with many couples who had long lives together prior to the enactment of the Domestic Partnership Act. Unless such couples have reached agreement on the division of assets that were jointly acquired prior to registration, judges will need to determine whether some form of look-back process should be used.

CHAPTER 16
LEGAL MATTERS

FINDING AND WORKING WITH AN ATTORNEY

Often times, people hesitate to seek out legal advice because they believe it will be expensive, or because they are embarrassed by their situation or their sexual orientation. Although there are attorneys, as in everything, who will overcharge and under serve, there are far more who give advice and time readily and often without charge.

The first thing to remember is that, as in medicine, there are fewer and fewer general practitioners. Because the law has become so complex, most attorneys specialize in a few areas of law, such as real estate or criminal law. Thus, you should look for someone, if possible, who specializes in the type of law you need help with.

A good place to begin looking for an attorney is a local bar association, which usually has an attorney referral network. When you call the referral number, an intake specialist will usually ask you a few questions to help you determine the type of attorney you need, then provide you with the name of one or more attorneys who specialize in that area. If you can't find a referral program in your area, you might check with one of the directories online, such as Findlaw Law Directory (*http://lawyers.findlaw.com*), or Martindale-Hubbell (*http://www.martindale.com*).

Second, when you discuss your case with an attorney, your conversation is normally governed by attorney-client privilege. Even if he or she does not take you on as a client, the information you provide during your initial meeting with the attorney may not be revealed by the lawyer except in very limited circumstances.

Not every attorney is going to meet your needs. First, call the attorney's office and schedule a preliminary meeting. You do not need to go into a great deal of detail over the telephone but ask if he or she has handled a similar matter before. Also, be sure to ask if there is any fee associated with the initial consultation so you're not surprised. It's not uncommon, particularly for non-litigation matters, for the attorney to charge their regular hourly fee for a brief consultation. At the first meeting, bring all of the documents, letters, and everything you can think of related to your case.

Once the attorney agrees to take you on as a client, he or she will provide you with some form of contract. Typically, there are three kinds of these: a straight hourly contract, a fixed fee contract, or a contingency contract. The kind of contract used will depend upon your lawyer, the type of matter, and the bar rules. Generally, hourly fee contracts are used when the attorney is representing you as a defendant in a criminal or civil matter or when there is an on-going project.

Fixed fee contracts are used when the work is something straightforward, such as a will or a living-to-gether agreement. These kinds of contracts are becoming more common and the attorney will usually require you to pay half or even the full amount in advance. Your attorney should specifically tell you what documents are going to be produced and when.

Contingent fee contracts are most commonly used with plaintiffs in litigation. These are fees that are "contingent" upon the outcome of the case and are most common in personal injury, medical malpractice or similar high-stakes cases. These contracts award the attorney a fee only if they are successful in winning your case. A few states regulate the percentages and some prohibit them. Some attorneys use a modified contingent fee, which requires you to pay a reduced fee during the litigation and a reduced percentage of the award if you are successful.

Most attorneys expect to get some of their fee in advance. There are two ways they can do this: as a non-refundable retainer or as an advance against fees. A non-refundable retainer is an earned fee paid to an attorney for simply agreeing to take a case. It's most often used by very high demand defense attorneys, like the late Johnny Cochran, and you are paying them this fee because they have their choice of clients.

Another type of retainer is a monthly fee for regular clients (usually businesses). It's really a flat fee that guarantees a certain amount of the attorney's time during a specific period of time.

An advance fee is sometimes called a retainer, but it's really an advance against earned fees. The amount will vary depending on the estimated length of time involved and the attorney's hourly or daily fee. The attorney will bill his or her time and expenses against this advance, and you may be expected to replenish the advance when it gets below a certain level. You will generally receive monthly bills detailing the fees for the prior month and the attorney or firm will only draw down these funds when you have approved the bill for that month. New Jersey has very strict rules for collecting, maintaining and disbursing these funds, which must be maintained in a client trust account separate from the attorney's other funds. The attorney's contract will provide details on how these funds, if any, are maintained.

There are basic expectations that are required when you hire an attorney. First, you will be entitled to make the big decisions, such as whether to settle, but let your attorney choose the strategy. You are paying for his or her advice so you should heed it. You are expected to cooperate with your attorney, providing him or her with whatever information they ask for, show up on time for appointments, depositions, court appearances, and respect their time. Many attorneys will charge for telephone consultations so be sure you understand that the clock is ticking when your on the telephone. On the other hand, you have a right to be adequately informed about developments in your case, and your attorney should return your telephone calls in a reasonable amount of time, let you know what's going on in the case, send you copies of all documents and letters received or sent on your behalf, and protect your interests. Don't second-guess your attorney but don't let him or her keep you in the dark. You have a right to fire your attorney and your attorney usually has a right to withdraw from representing you. Finally, when you and an attorney part ways, hopefully because your case has finished, you have a right to the return of your files in a reasonable time, although the attorney has a right to retain copies of everything for his or her files.

MAKING AND ENFORCING AGREEMENTS

Throughout this book, I have made frequent reference to different types of agreements you and your partner should have or may want to consider having. For example, you and your partner may sign a living-together or domestic partnership agreement as a way of adding to or modifying the rights and responsibilities acquired from registering your partnership, or you may decide how to split up parenting responsibilities.

Written or Oral Agreements

Most agreements must be in writing. Oral agreements can become enforceable if they can be established with sufficient certainty, such as testimony of witnesses, or by demonstrating a course of conduct that both parties have followed.

However, in the context of same-sex relationships, where there are often family or others who are hostile to the relationship, nearly every aspect of your partnership should be supported by signed, written agreements.

Authenticating Documents

It is frequently not enough to have documents signed by you and your partner in order to prove they are authentic. Many documents benefit from being notarized or witnessed, and some require this step. Although the requirements for authentication of documents depend upon the kind of document, there are certain general considerations you should be aware of.

Using Witnesses

In New Jersey, any person who is competent to testify in court is also competent to act as a witness. For most documents, you will only need two witnesses. A Will is not invalid if one or both witnesses have an interest in the Will.

Self-Proving Documents

Some documents, particularly Wills, can be made less susceptible to challenge by others if the witnesses signatures are accompanied by a sworn affidavit attesting to their authenticity. In the event that the document is challenged, you will not be required to produce the witnesses.

Notarizing Documents

Usually reserved for official documents or documents that go before a court, having a document notarized is generally recommended for documents that require a signature but not witnesses. A notary is also used when an oath or other formal statement needs to be recited, in which case the notary will swear you in, will listen to your statement, and then sign the document. In New Jersey, your attorney can authenticate the document instead of a notary.

In New Jersey, attorneys have the same powers as notaries and it is frequently the practice for an attorney to attest to your signature after you've signed a document. However, this is not the case in all U.S. states and for documents that you should have with you when you travel, you may want to have them notarized to avoid having to explain New Jersey law in an emergency.

Where to Keep Documents

The documents recommended in this section provide important legal rights to you and your partner, rights you might not otherwise have if they were lost. Obviously, you need to keep these valuable documents in a safe place but have them readily available when you need them.

For some documents, such as Wills, it is particularly important that you keep original documents in a safe place. If you are unable to produce an original document when it is needed, such as providing an original Will at probate, you will have to undergo the added steps of proving that your copy is a valid one and that the document has not been subsequently revoked.

Do-it-Yourself or Boilerplate Documents

A lot of bookstores and web sites will have books and other information on Wills and other legal topics for New Jersey. Often, these sources have examples of forms you can use. Many of these forms are directed at people with simple legal needs, or are tailored to opposite-sex couples.

Given that same-sex couples are more likely to encounter difficulties protecting and enforcing their rights, I don't recommend these boilerplate Will kits or software. If you shop around, you should be able to find an attorney who will prepare a simple Will, powers of attorney, disposition of remains, declaration of guardianship and physicians directive for a reasonable, flat fee. If you are poverty-stricken, most local bar associations have lists of attorneys who will do this for free.

Do-it-yourself law is like do-it-yourself surgery -- you may save a lot of money but the outcome may be fatal. For same-sex couples, there is a greater likelihood that documents may be challenged, so it is particularly important that they be well drafted.

CHOOSING A FIDUCIARY

Although last year's sad events involving Terri Schiavo demonstrated the need for advance directives, such as living wills, powers of attorney, and medical proxy designations, there has been little discussion regarding an equally important matter: selecting the person (or persons) who will act on your behalf in these and other estate planning documents. Choosing wisely can ensure that your wishes are carried out and your affairs are managed well. A poor choice can result in the wasting of your assets, the failure to manage your financial affairs as you would have wanted, and an often protracted, and expensive, legal battle.

Your will, trusts (if any), and advance directives designate someone to carry out your wishes as expressed in these documents. For a will, the designee is called the "executor," for a trust, a "trustee", and for advance directives, the most commonly used term is "agent". Regardless of the title, your designee is a "fiduciary," who has the duty to act primarily for another's benefit in all matters in which they are involved in that capacity. The executor's and the trustee's fiduciary responsibility is to the beneficiaries. The agent's fiduciary responsibility, under the power of attorney and the medical proxy, are to the incapacitated person who has designated them. If a fiduciary breaches his or her duties, he or she is liable to the person(s) to whom they owe the duty.

There is a natural tendency, when choosing someone to act in one of these special fiduciary roles, to choose an immediate family member, such as a spouse or domestic partner, or one or more children. After all, we often place the greatest trust in those we hold closest to us. However, it is important to candidly evaluate the person(s) you designate as your executor or your agent, to ensure that they are both capable of and willing to act in a way that is consistent with their fiduciary duties. If you appoint someone as your executor, trustee, or agent, simply out of loyalty or because you are unwilling to hurt the feelings of a loved one or friend, then you are inviting disaster.

When choosing an individual as executor, trustee, or agent, you should consider the following questions:

- Is he or she mentally and physically capable of carrying out their duties? An aging spouse may not be as sharp as they once were, or may have become quite frail, and are therefore unable to manage the estate or look after your affairs.

- Does he or she have an alcohol or substance abuse problem? Such a person may, at best, neglect your care or your estate, and at worst, actively steal from you or your estate to support their habit.

- Is he or she incapable of abiding by your wishes? For example, a child with a different set of religious or ethical beliefs than yours may substitute their wishes for yours, when acting as your medical proxy.

- Is he or she financially irresponsible or reckless? No matter how well meaning they may be, such a person would not be a good choice when handling your finances or your estate.

- Does he or she possess special education or training that would be beneficial? For example, a daughter who is a doctor or nurse may be an excellent choice as your medical proxy. A close cousin who is a financial planner or CPA may make a better executor than a child with no such training or experience.

- Does he or she live near or far away from you? Someone living nearby is generally preferable to someone living further away, particularly when it comes to making life-threatening decisions.

The answers to these questions should help guide your decision-making process, but may not be fatal to the choice of one person or another. For instance, if a spouse lacks particular financial expertise, a co-trustee or co-executor with the requisite experience could be named, or the fiduciary could be directed to seek advice from a particular person or persons before making an important decision. In some cases, decision making duties could be split, for example, by naming a child with financial expertise as your agent under a power of attorney and naming a close friend with medical knowledge as your medical proxy. For trusts, it is common, and frequently prudent, to either name a corporate trustee as a co-fiduciary, or to allow a trustee to name a corporate trustee if he or she needs the additional expertise. Corporate trustees may be particularly useful if, after evaluating family or friends, you conclude there is no suitable trustee among them.

Regardless of whom you choose, you should also name a second, and even a third choice for each fiduciary role. Many people choose their spouse as their first designee, followed by a son or daughter, or a close friend. In this way, if your first or second choice is unwilling or unable to act, you avoid the necessity of court intervention. I generally recommend against the use of co-fiduciaries, unless you specify some mechanism for breaking an impasse. In any case, you should speak with your chosen fiduciaries to ensure that they are willing to act as such and understand their duties.

No matter what choices you make when naming your fiduciaries, you should let your family members know who you have chosen and, to the extent you can be honest without being hurtful, why you have made these choices. By doing so, you will have conveyed two important pieces of information. First, your family will know who to turn to when you become disabled or die. Second, any anger and resentment your choices may provoke can more easily be assuaged while you are alive than later.

The responsibilities and trusts that you place upon someone by naming them as your fiduciary are too important for you to make the choice of fiduciary lightly. By taking the time to choose your fiduciaries wisely, you can help ensure that you and your family are left in the best of hands.

ABOUT THE AUTHOR

Stephen J. Hyland is partner-in-charge of the Trusts and Estates Group at Hill Wallack, a Princeton, New Jersey law firm. He is licensed to practice in all courts in New Jersey, as well as in Pennsylvania, New York and Texas. His practice focuses on estate planning, probate, trusts, elder law, and the law of same-sex relationships.

Mr. Hyland has authored numerous articles on gay and lesbian legal issues, as well as estate planning and related subjects, and is a frequent speaker on such legal issues. He is an active member of various community and professional organizations, including the GLBT Law Committee of the New Jersey State Bar Association and the Individual Rights and Responsibilities Section of the American Bar Association.

Born and raised in Camden County, New Jersey, Mr. Hyland is a graduate of Pennsylvania State University and South Texas College of Law, and is currently pursuing an LLM degree in Tax and Estate Planning at Temple Law School. He resides by the banks of the Delaware River with his domestic partner of over 18 years, and their two dogs. In October 2004, he and his partner registered as domestic partners.

Using many of the skills he acquired in his prior career in the software field, Mr. Hyland has developed and continues to maintain the guide's companion blog and web site, www.njdomesticpartnership.com, where updates, corrections, related articles, and news may be found.

UPDATES AND ERRATA

I have endeavored to make this guide as complete and up-to-date as possible. However, New Jersey law, in general, is constantly evolving, and the law affecting same-sex couples is particularly fast moving. Thus, it is practically impossible to guarantee that some parts of this book have not been made irrelevant or outdated by changes in state or federal law. Please let me know if you find errors or omissions, or if you have suggestions for future editions by writing to me at:

Stephen J. Hyland, Esq.
Hill Wallack
202 Carnegie Center
Princeton, NJ 08543
Telephone: (609) 924-0808
Fax: (609) 452-1888

There is a web page for this book, which lists errata, changes in the law, updates, and additional information. You can access this page at:

http://www.njdomesticpartnership.com/guide/

From time-to-time, I present seminars on various legal topics of interest to same-sex couples and to the GLBT community. For a list of upcoming seminars and speaking engagements, or if you would like me to speak at your company, conference, or other event, please check the events page at:

http://www.njdomesticpartnership.com/events/

To comment or ask questions about this book, send e-mail to:

comments@njdomesticpartnership.com

However, please be advised that I cannot answer legal questions or provide legal advice to you, except to refer you to an attorney.

For more information about the legal services offered by my law firm, Hill Wallack, see the firm's web site at:

http://www.hillwallack.com

GLOSSARY

administration. The process by which an intestate estate is probated.

adoption. This is a legal process by which a court terminates a child's legal rights and duties toward his or her natural parents and creates a new parent-child relationship in its place.

advance directive. A written document, such as a living will, power of attorney or medical proxy that expresses a person's wishes and appoints an individual to carry out those wishes. An advance directive is written and signed in advance of a person becoming incapacitated and usually only comes into effect when needed.

alimony. See *support*.

annuity. A contract that guarantees a series of payments in return for a lump sum initial investment.

annulment. See *nullification*.

ante-nuptial agreement. See *prenuptial agreement*.

arbitration. A form of alternative dispute resolution that involves presentation of a case to an individual who renders a decision that is binding on all parties. See *mediation*.

assets. Everything owned by a person that has monetary value and can be used to pay a debt.

assisted reproductive technology. Medical procedures, such as retrieval of eggs and in vitro fertilization, that are used to assist in achieving pregnancy.

attorney in fact. A person who is appointed to act (as agent) for another person under a power of attorney.

autopsy. Examination of tissues and organs of the body following death; a postmortem examination usually performed to determine the cause of death.

beneficiary. In a life insurance or other type of account, the person designated to receive payment of the funds. In a trust, the person designated to receive the income or principal from the trust. In a Will, the person who is named to receive property from the estate.

bequest. A gift (transfer) of personal property through a will. See *devise*.

birth parent. The mother who carries a child to term.

charitable remainder trust. An irrevocable tax-exempt trust that provides income distributions only to a beneficiary and pays the principal of the trust to a charity when the trust is dissolved.

child support. Financial and other support for children.

Civil Rights Act. New Jersey law that gives individuals a cause of action for interference with state or federal constitutional or statutory rights.

civil union. A legally recognized and voluntary union of adult parties of the same sex. See *marriage*.

codicil. A supplement or an addition to an existing will for purposes of explaining, modifying, adding to, subtracting clauses.

cohabitation. To live together with the mutual assumption of the rights, duties and obligations which are usually manifested by married people. See *palimony*.

common law. The body of law that is not found in statutory law, which derives from usage, custom, and the decrees of courts. For example, until the Domestic Partnership Act, the term "spouse" was not defined anywhere in New Jersey law but it has a common law definition meaning "husband" or "wife."

Consolidated Omnibus Budget Reconciliation Act (COBRA). A statute that gives workers and their families who lose their health benefits the right to choose to continue group health benefits provided by their group health plan for limited periods of time under certain circumstances such as voluntary or involuntary job loss, reduction in the hours worked, transition between jobs, death, divorce, and other life events.

co-parenting. An arrangement by which two persons share the obligations of raising a child or children

co-respondent. In a domestic partnership termination proceeding based on sexual infidelity, the person outside the relationship with whom the defendant partner is having sex.

Crummey letter. A written notification to the beneficiaries of a trust, typically an irrevocable life insurance trust, that money has been received on their behalf and that they may withdraw such sum.

custody. The care and control of a child or children.

death tax. See *inheritance tax*.

deed. A written instrument that conveys title of real estate from one party to another and that, once officially recorded, shows legal right to possess that real estate. The deed contains an accurate, specific and legal description of the property and it is delivered at closing.

Defense Of Marriage Act (DOMA). A federal law that purports to allow each state to deny recognition of any marriage or marriage-like relationship between persons of the same sex that has been recognized in another state, and which prohibits federal recognition of same-sex marriage.

> *State Defense of Marriage Act*. A state law or state constitutional amendment prohibiting same-sex marriage or other marriage-like relationships.

devise. A gift of real estate in the last will and testament of a person.

disclaimer. The disavowal, denial, or renunciation of an interest, right or property imputed to a person, usually of a gift in a will.

disposition of remains. An advance directive in which a person appoints another person to take control of their remains and provides instructions for the disposition of their body including cremation, organ donations, funeral arrangements, and grave marker inscriptions.

dissolution. The act or process of terminating, dissolving, or winding up a marriage. Contrast *termination*.

DOMA. See *Defense of Marriage Act*.

domestic partnership. A voluntary union of adult parties of the same or opposite sex, which in some states is legally recognized.

Domestic Partnership Act. In New Jersey, the statute which provides broad rights and benefits in many areas to persons in domestic partnerships similar to those afforded to spouses or married couples.

domicile. Having a bona fide connection with some fixed home; the place in which you have a permanent, rather than temporary home. Contrast *residence*.

donor. One who makes a gift or confers a power to another.

durable power of attorney. See *power of attorney*.

elective share. A statutory provision that permits a surviving spouse to take a one-third share of the decedent's estate. The elective share is intended to prevent a surviving spouse to be impoverished if the decedent has intentionally or unintentionally failed to provide for the surviving spouse in a will.

equitable distribution. The distribution of all property legally and beneficially acquired by both partners during a domestic partnership in a manner that avoids impoverishment of one partner to the benefit of another.

equity. Justice based upon what is fair as opposed to what is strictly written in the law. A court's equitable powers allow it to bring about a result that is fair to all parties and to overcome what may otherwise be an unjust result.

estate. The entire assets and liabilities of a person, including all property, that he or she will give to others at death. The gross estate is the full value of the estate. The net estate is the value of the entire less all liabilities. The taxable estate is that property subject to federal and state estate taxes. The probate estate is that portion of the decedent's estate that passes via their will or intestate distribution.

executor (executrix). A person appointed by a testator to carry out the directions and requests in his or her will, and to dispose of the property according to the testamentary provisions after his or her death.

Family Leave Act (FLA). In New Jersey, a statute that requires certain employers to grant eligible employees time off from work in connection with the birth or adoption of a child, or the serious illness of a parent, child or spouse. Definition of "parent" includes step-parent and parent-in-law.

Family and Medical Leave Act (FMLA). A federal statute similar to the New Jersey Family Leave Act. This statute allows employees time off from work due to an employee's own disability while the FLA does not.

fiduciary. A person having a legal duty to act primarily for another's benefit in certain matters, such as appointment as an executor or trustee.

generation skipping tax (GST). This is an additional federal transfer tax if a transfer "skips" a generation, for example, from parent to grandchildren.

genetic parent. The parent who is genetically related to a child. Contrast *birth parent*.

gift. A gratuitous transfer of an asset for less than fair market value. An inter vivos gift is a gift made during the donor's life. A testamentary gift is a gift made after death pursuant to a provision in a Will.

gift in contemplation of death. A gift made at a time when the donor reasonably believed that his or her death was imminent.

gift tax. A tax on the transfer of a gift.

grantor. The person who grants something.

grantor retained annuity trust (GRAT). A GRAT is an irrevocable trust funded with a single contribution of assets, which pays a percentage of the initial contribution, either fixed or with a predetermined increase (the annuity), back to the donor for a term of years, and then distributes the assets remaining at the end of the term to beneficiaries other than the donor.

grantor retained income trust (GRIT). An irrevocable trust in which a grantor transfers property to a beneficiary but receives income until its termination, at which time the beneficiary begins receiving the income.

gross estate. See *estate*.

guardian. A person lawfully invested with the power, and charged with the duty, or taking care of the person and managing the property and rights of another person, who, for defect of age, understanding, or self-control, is considered incapable of administering his own affairs.

health care directive. A written statement made by a person about his or her preferences for future medical treatment in the event that the person is unable to make decisions at the time of treatment

health care power of attorney. An written advance directive whereby a person authorizes another person to act on his or her behalf in making health care decisions.

holographic will. A will written out in the hand of the testator and accepted as valid in New Jersey if it meets certain statutory requirements.

imputed income. Value assigned to certain types of income for tax purposes, for instance, payment by an employer of premiums for a domestic partner's health insurance.

inheritance. The acquisition of property through intestacy or by will.

inheritance tax. Tax imposed for the privilege of receiving property from a decedent at death.

intervivos. Conveying or transferring property from one living person to another.

intervivos gift. See *gift*.

intervivos trust. See *trust*.

intestate. To die without a will.

intestate share. The share of deceased's property that goes to his or her heirs in the absence of a valid will. Domestic partners are not recognized as heirs in most states.

in vitro fertilization. Fertilization of an egg outside the body of a female.

irrevocable life insurance trust. An irrevocable trust which can remove life insurance proceeds from an estate and hence from estate tax liability.

irrevocable trust. A trust that, once created, cannot be modified or revoked.

joint adoption. A form of adoption wherein two person adopt a child in one proceeding.

joint ownership. A form of property ownership where two or more persons hold joint title to specific property, usually in equal shares.

joint tenancy. A form of property ownership where two or more persons hold title to real property. Without a right of survivorship, joint tenancy is also called tenancy in common.

joint tenancy with rights of survivorship. A form of joint tenancy where a joint tenant's title in the property passes automatically at death to the other tenants. In New Jersey, rights of survivorship must be explicitly stated on the deed for any property to pass to the surviving tenants.

legacy. A gift or bequest of personal property in a will.

Law Against Discrimination (LAD). New Jersey state law prohibiting discrimination in housing, employment, credit and other areas, based on specific protected categories including sexual orientation and domestic partnership.

lien. A lien is a claim against property that arises out of a debt or a judgment.

living trust. A revocable trust that is created and operative during the life of the person creating the trust (the "settlor") and which is sometimes used to avoid probate. Also called a revocable living trust.

living will. See *health care directive*.

long-term care insurance. A form of insurance that pays for in-home care, nursing home care and hospice care.

look-back period. A length of time during which a court or agency can review and, sometimes, reverse property transfers, particularly gifts or other transfers for less than fair market value.

maintenance. Financial support provided to a separated or divorced spouse, usually as a result of a property settlement agreement or court order.

mediation. A form of alternate dispute resolution in which a neutral third party, called a mediator, assists parties to a dispute to resolve their differences. Unlike arbitration, mediation is non-binding.

Medicaid. A federal and state-funded form of medical assistance provided to those who have insufficient income for their own care.

medical proxy designation. An advance directive that appoints an agent to make medical decisions on behalf of the principal. Also referred to as a medical power of attorney or power of attorney for health care.

Medicare. A federal act that provides health insurance to the elderly.

municipal employer. See *public employer*.

necropsy. A post-mortem examination of a body, particularly tissue examination.

net estate. See *estate*.

nullification. A state procedure by which a marriage or domestic partnership is declared invalid.

palimony. A form of alimony awarded to unmarried cohabitants.

partition. A procedure by which joint property is divided into individual shares. The result is tenancy in common.

payable on death (POD). A bank account that is closed upon proof of death of the owner and the funds are transferred to a named beneficiary.

pendente lite. A court proceeding brought prior to dissolution or termination for interim maintenance and support.

pet directive. An advanced directive that provides for the care and custody of pets when the owner is incapacitated or deceased.

pour-over will. A will that directs the distribution of property into a trust.

power of attorney. An advance directive in which a person (the "principal") authorizes another person (the "attorney-in-fact" or "agent,") to act on the principal's behalf in the event the principal becomes disabled or incapacitated. Powers of attorney can be durable, that is, in effect as soon as they are signed, or springing, meaning they become effective only when the principal has been determined to be incapacitated.

power of attorney for health care. See *medical proxy designation*.

probate. The legal proceeding that provides for the administration and settlement of a decedent's estate. Probate begins with the filing of the death certificate, the Will, and application for letters testamentary or letters of administration, and ends with the distribution of the estate.

probate estate. See *estate*.

public employer. An publicly-funded employer other than the State or federal government, including school districts, municipalities, and state and county colleges.

psychological parent. A person whom a child considers to be his or her parent, even though that individual may not be a biological or adoptive parent.

real property. Real estate.

reciprocal beneficiary. A legally recognized and voluntary union of adult parties of the same or opposite sex, but with limited rights.

reciprocal will. Wills made by two persons which make reciprocal provisions for each other.

residence. Any address at which you live more than temporarily. You may have several residences. Compare *domicile*.

resident. A person who occupies a residence in a state, has a present intent to occupy that residence for some period of time, and establishes an on-going relationship with that state.

remainderman. The person or organization who receives the remaining assets of a trust when the trust is terminated.

revocable trust. A trust in which the settlor reserves the right to terminate the trust.

right of survivorship. A joint tenant's automatic right to the decedent joint tenant's property.

second parent adoption. A form of adoption in which the same-sex partner of a child's natural or legal parent may adopt the child without terminating the natural parent's rights. Based upon stepparent adoption.

settlor. The person who creates a trust.

State Health Benefits Program (SHBP). The New Jersey medical and dental plan for state employees.

springing power of attorney. See *power of attorney*.

step-up in basis. An increase in the value of property for tax purposes. Capital gains tax is based upon the difference between the sale price of an asset and the basis.

successor trustee. The person or entity that follows or succeeds an earlier trustee.

surrogacy. Having to do with the use of a surrogate mother to conceive and carry a child to term.

surrogate. A woman who, on behalf of another couple, consents to being inseminated by a person other than her husband, and who intends to give up parental rights to the child subsequently born. The surrogate is both the birth mother and the genetic mother of the child.

taxable estate. See *estate*.

tenants by the entirety. A tenancy that is created between spouses and which has automatic rights of survivorship. Dissolution of the marriage converts the ownership to tenancy in common.

tenancy in common. A form of property ownership where each owner holds an undivided interest in the property. The share of a deceased tenant in common is part of his or her estate. Contrast *joint tenancy with rights of survivorship*.

termination. The legal proceeding by which a registered domestic partnership is formally ended in New Jersey.

testamentary gift. See *gift*.

testamentary trust. See *trust*.

testator. A person who makes a will or who dies leaving a valid will.

title. In regard to property, the formal right of ownership in property.

tort. A private wrong or injury, such as assault, wrongful death, or intentional infliction of emotional distress.

Totten trust. See *payable on death (POD)*.

transfer on death. The automatic transfer of title to a beneficiary upon the death of the title holder.

transfer tax. A tax on the transfer of property. The primary transfer taxes are the estate tax, gift tax and generation-skipping tax.

transgender. A person who physically changes his or her gender to its opposite gender via hormone treatment and sexual reassignment surgery.

trust. A legal entity created by a person, called the grantor or settlor, into which assets are transferred for the benefit of specific beneficiaries. Trusts are created by a trust document, called an instrument, under the laws of a particular state and are subject to tax regulations.

trust property. The property held in trust by the trustee. It may also be called the *corpus, res* or *subject matter of the trust*.

trustee. The person who holds title to the trust property. A person who is appointed to administer and execute a trust.

visitation rights. The permission granted by a court to a noncustodial parent, including psychological parent, to visit or have visits by a child or children of the marriage or partnership.

void. Having no legal force or binding effect.

void ab initio. Void from the beginning or inception.

will. A written document containing the disposition of a person's property, to take effect upon the person's death.

APPENDICES

APPENDIX A
DOMESTIC PARTNERSHIP ACT

This appendix contains the twelve sections of the Domestic Partnership Act that create the status of domestic partnership. The remaining sections of the Act consist of modifications to other statutes to conform to the Act.

TITLE 26
HEALTH AND VITAL STATISTICS
CHAPTER 8A
DOMESTIC PARTNERS

26:8A-1. Short title

This act shall be known and may be cited as the "Domestic Partnership Act."

26:8A-2. Legislative findings; declarations

The Legislature finds and declares that:

a. There are a significant number of individuals in this State who choose to live together in important personal, emotional and economic committed relationships with another individual;

b. These familial relationships, which are known as domestic partnerships, assist the State by their establishment of a private network of support for the financial, physical and emotional health of their participants;

c. Because of the material and other support that these familial relationships provide to their participants, the Legislature believes that these mutually supportive relationships should be formally recognized by statute, and that certain rights and benefits should be made available to individuals participating in them, including: statutory protection against various forms of discrimination against domestic partners; certain visitation and decision-making rights in a health care setting; and certain tax-related benefits; and, in some cases, health and pension benefits that are provided in the same manner as for spouses;

d. All persons in domestic partnerships should be entitled to certain rights and benefits that are accorded to married couples under the laws of New Jersey, including: statutory protection through the "Law Against Discrimination," P.L.1945, c. 169 (C.10:5-1 et seq.) against various forms of discrimination based on domestic partnership status, such as employment, housing and credit discrimination; visitation rights for a hospitalized domestic partner and the right to make medical or legal decisions for an incapacitated partner; and an additional exemption from the personal income tax and the transfer inheritance tax on the same basis as a spouse. The need for all persons who are in domestic partnerships, regardless of their sex, to have access to these rights and benefits is paramount in view of their essential relationship to any reasonable conception of basic human dignity and autonomy, and the extent to which they will play an integral role in enabling these persons to enjoy their familial relationships as domestic partners and to cope with adversity when a medical emergency arises that affects a domestic partnership, as was painfully but graphically illustrated on a large scale in the aftermath of the tragic events that befell the people of our State and region on September 11, 2001;

e. The Legislature, however, discerns a clear and rational basis for making certain health and pension benefits available to dependent domestic partners only in the case of domestic partnerships in which both persons are of the same sex and are therefore unable to enter into a marriage with each other that is recognized by New Jersey law, unlike persons of the opposite sex who are in a domestic partnership but have the right to enter into a marriage that is recognized by State law and thereby have access to these health and pension benefits; and

f. Therefore, it is the public policy of this State to hereby establish and define the rights and responsibilities of domestic partners.

26:8A-3.   Definitions

As used in sections 1 through 9 of P.L.2003, c. 246 (C.26:8A-1 through 26:8A-9) and in R.S. 26:8-1 et seq.:

"Affidavit of Domestic Partnership" means an affidavit that sets forth each party's name and age, the parties' common mailing address, and a statement that, at the time the affidavit is signed, both parties meet the requirements of this act for entering into a domestic partnership and wish to enter into a domestic partnership with each other.

"Basic living expenses" means the cost of basic food and shelter, and any other cost, including, but not limited to, the cost of health care, if some or all of the cost is paid as a benefit because a person is another person's domestic partner.

"Certificate of Domestic Partnership" means a certificate that includes: the full names of the domestic partners, a statement that the two individuals are members of a registered domestic partnership recognized by the State of New Jersey, the date that the domestic partnership was entered into, and a statement that the partners are entitled to all the rights, privileges and responsibilities accorded to domestic partners under the law. The certificate shall bear the seal of the State of New Jersey.

"Commissioner" means the Commissioner of Health and Senior Services.

"Domestic partner" or "partner" means a person who is in a relationship that satisfies the definition of a domestic partnership as set forth in this act.

"Have a common residence" means that two persons share the same place to live in this State, or share the same place to live in another jurisdiction when at least one of the persons is a member of a State-administered retirement system, regardless of whether or not: the legal right to possess the place is in both of their names; one or both persons have additional places to live; or one person temporarily leaves the shared place of residence to reside elsewhere, on either a short-term or long-term basis, for reasons that include, but are not limited to, medical care, incarceration, education, a sabbatical or employment, but intends to return to the shared place of residence.

"Jointly responsible" means that each domestic partner agrees to provide for the other partner's basic living expenses if the other partner is unable to provide for himself.

"Notice of Rights and Obligations of Domestic Partners" means a form that advises domestic partners, or persons seeking to become domestic partners, of the procedural requirements for establishing, maintaining, and terminating a domestic partnership, and includes information about the rights and responsibilities of the partners.

26:8A-4.   Establishment of domestic partnership; requirements; affidavit

a. Two persons who desire to become domestic partners and meet the requirements of subsection b. of this section may execute and file an Affidavit of Domestic Partnership with the local registrar upon payment of a fee, in an amount to be determined by the commissioner, which shall be deposited in the General Fund. Each person shall receive a copy of the affidavit marked "filed."

b. A domestic partnership shall be established when all of the following requirements are met:

(1) Both persons have a common residence and are otherwise jointly responsible for each other's common welfare as evidenced by joint financial arrangements or joint ownership of real or personal property, which shall be demonstrated by at least one of the following:

(a) a joint deed, mortgage agreement or lease;

(b) a joint bank account;

(c) designation of one of the persons as a primary beneficiary in the other person's will;

(d) designation of one of the persons as a primary beneficiary in the other person's life insurance policy or retirement plan; or

(e) joint ownership of a motor vehicle;

(2) Both persons agree to be jointly responsible for each other's basic living expenses during the domestic partnership;

(3) Neither person is in a marriage recognized by New Jersey law or a member of another domestic partnership;

(4) Neither person is related to the other by blood or affinity up to and including the fourth degree of consanguinity;

(5) Both persons are of the same sex and therefore unable to enter into a marriage with each other that is recognized by New Jersey law, except that two persons who are each 62 years of age or older and not of the same sex may establish a domestic partnership if they meet the requirements set forth in this section;

(6) Both persons have chosen to share each other's lives in a committed relationship of mutual caring;

(7) Both persons are at least 18 years of age;

(8) Both persons file jointly an Affidavit of Domestic Partnership; and

(9) Neither person has been a partner in a domestic partnership that was terminated less than 180 days prior to the filing of the current Affidavit of Domestic Partnership, except that this prohibition shall not apply if one of the partners died; and, in all cases in which a person registered a prior domestic partnership, the domestic partnership shall have been terminated in accordance with the provisions of section 10 of P.L.2003, c. 246 (C.26:8A-10).

c. A person who executes an Affidavit of Domestic Partnership in violation of the provisions of subsection b. of this section shall be liable to a civil penalty in an amount not to exceed $1,000. The penalty shall be sued for and collected pursuant to the "Penalty Enforcement Law of 1999," P.L.1999, c. 274 (C.2A:58-10 et seq.).

26:8A-5. Termination of domestic partnership; notification of termination; requirements

a. A former domestic partner who has given a copy of the Certificate of Domestic Partnership to any third party to qualify for any benefit or right and whose receipt of that benefit or enjoyment of that right has not otherwise terminated, shall, upon termination of the domestic partnership, give or send to the third party, at the last known address of the third party, written notification that the domestic partnership has been terminated. A third party that suffers a loss as a result of failure by a domestic partner to provide this notice shall be entitled to seek recovery from the partner who was obligated to send the notice for any actual loss resulting thereby.

b. Failure to provide notice to a third party, as required pursuant to this section, shall not delay or prevent the termination of the domestic partnership.

26:8A-6. Obligations of domestic partners

a. The obligations that two people have to each other as a result of creating a domestic partnership shall be limited to the provisions of this act, and those provisions shall not diminish any right granted under any other provision of law.

b. Upon the termination of a domestic partnership, the domestic partners, from that time forward, shall incur none of the obligations to each other as domestic partners that are created by this or any other act.

c. A domestic partnership, civil union or reciprocal beneficiary relationship entered into outside of this State, which is valid under the laws of the jurisdiction under which the partnership was created, shall be valid in this State.

d. Any health care or social services provider, employer, operator of a place of public accommodation, property owner or administrator, or other individual or entity may treat a person as a member of a domestic partnership, notwithstanding the absence of an Affidavit of Domestic Partnership filed pursuant to this act.

e. Domestic partners may modify the rights and obligations to each other that are granted by this act in any valid contract between themselves, except for the requirements for a domestic partnership as set forth in section 4 of P.L.2003, c. 246 (C.6:8A-4).

f. Two adults who have not filed an Affidavit of Domestic Partnership shall be treated as domestic partners in an emergency medical situation for the purposes of allowing one adult to accompany the other adult who is ill or injured while the latter is being transported to a hospital, or to visit the other adult who is a hospital patient, on the same basis as a member of the latter's immediate family, if both persons, or one of the persons in the event that the other person is legally or medically incapacitated, advise the emergency care provider that the two persons have met the other requirements for establishing a domestic partnership as set forth in section 4 of P.L.2003, c. 246 (C.26:8A-4); however, the provisions of this section shall not be construed to permit the two adults to be treated as domestic partners for any other purpose as provided in P.L.2003, c. 246 (C.26:8A-1 et al.) prior to their having filed an Affidavit of Domestic Partnership.

g. A domestic partner shall not be liable for the debts of the other partner contracted before establishment of the domestic partnership, or contracted by the other partner in his own name during the domestic partnership. The partner who contracts for the debt in his own name shall be liable to be sued separately in his own name, and any property belonging to that partner shall be liable to satisfy that debt in the same manner as if the partner had not entered into a domestic partnership.

26:8A-7.   Forms and notices; preparation

a. The commissioner shall cause to be prepared, in such a manner as the commissioner determines appropriate:

(1) blank forms, in quadruplicate, of Affidavits of Domestic Partnership and Certificates of Domestic Partnership corresponding to the requirements of this act; and

(2) copies of the Notice of the Rights and Obligations of Domestic Partners.

b. The commissioner shall ensure that these forms and notices, along with such sections of the laws concerning domestic partnership and explanations thereof as the commissioner may deem useful to persons having duties to recognize domestic partners under those laws, are printed and supplied to each local registrar, and made available to the public upon request.

26:8A-8.   Requirements of local registrar

a. The local registrar shall:

(1) stamp each completed Affidavit of Domestic Partnership received with the date of its receipt and the name of the registration district in which it is filed; and

(2) immediately provide two copies of the stamped Affidavit of Domestic Partnership to the person who files that document.

b. Upon the filing of an Affidavit of Domestic Partnership and payment of the appropriate filing fee, the local registrar shall immediately complete a Certificate of Domestic Partnership with the domestic partners' relevant information and the date that the domestic partnership was established. The local registrar shall then issue to the domestic partners two copies of the certificate and two copies of the Notice of the Rights and Obligations of Domestic Partners. Copies of the Certificate of Domestic Partnership shall be prepared and recorded in the local registrar's records and with the State registrar.

c. Each local registrar shall, on or before the 10th day of each calendar month, or sooner if requested by the Department of Health and Senior Services, transmit to the State registrar the original of all the Affidavits of Domestic Partnership and Certificates of Domestic Partnership received or prepared by the local registrar for the preceding month.

26:8A-9. Duties of State registrar

The State registrar shall cause all Affidavits of Domestic Partnership and Certificates of Domestic Partnership received to be alphabetically indexed by the surname of one of the partners, and shall establish a cross-referencing system to allow the records to be identified by the surname of the second partner. The State registrar shall also cause to be transcribed or otherwise recorded from the certificates any of the vital facts appearing thereon as the commissioner may deem necessary or useful.

26:8A-10. Jurisdiction of Superior Court over proceedings to terminate domestic partnership

a. (1) The Superior Court shall have jurisdiction over all proceedings relating to the termination of a domestic partnership established pursuant to section 4 of P.L.2003, c. 246 (C.26:8A-4), including the division and distribution of jointly held property. The fees for filing an action or proceeding for the termination of a domestic partnership shall be the same as those for filing an action or proceeding for divorce pursuant to N.J.S.A. 22A:2-12.

(2) The termination of a domestic partnership may be adjudged for the following causes:

(a) voluntary sexual intercourse between a person who is in a domestic partnership and an individual other than the person's domestic partner as defined in section 3 of P.L.2003, c. 246 (C.26:8A-3);

(b) willful and continued desertion for a period of 12 or more consecutive months, which may be established by satisfactory proof that the parties have ceased to cohabit as domestic partners;

(c) extreme cruelty, which is defined as including any physical or mental cruelty that endangers the safety or health of the plaintiff or makes it improper or unreasonable to expect the plaintiff to continue to cohabit with the defendant; except that no complaint for termination shall be filed until after three months from the date of the last act of cruelty complained of in the complaint, but this provision shall not be held to apply to any counterclaim;

(d) separation, provided that the domestic partners have lived separate and apart in different habitations for a period of at least 18 or more consecutive months and there is no reasonable prospect of reconciliation; and provided further that, after the 18-month period, there shall be a presumption that there is no reasonable prospect of reconciliation;

(e) voluntarily induced addiction or habituation to any narcotic drug, as defined in the "New Jersey Controlled Dangerous Substances Act," P.L.1970, c. 226 (C. 24:21-2) or the "Comprehensive Drug Reform Act of 1987," N.J.S.C. 2C:35-1 et al., or habitual drunkenness for a period of 12 or more consecutive months subsequent to establishment of the domestic partnership and next preceding the filing of the complaint;

(f) institutionalization for mental illness for a period of 24 or more consecutive months subsequent to establishment of the domestic partnership and next preceding the filing of the complaint; or

(g) imprisonment of the defendant for 18 or more consecutive months after establishment of the domestic partnership, provided that where the action is not commenced until after the defendant's release, the parties have not resumed cohabitation following the imprisonment.

(3) In all such proceedings, the court shall in no event be required to effect an equitable distribution of property, either real or personal, which was legally and beneficially acquired by both domestic partners or either domestic partner during the domestic partnership.

(4) The court shall notify the State registrar of the termination of a domestic partnership pursuant to this subsection.

b. In the case of two persons who are each 62 years of age or older and not of the same sex and have established a domestic partnership pursuant to section 4 of P.L.2003, c. 246 (C.26:8A-4), the domestic partnership shall be deemed terminated if the two persons enter into a marriage with each other that is recognized by New Jersey law.

c. The State registrar shall revise the records of domestic partnership provided for in section 9 of P.L.2003, c. 246

(C.26:8A-9) to reflect the termination of a domestic partnership pursuant to this section.

26:8A-11. Applicability of act

a. The provisions of sections 41 through 56, inclusive, of P.L.2003, c. 246 shall only apply in the case of two persons who are of the same sex and have established a domestic partnership pursuant to section 4 of P.L.2003, c. 246 (C.26:8A-4).

b. Notwithstanding any other provisions of law to the contrary, the provisions of subsection a. of this section shall not be deemed to be an unlawful discrimination under the "Law Against Discrimination," P.L.1945, c. 169 (C.10:5-1 et seq.).

26:8A-12. Rules and regulations

a. The Commissioner of Health and Senior Services, pursuant to the "Administrative Procedure Act," P.L.1968, c. 410 (C.52:14B-1 et seq.), shall adopt rules and regulations to effectuate the purposes of sections 1 through 10 and 13 through 35 of this act.

b. The Commissioner of Banking and Insurance, pursuant to the "Administrative Procedure Act," P.L.1968, c. 410 (C.52:14B-1 et seq.), shall adopt rules and regulations to effectuate the purposes of sections 47 through 52, 55 and 56 of this act.

c. The New Jersey Individual Health Coverage Program Board, pursuant to the "Administrative Procedure Act," P.L.1968, c. 410 (C.52:14B-1 et seq.), shall adopt rules and regulations to effectuate the purposes of section 53 of this act.

d. The New Jersey Small Employer Health Benefits Program Board, pursuant to the "Administrative Procedure Act," P.L.1968, c. 410 (C.52:14B-1 et seq.), shall adopt rules and regulations to effectuate the purposes of section 54 of this act.

APPENDIX B
DEFENSE OF MARRIAGE ACT

The Defense of Marriage Act (DOMA) was passed by Congress in 1996 and signed into law by President Clinton on September 21, 1996 as Pub. L. 104-199. DOMA added the following sections to the United States Code:

TITLE 1
GENERAL PROVISIONS
CHAPTER 1
RULES OF CONSTRUCTION

§ 7. Definition of "marriage" and "spouse"

In determining the meaning of any Act of Congress, or of any ruling, regulation, or interpretation of the various administrative bureaus and agencies of the United States, the word "marriage" means only a legal union between one man and one woman as husband and wife, and the word "spouse" refers only to a person of the opposite sex who is a husband or a wife.

TITLE 28
JUDICIARY AND JUDICIAL PROCEDURE
PART V. PROCEDURE
CHAPTER 115

EVIDENCE; DOCUMENTARY

§ 1738C. Certain acts, records, and proceedings and the effect thereof.

No State, territory, or possession of the United States, or Indian tribe, shall be required to give effect to any public act, record, or judicial proceeding of any other State, territory, possession, or tribe respecting a relationship between persons of the same sex that is treated as a marriage under the laws of such other State, territory, possession, or tribe, or a right or claim arising from such relationship.

APPENDIX C
AFFIDAVIT OF DOMESTIC PARTNERSHIP

REG- 71
MAY 04

NEW JERSEY DEPARTMENT OF HEALTH AND SENIOR SERVICES
AFFIDAVIT OF DOMESTIC PARTNERSHIP

STATE FILE NUMBER

A person who unlawfully executes an Affidavit of Domestic Partnership shall be subject to a civil penalty of up to $1000.

1a. Full Name of Domestic Partner A *(First, Middle, Last)*			2a. Full Name of Domestic Partner B *(First, Middle, Last)*		
b. Birthdate *(Mo/Day/Yr)*	c. Age	d. Sex	b. Birthdate *(Mo/Day/Yr)*	c. Age	d. Sex

3a. Common Residence Street Address		b. County
c. City	d. State	e. Zip Code

We, the undersigned, do declare that we meet the requirements of N.J.S.A. 26:8A-4, for entering into a domestic partnership at this time and that we wish to enter into a domestic partnership with each other:

- we share a common residence;
- we are jointly responsible for each other's common welfare as evidenced by joint financial arrangements or joint ownership of real or personal property;
- we agree to be jointly responsible for each other's basic living expenses during the domestic partnership;
- neither of us is in a marriage recognized by New Jersey law or a member of another domestic partnership;
- we are not related to each other by blood or affinity up to and including the fourth degree of consanguinity (see Note below);
- we are both members of the same sex -OR- each of us is over the age of 62 and not of the same sex;
- we have chosen to share each other's lives in a committed relationship of mutual caring;
- we are both at least 18 years of age; and
- neither of us has terminated another domestic partnership within the last 180 calendar days, except that this prohibition shall not apply if one of the partners died.

The representations herein are true, correct and contain no material omissions of fact to the best of our knowledge and belief.

Both partners must appear together in the presence of a Notary Public to record their signatures below.

Signature of Domestic Partner A	Signature of Domestic Partner B
Date	Date

Sworn to and subscribed before me this _____ day of _____ ,in the year _____.

Signature of Notary Public _____ My Commission Expires on: _____.

LOCAL REGISTRAR USE ONLY		
☐ Affidavit of Domestic Partnership Filed	Date Filed	Registration Number Assigned
Name of Local Registrar Receiving Affidavit of Domestic Partnership	Signature	
Name of Municipality	County	

H5175

Note: Consanguinity is generally used to refer to someone who is related by blood, while affinity is normally used to describe someone who is related by marriage. Applicants are advised to make their own determination or seek legal counsel as to whether they are related, up to and including the fourth degree of consanguinity, before they take the oath for the affidavit.

State Registrar Copy

Local Registrar Copy

Domestic Partner Copy

Domestic Partner Copy

167

NEW JERSEY DEPARTMENT OF HEALTH AND SENIOR SERVICES
AFFIDAVIT OF DOMESTIC PARTNERSHIP

(FORM VALID FOR USE ONLY WITHIN THE STATE OF NEW JERSEY)

To register a domestic Partnership in the State of New Jersey, applicants must:

- Execute the attached Affidavit of Domestic Partnership form together in the presence of a Notary Public.

- File the notarized Affidavit of Domestic Partnership form with the Local Registrar of Vital Statistics in any municipality in New Jersey to obtain a Certificate of Domestic Partnership; and

- Remit payment of the registration fee as established by the appropriate New Jersey Regulations

- Provide valid identification for each applicant that establishes name, age, and date of birth.

- identify a common residence in the State of New Jersey or share a common residence in another jurisdiction if at least one of the applicants is a member of a New Jersey State-administered retirement system.

- (FOR NON-NJ RESIDENTS:) Provide proof of membership in a New Jersey state-administered retirement system as evidenced by one or more of the following documents issued by the New Jersey Division of Pension and Benefits:

  - Personal Benefits Statement from the previous year

  - 1099R from the previous calendar year

  - Certificate of Pension Membership

- Provide proof of joint financial responsibility as evidenced by one or more of the following:

  - Joint deed, mortgage agreement or lease;

  - Joint bank account

  - Designation of one of the persons as primary beneficiary in the other person's will;

  - Designation of one of the persons as primary beneficiary in the other person's life insurance policy or retirement plan; or

  - Joint ownership of a motor vehicle.

A DOMESTIC PARTNERSHIP IS NOT CONSIDERED REGISTERED UNTIL THE ABOVE REQUIREMENTS HAVE BEEN SATISFIED.

APPENDIX D
CERTIFICATE OF PENSION MEMBERSHIP

CP-0696-0404

STATE OF NEW JERSEY
DEPARTMENT OF THE TREASURY
DIVISION OF PENSIONS AND BENEFITS
PO BOX 295
TRENTON, NJ 08625-0295

CERTIFICATE OF PENSION MEMBERSHIP

Chapter 246, P.L. 2003, the Domestic Partnership Act, permits out-of-state residents to file for a *Certificate of Domestic Partnership* when at least one of the partners is a member of a New Jersey State-administered pension system (the partners must also meet all other requirements of the law for entering into a domestic partnership and share the same place of residence in the out-of-state jurisdiction).

Applicants using this form to certify pension membership should have their employer complete and certify the required information, and submit the completed form to a Local Registrar along with their *Affidavit of Domestic Partnership.* A list of Local Registrars is available from the Department of Health and Social Services Web site: *www.state.nj.us/health/vital/regbycnty.shtml*

TO BE COMPLETED BY EMPLOYEE/RETIREE

Employee Name: _____

Daytime Phone Number: _____

Pension Fund: ☐ PERS ☐ TPAF ☐ PFRS ☐ SPRS ☐ JRS ☐ ABP

Pension Membership Number: _____

TO BE COMPLETED BY EMPLOYER OR THE DIVISION OF PENSION AND BENEFITS

Employer Name: _____

Name and Title of Verifying Official: _____

Signature of Verifying Official:_____ Date: _____

Phone Number of Verifying Official: _____

In lieu of this *Certificate of Pension Membership,* issued by the employer or the Division of Pensions and Benefits, Local Registrars may also accept the following documentation as evidence of participation in a New Jersey State-administered pension fund:

An employee's Personal Benefit Statement from the:

- Public Employees' Retirement System (PERS)
- Teachers' Pension and Annuity Fund (TPAF)
- Police and Firemen's Retirement System (PFRS)
- State Police Retirement System (SPRS)
- Judicial Retirement System (JRS)
- Alternate Benefits Program (ABP)

A Form1099R issued by the Division of Pensions and Benefits for the :

- Public Employees' Retirement System (PERS)
- Teachers' Pension and Annuity Fund (TPAF)
- Police and Firemen's Retirement System (PFRS)
- State Police Retirement System (SPRS)
- Judicial Retirement System (JRS)

169

APPENDIX E
NOTICE OF RIGHTS AND OBLIGATIONS

New Jersey Department of Health and Senior Services
Bureau of Vital Statistics
P. O. Box 370
Trenton, NJ 08625-0370

NOTICE OF RIGHTS AND OBLIGATIONS OF DOMESTIC PARTNERS

Procedural Requirements:

Establish Eligibility

A domestic partnership shall be established when all of the following requirements are met:

1. Both persons have a common residence within the State of New Jersey, or have a common residence in another jurisdiction and at least one of the persons is a member of a New Jersey State-administered retirement system, and both persons are otherwise jointly responsible for each other's common welfare as evidenced by joint financial arrangements or joint ownership of real or personal property, which shall be demonstrated by at least one of the following:

   a. a joint deed, mortgage agreement or lease;
   b. a joint bank account;
   c. designation of one of the persons as a primary beneficiary in the other person's will;
   d. designation of one of the persons as a primary beneficiary in the other person's life insurance policy or retirement plan; or
   e. joint ownership of a motor vehicle;

2. Both persons agree to be jointly responsible for each other's basic living expenses during the domestic partnership;

3. Neither person is in a marriage recognized by New Jersey law or a member of another domestic partnership;

4. Neither person is related to the other by blood or affinity up to and including the fourth degree of consanguinity;

5. Both persons are of the same sex and therefore unable to enter into a marriage with each other that is recognized by New Jersey law, except that two persons who are each 62 years of age or older and not of the same sex may establish a domestic partnership if they meet the requirements of this section.

6. Both persons have chosen to share each other's lives in a committed relationship of mutual caring;

7. Both persons are at least 18 years of age;

8. Both persons file jointly an Affidavit of Domestic Partnership; and

9. Neither person has been a partner in a domestic partnership that was terminated less than 180 days prior to filing of the current Affidavit of Domestic Partnership, except that this prohibition shall not apply if one of the partners died; and, in all cases in which a person registered a prior domestic partnership, the domestic partnership shall have been terminated in accordance with the provisions shown below under terminating a Domestic Partnership.

10. A person who unlawfully executes an Affidavit of Domestic Partnership shall be subject to a civil penalty of up to $1000.

Complete an Affidavit of Domestic Partnership

Affidavits of Domestic Partnership can be obtained from any local registrar's office of vital statistics at any municipality within the State of New Jersey.

An Affidavit of Domestic Partnership requires the applicants to provide their full name, date of birth, age, sex, and common residence.

Both applicants must present the completed Affidavit of Domestic Partnership and identification to a notary public and sign in the presence of the notary attesting that they meet the requirements for establishing a domestic partnership.

Filing the Affidavit of Domestic Partnership

The signed and notarized Affidavit of Domestic Partnership shall be presented to any local registrar of vital statistics at any municipality within the State of New Jersey. The Affidavit of Domestic Partnership must be accompanied by proof of at least one of the following:

1. a joint deed, mortgage agreement or lease;

2. a joint bank account;

3. designation of one of the persons as a primary beneficiary in the other person's will;

4. designation of one of the persons as a primary beneficiary in the other person's life insurance policy or retirement plan; or

5. joint ownership of a motor vehicle;

Applicants whose common residence is not within the State of New Jersey must provide proof, by at least one applicant, of membership in a New Jersey state-administered retirement system as evidenced by one or more of the following documents issued by the New Jersey Division of Pension and Benefits:

1. Personal Benefits Statement from the current or previous calendar year;

2. 1099R from the current or previous calendar year; or

3. Certificate of Pension Membership.

Upon filing of the Affidavit of Domestic Partnership and payment of the appropriate fee the local registrar shall immediately complete a Certificate of Domestic Partnership.

Terminating A Domestic Partnership

The Superior Court of New Jersey shall have jurisdiction over all proceedings relating to the termination of a domestic partnership. The fees for filing an action or proceeding for the termination of a domestic partnership shall be the same as those for filing an action or proceeding for divorce.

Termination of a domestic partnership may be adjudged for the following causes:

a. voluntary sexual intercourse between a person who is in a domestic partnership and an individual other than the person's domestic partner;

b. willful and continued desertion for a period of 12 or more consecutive months, which may be established by satisfactory proof that the parties have ceased to cohabit as domestic partners;

c. extreme cruelty, which is defined as including any physical or mental cruelty that endangers the safety or health of the plaintiff or makes it

improper or unreasonable to expect the plaintiff to continue to cohabit with the defendant; except that no complaint for termination shall be filed until after three months from the date of the last act of cruelty complained of in the complaint, but this provision shall not be held to apply to any counterclaim;

d. separation, provided that the domestic partners have lived separate and apart in different habitations for a period of at least 18 or more consecutive months and there is no reasonable prospect of reconciliation; and provided further that, after the 18 month period, there shall be a presumption that there is no reasonable prospect of reconciliation;

e. voluntarily induced addiction or habituation to any narcotic drug, as defined in the "New Jersey Controlled Dangerous Substances Act" or the "Comprehensive Drug Reform Act of 1987," or habitual drunkenness for a period of 12 or more consecutive months subsequent to establishment of the domestic partnership and next preceding the filing of the complaint;

f. institutionalization for mental illness for a period of 24 or more consecutive months subsequent to establishment of the domestic partnership and next preceding the filing of the complaint; or

g. imprisonment of the defendant for 18 or more consecutive months after establishment of the domestic partnership, provided that where the action is not commenced until after the defendant's release, the parties have not resumed cohabitation following imprisonment.

In the case of two persons who are each 62 years of age or older and not of the same sex and have established a domestic partnership, the domestic partnership shall be deemed terminated if the two persons enter into a marriage with each other that is recognized by New Jersey law.

In all such proceedings, the court shall in no event be required to effect an equitable distribution of property, either real or personal, which was legally and beneficially acquired by both domestic partners or either domestic partner during the domestic partnership.

The court shall notify the State Registrar of the termination of a domestic partnership.

Rights and Obligation of Domestic Partners

Pursuant to N.J.S.A. 26:8A-1 et seq., all persons in domestic partnerships shall be entitled to certain rights and benefits that are accorded to married couples under the laws of New Jersey, including statutory protection through the "Law Against Discrimination" against various forms of discrimination based on domestic partnership status, such as employment, housing and credit discrimination, visitation rights for a hospitalized domestic partner and the right to make medical or legal decisions for an incapacitated partner; and an additional exemption from the personal income tax and the transfer inheritance tax on the same basis as a spouse.

The obligations that two people have to each other as a result of creating a domestic partnership shall be limited to the provisions of the Domestic Partnership Act and those provisions shall not diminish any right granted under any other provision of law.

Upon termination of a domestic partnership, the domestic partners, from that time forward, shall incur none of the obligations to each other as domestic partners that are created by the Domestic Partnership Act or any other act.

A domestic partnership, civil union or reciprocal beneficiary relationship entered into outside of this State, which is valid under the laws of the jurisdiction under which the partnership was created, shall be valid in this State.

Any health care or social services provider, employer, operator of a place of public accommodation, property owner or administrator, or other individual or entity may treat a person as a member of a domestic partnership, notwithstanding the absence of an Affidavit of Domestic Partnership filed pursuant to the Domestic Partnership Act.

Domestic Partners may modify the rights and obligations to each other that are granted by the Domestic Partnership Act in any valid contract between themselves, except for the requirements for a domestic partnership as set forth in the section of the Domestic Partnership Act governing eligibility to establish a domestic partnership.

Two adults who have not filed an Affidavit of Domestic Partnership shall be treated as domestic partners in an emergency medical situation for the purposes of allowing one adult to accompany the other adult who is ill or injured while the latter is being transported to a hospital, or to visit the other adult who is a hospital patient, on the same basis as a member of the latter's immediate family, if both persons, or one of the persons in the event that the other person is legally or medically incapacitated, advise the emergency care provider that the two persons have met the other requirements for establishing a domestic partnership as set forth in the Domestic Partnership Act; however, the provisions of this section shall not be construed to permit the two adults to be treated as domestic partners for any other purpose as provided in the Domestic Partnership Act prior to their having filed an Affidavit of Domestic Partnership.

A domestic partner shall not be liable for the debts of the other partner contracted before establishment of the domestic partnership, or contracted by the other partner in his/her own name during the domestic partnership. The partner who contracts for the debt in his/her own name shall be liable to be sued separately in his/her own name, and any property belonging to that partner shall be liable to satisfy that debt in the same manner as if the partner had not entered into a domestic partnership.

Pursuant to N.J.S.A. 26:8A-5, a former domestic partner who has given a copy of the Certificate of Domestic Partnership to any third-party to qualify for any benefit or right and whose receipt of that benefit or enjoyment of that right has not otherwise terminated, shall upon termination of the domestic partnership, give or send to the third-party at last known address of third-party, written notification that the domestic partnership has been terminated. A third-party that suffers a loss as a result of failure by the domestic partner to provide this notice, shall be entitled to seek recovery from the partner who was obligated to send notice for any actual loss resulting thereby. Failure to provide notice to a third party shall not delay or prevent the termination of a domestic partnership.

APPENDIX F

APPLICATION FOR CERTIFICATION

New Jersey Department of Health and Senior Services
Vital Statistics and Registration

APPLICATION FOR A *CERTIFICATION* OR A *CERTIFIED COPY* OF A VITAL RECORD

A ***Certification*** of a vital record event is issued to those individuals with a distant or no relationship to the individual(s) listed on the vital record. It is issued for informational purposes only and cannot be used for legal or identification purposes.

A ***Certified Copy*** of a vital record event is issued to those individuals who have a direct link to the individual(s) named on the vital record event, as identified in Governor McGreevey's Executive Order 18, and provided that the requestor is able to identify the vital record and can provide proof of his identity and relationship. A Certified Copy will contain the raised Great Seal of the State of New Jersey and can be used for legal or identification purposes.

PLEASE TYPE OR PRINT CLEARLY! ALL ITEMS ARE REQUIRED UNLESS NOTED OTHERWISE.* PROOF OF IDENTITY IS REQUIRED. MAKE CHECK OR MONEY ORDER PAYABLE TO "STATE TREASURER." DO NOT MAIL CASH.

Name of Applicant	Relationship to Person Named On Requested Record *(Proof may be required.)*	Why is record being requested? ☐Passport ☐Driver License
Street Address		☐School/Sports ☐Social Security Card ☐Soc. Sec. Disability ☐Other Soc. Sec. Benefits
City State Zip Code	Telephone Number	☐Veterans Benefits ☐Medicare ☐Welfare
Signature of Applicant	Date of Application	☐Genealogy ☐Other:

B I R T H	Full Name of Child at Time of Birth	No. of Copies Requested
	Place of Birth (City, Town or Township) County	
	Exact Date of Birth Name of Hospital (Optional)	
	Mother's Full Maiden Name Father's Name (if recorded on the record)	
	If Child's Name Was Changed, Indicate New Name and How It Was Changed	

DO NOT use this form to request a <u>Certified Copy of a Certificate of Birth Resulting in Stillbirth</u>. Use form REG-68 which is available on the Department's website at: www.state.nj.us/health/vital/vital.shtml. Follow the instructions carefully.

M A R R I A G E	Name of Husband	No. of Copies Requested
	Maiden Name of Wife	Exact Date of Marriage
	Place of Marriage (City, Town or Township) County	
DOMESTIC PARTNERSHIP	Name of Partner	No. of Copies Requested
	Name of Partner	Exact Date Registered
	Place Where Domestic Partnership Registered (City, Town or Township) County	
D E A T H	Name of Deceased	No. of Copies Requested
	Exact Date of Death Place of Death (City, Town or Township) County	
	Mother's Full Maiden Name Father's Name (if recorded on the record)	

* Births occurring over 80 years ago, marriages occurring over 50 years ago and deaths occurring over 40 years ago are considered genealogical and therefore exact information is not required. You may provide only the name of the individual recorded on the vital record, the county where the event occurred and the year the event occurred. Multiple years may be searched at a fee of $1.00 per additional year searched.

REG-3
FEB 05

FOR STATE USE ONLY			
Payment Type: ☐Cash ☐M/O ☐Check ☐Waived	Payment Amount: $	ID Viewed:	Processed By:

New Jersey Department of Health and Senior Services
Bureau of Vital Statistics
P. O. Box 370, Trenton, NJ 08625-0370

	STATE USE ONLY
	Co/Mun Code

REQUEST TO PURCHASE CERTIFIED COPY OF VITAL RECORDS FORMS

Please mail this completed form along with the <u>original copy</u> of your Purchase Order to the attention
of the State Registrar at the above address. See other important instructions on the reverse side.

Name of Municipality	County	Date

SHIPPING	Ship To Name (Registrar Only)	BILLING	Bill To (Name and Address)
	Alternate Ship To Name (Deputy or Alternate Deputy)		
	Ship To Address		

Telephone Number	Fax Number	E-Mail Address
( )	( )	

Form Number / Description of Item	Quantity Per Pkg.	Cost Per Package	Packages Requested	Total Cost
REG-42A	Certified Copy of Vital Record [Computer-Generated Certified Copies or Photocopies of Births, Marriages and Deaths (Prior to 2004)] Size: 8-1/2 x 11"	500	$66.58		
REG-42B	Certified Copy of Vital Record (Photocopied 2004 or Newer Death Records) Size: 8-1/2 x 14"	500	$66.58		
REG-42C	Certified Copy of Vital Record (Microfilmed or Imaged Records / Image on Back) Size: 8-1/2 x 11"	500	$66.58		
REG-42D	Certified Copy of Vital Record (Typed Birth Record WITH Parents' Names) Size: 8-1/2 x 11"	50	$6.65		
REG-42E	Certified Copy of Vital Record (Typed Birth Record WITHOUT Parents' Names) Size: 8-1/2 x 11"	50	$6.65		
REG-42F	Certified Copy of Vital Record (Typed Marriage Records) Size: 8-1/2 x 11"	50	$6.65		
REG-42G	Certified Copy of Vital Record (**Typed** Death Records) Size: 8-1/2 x 11"	50	$6.65		
REG-42H	Certified Copy of Vital Record (**Typed** Domestic Partnership Records) Size: 8-1/2 x 11"	50	$6.65		
	TOTAL COST FOR FORMS:				

FOR STATE USE ONLY→	NJDHSS Authorization Signature	Date

REG-62
NOV 04

INSTRUCTIONS FOR COMPLETION

The following instructions are intended to help you complete the order form properly:

Ship To Name/ Alternate
Provide the name of the Registrar who will be responsible to accept and sign for the forms when they are delivered. The name of the Deputy or Alternate Deputy Registrar must be provided as a back up, in the event that the Registrar is unavailable to accept delivery of the forms.

Ship To Address
Provide a physical location address since these forms are shipped via express courier, with a receiving signature required. Do not provide a post office box.

Bill To (Name and Address)
Provide the name and address of the individual to whom the bill should be mailed. Please enter complete information even if it is the same as the Ship To Address.

Quantity Per Package
Please note that some of the forms are sold in packages of 500 forms, while others are sold in smaller packages of only 50 forms.

Packages Requested
Enter the number of _packages_ requested, **NOT** the number of forms.

Total Cost
Multiply the cost per package by the number of packages requested. Add all entries in this column and enter it at the bottom. This will be the total cost for your order.

Purchase Orders
MUST be approved by the Office of the State Registrar, Bureau of Vital Statistics, **BEFORE** being submitted to Moore-Wallace.

Mail directly to:

Office of the State Registrar
Bureau of Vital Statistics
P. O. Box 370
Trenton, NJ 08625-0370

Vendor Information:

Moore-Wallace North America Inc.

Contract Number A55230
FEIN: 160331690

Payment for Processed PO's
You MUST include the Invoice Number on your check when you remit payment, or attach a copy of the Invoice to your check. If space permits, also include the purchase order number, name of municipality and name of county on your check.

Send payment directly to Moore-Wallace North America, at the address provided on the Invoice.

****

IMPORTANT!

It is important to remit prompt payment for the forms ordered.

Outstanding balances due may result in future orders being delayed.

Moore Wallace can refuse to ship additional forms to any municipality with an outstanding balance due.

Please direct all **questions** about the forms to the **Office of the State Registrar** at 609-292-4087, Ext. 505 or 506.

APPENDIX G
LAW AGAINST DISCRIMINATION

The Domestic Partnership Act added protection for registered domestic partners in certain categories. This appendix contains the excerpts from the LAD that apply to domestic partners, including prohibitions against discrimination on the basis of affectional or sexual orientation.

TITLE 10
CIVIL RIGHTS
CHAPTER 5
LAW AGAINST DISCRIMINATION

10:5-1.   Short title.

This act shall be known as "Law Against Discrimination."

10:5-2.   Police power, enactment deemed exercise of

The enactment hereof shall be deemed an exercise of the police power of the State for the protection of the public safety, health and morals and to promote the general welfare and in fulfillment of the provisions of the Constitution of this State guaranteeing civil rights.

10:5-3.   Findings and declarations

The Legislature finds and declares that practices of discrimination against any of its inhabitants, because of race, creed, color, national origin, ancestry, age, sex, affectional or sexual orientation, marital status, familial status, liability for service in the Armed Forces of the United States, disability or nationality, are matters of concern to the government of the State, and that such discrimination threatens not only the rights and proper privileges of the inhabitants of the State but menaces the institutions and foundation of a free democratic State; provided, however, that nothing in this expression of policy prevents the making of legitimate distinctions between citizens and aliens when required by federal law or otherwise necessary to promote the national interest.

The Legislature further declares its opposition to such practices of discrimination when directed against any person by reason of the race, creed, color, national origin, ancestry, age, sex, affectional or sexual orientation, marital status, liability for service in the Armed Forces of the United States, disability or nationality of that person or that person's spouse, partners, members, stockholders, directors, officers, managers, superintendents, agents, employees, business associates, suppliers, or customers, in order that the economic prosperity and general welfare of the inhabitants of the State may be protected and ensured.

The Legislature further finds that because of discrimination, people suffer personal hardships, and the State suffers a grievous harm. The personal hardships include: economic loss; time loss; physical and emotional stress; and in some cases severe emotional trauma, illness, homelessness or other irreparable harm resulting from the strain of employment controversies; relocation, search and moving difficulties; anxiety caused by lack of information, uncertainty, and resultant planning difficulty; career, education, family and social disruption; and adjustment problems, which particularly impact on those protected by this act. Such harms have, under the common law, given rise to legal remedies, including compensatory and punitive damages. The Legislature intends that such damages be available to all persons protected by this act and that this act shall be liberally construed in combination with other protections available under the laws of this State.

10:5-4.   Obtaining employment, accommodations and privileges without discrimination; civil right

All persons shall have the opportunity to obtain employment, and to obtain all the accommodations, advantages, facilities, and privileges of any place of public accommodation, publicly assisted housing accommodation, and other real property without discrimination because of race, creed, color, national origin, ancestry, age, marital status, affectional or sexual orientation, familial status, disability, nationality, sex or source of lawful income used for rental or mortgage payments, subject only to conditions and limitations applicable alike to all persons. This opportunity is recognized as and declared to be a civil right.

10:5-5.   Definitions

As used in this act, unless a different meaning clearly appears from the context:

a. "Person" includes one or more individuals, partnerships, associations, organizations, labor organizations, corporations, legal representatives, trustees, trustees in bankruptcy, receivers, and fiduciaries.

b. "Employment agency" includes any person undertaking to procure employees or opportunities for others to work.

c. "Labor organization" includes any organization which exists and is constituted for the purpose, in whole or in part, of collective bargaining, or of dealing with employers concerning grievances, terms or conditions of employment, or of other mutual aid or protection in connection with employment.

d. "Unlawful employment practice" and "unlawful discrimination" include only those unlawful practices and acts specified in section 11 of this act. [FN1]

e. "Employer" includes all persons as defined in subsection a. of this section unless otherwise specifically exempt under another section of this act, and includes the State, any political or civil subdivision thereof, and all public officers, agencies, boards or bodies.

f. "Employee" does not include any individual employed in the domestic service of any person.

g. "Liability for service in the Armed Forces of the United States" means subject to being ordered as an individual or member of an organized unit into active service in the Armed Forces of the United States by reason of membership in the National Guard, naval militia or a reserve component of the Armed Forces of the United States, or subject to being inducted into such armed forces through a system of national selective service.

h. "Division" means the "Division on Civil Rights" created by this act.

i. "Attorney General" means the Attorney General of the State of New Jersey or his representative or designee.

j. "Commission" means the Commission on Civil Rights created by this act.

k. "Director" means the Director of the Division on Civil Rights.

l. "A place of public accommodation" shall include, but not be limited to: any tavern, roadhouse, hotel, motel, trailer camp, summer camp, day camp, or resort camp, whether for entertainment of transient guests or accommodation of those seeking health, recreation or rest; any producer, manufacturer, wholesaler, distributor, retail shop, store, establishment, or concession dealing with goods or services of any kind; any restaurant, eating house, or place where food is sold for consumption on the premises; any place maintained for the sale of ice cream, ice and fruit preparations or their derivatives, soda water or confections, or where any beverages of any kind are retailed for consumption on the premises; any garage, any public conveyance operated on land or water, or in the air, any stations and terminals thereof; any bathhouse, boardwalk, or seashore accommodation; any auditorium, meeting place, or hall; any theatre, motion-picture house, music hall, roof garden, skating rink, swimming pool, amusement and recreation park, fair, bowling alley, gymnasium, shooting gallery, billiard and pool parlor, or other place of amusement; any comfort station; any dispensary, clinic or hospital; any public library; any kindergarten, primary and secondary school, trade or business school, high school, academy, college and university, or any educational institution under the supervision of the State Board of Education, or the Commissioner of Education of the State of New Jersey. Nothing herein contained shall be construed to include or to apply to any institution, bona fide club, or place of accommodation, which is in its nature distinctly private; nor shall anything herein contained apply to any educational facility operated or maintained by a bona fide religious or sectarian institution, and the right of a natural parent or one in loco parentis to direct the education and upbringing of a child under his control is hereby affirmed; nor shall anything herein contained be construed to bar any private secondary or post secondary school from using in good faith criteria other than race, creed, color, national origin, ancestry or affectional or sexual orientation in the admission of students.

m. "A publicly assisted housing accommodation" shall include all housing built with public funds or public assistance pursuant to P.L.1949, c. 300 [FN2], P.L.1941, c. 213 [FN3], P.L.1944, c. 169 [FN4], P.L.1949, c. 303 [FN5], P.L.1938, c. 19 [FN6], P.L.1938, c. 20 [FN7], P.L.1946, c. 52 [FN8], and P.L.1949, c. 184 [FN9], and all housing financed in whole or in part by a loan, whether or not secured by a mortgage, the repayment of which is guaranteed or insured by the federal government or any agency thereof.

n. The term "real property" includes real estate, lands, tenements and hereditaments, corporeal and incorporeal, and leaseholds, provided, however, that, except as to publicly assisted housing accommodations, the provisions of this act shall not apply to the rental: (1) of a single apartment or flat in a two-family dwelling, the other occupancy unit of which is occupied by the owner as a residence; or (2) of a room or rooms to another person or persons by the owner or occupant of a one-family dwelling occupied by the owner or occupant as a residence at the time of such rental. Nothing herein contained shall be construed to bar any religious or denominational institution or organization, or any organization operated for charitable or educational purposes, which is operated, supervised or controlled by or in connection with a religious organization, in the sale, lease or rental of real property, from limiting admission to or giving preference to persons of the same religion or denomination or from making such selection as is calculated by such organization to promote the religious principles for which it is established or maintained. Nor does any provision under this act regarding discrimination on the basis of familial status apply with respect to housing for older persons.

o. "Real estate broker" includes a person, firm or corporation who, for a fee, commission or other valuable consideration, or by reason of promise or reasonable expectation thereof, lists for sale, sells, exchanges, buys or rents, or offers or attempts to negotiate a sale, exchange, purchase, or rental of real estate or an interest therein, or collects or offers or attempts to collect rent for the use of real estate, or solicits for prospective purchasers or assists or directs in the procuring of prospects or the negotiation or closing of any transaction which does or is contemplated to result in the sale, exchange, leasing, renting or auctioning of any real estate, or negotiates, or offers or attempts or agrees to negotiate a loan secured or to be secured by mortgage or other encumbrance upon or transfer of any real estate for others; or any person who, for pecuniary gain or expectation of pecuniary gain conducts a public or private competitive sale of lands or any interest in lands. In the sale of lots, the term "real estate broker" shall also include any person, partnership, association or corporation employed by or on behalf of the owner or owners of lots or other parcels of real estate, at a stated salary, or upon a commission, or upon a salary and commission or otherwise, to sell such real estate, or any parts thereof, in lots or other parcels, and who shall sell or exchange, or offer or attempt or agree to negotiate the sale or exchange, of any such lot or parcel of real estate.

p. "Real estate salesperson" includes any person who, for compensation, valuable consideration or commission, or other thing of value, or by reason of a promise or reasonable expectation thereof, is employed by and operates under the supervision of a licensed real estate broker to sell or offer to sell, buy or offer to buy or negotiate the purchase, sale or exchange of real estate, or offers or attempts to negotiate a loan secured or to be secured by a mortgage or other encumbrance upon or transfer of real estate, or to lease or rent, or offer to lease or rent any real estate for others, or to collect rents for the use of real estate, or to solicit for prospective purchasers or lessees of real estate, or who is employed by a licensed real estate broker to sell or offer to sell lots or other parcels of real estate, at a stated salary, or upon a commission, or upon a salary and commission, or otherwise to sell real estate, or any parts thereof, in lots or other parcels.

q. "Disability" means physical disability, infirmity, malformation or disfigurement which is caused by bodily injury, birth defect or illness including epilepsy and other seizure disorders, and which shall include, but not be limited to, any degree of paralysis, amputation, lack of physical coordination, blindness or visual impediment, deafness or hearing impediment, muteness or speech impediment or physical reliance on a service or guide dog, wheelchair, or other remedial appliance or device, or any mental, psychological or developmental disability resulting from anatomical, psychological, physiological or neurological conditions which prevents the normal exercise of any bodily or mental functions or is demonstrable, medically or psychologically, by accepted clinical or laboratory diagnostic techniques. Disability shall also mean AIDS or HIV infection.

r-t. (Omitted).

u. "Housing accommodation" means any publicly assisted housing accommodation or any real property, or portion thereof, which is used or occupied, or is intended, arranged, or designed to be used or occupied, as the home, residence or sleeping place of one or more persons, but shall not include any single family residence the occupants of which rent, lease, or furnish for compensation not more than one room therein.

v. "Public facility" means any place of public accommodation and any street, highway, sidewalk, walkway, public building, and any other place or structure to which the general public is regularly, normally or customarily permitted or invited.

w-dd. (Omitted).

ee. "Qualified Medicaid applicant" means an individual who is a qualified applicant pursuant to P.L.1968, c. 413 (C.30:4D-1 et seq.).

ff. "AIDS" means acquired immune deficiency syndrome as defined by the Centers for Disease Control and Prevention of the United States Public Health Service.

gg. "HIV infection" means infection with the human immunodeficiency virus or any other related virus identified as a probable causative agent of AIDS.

hh. "Affectional or sexual orientation" means male or female heterosexuality, homosexuality or bisexuality by inclination, practice, identity or expression, having a history thereof or being perceived, presumed or identified by others as having such an orientation.

ii. "Heterosexuality" means affectional, emotional or physical attraction or behavior which is primarily directed towards persons of the other gender.

jj. "Homosexuality" means affectional, emotional or physical attraction or behavior which is primarily directed towards persons of the same gender.

kk. "Bisexuality" means affectional, emotional or physical attraction or behavior which is directed towards persons of either gender.

ll. "Familial status" means being the natural parent of a child, the adoptive parent of a child, the resource family parent of a child, having a "parent and child relationship" with a child as defined by State law, or having sole or joint legal or physical custody, care, guardianship, or visitation with a child, or any person who is pregnant or is in the process of securing legal custody of any individual who has not attained the age of 18 years.

mm. "Housing for older persons" means housing:

(1) provided under any State program that the Attorney General determines is specifically designed and operated to assist elderly persons (as defined in the State program); or provided under any federal program that the United States Department of Housing and Urban Development determines is specifically designed and operated to assist elderly persons

(as defined in the federal program); or

(2) intended for, and solely occupied by persons 62 years of age or older; or

(3) intended and operated for occupancy by at least one person 55 years of age or older per unit. In determining whether housing qualifies as housing for older persons under this subsection, the Attorney General shall adopt regulations which require at least the following factors:

(a) the existence of significant facilities and services specifically designed to meet the physical or social needs of older persons, or if the provision of such facilities and services is not practicable, that such housing is necessary to provide important housing opportunities for older persons; and

(b) that at least 80 percent of the units are occupied by at least one person 55 years of age or older per unit; and

(c) the publication of, and adherence to, policies and procedures which demonstrate an intent by the owner or manager to provide housing for persons 55 years of age or older.

Housing shall not fail to meet the requirements for housing for older persons by reason of: persons residing in such housing as of September 13, 1988 not meeting the age requirements of this subsection, provided that new occupants of such housing meet the age requirements of this subsection; or unoccupied units, provided that such units are reserved for occupancy by persons who meet the age requirements of this subsection.

nn. "Genetic characteristic" means any inherited gene or chromosome, or alteration thereof, that is scientifically or medically believed to predispose an individual to a disease, disorder or syndrome, or to be associated with a statistically significant increased risk of development of a disease, disorder or syndrome.

oo-pp. (Omitted).

qq. "Domestic partnership" means a domestic partnership established pursuant to section 4 of P.L.2003, c. 246 (C.26:8A-4).

10:5-12. Unlawful employment practice or unlawful discrimination

It shall be an unlawful employment practice, or, as the case may be, an unlawful discrimination:

a. For an employer, because of the race, creed, color, national origin, ancestry, age, marital status, domestic partnership status, affectional or sexual orientation, genetic information, sex, disability or atypical hereditary cellular or blood trait of any individual, or because of the liability for service in the Armed Forces of the United States or the nationality of any individual, or because of the refusal to submit to a genetic test or make available the results of a genetic test to an employer, to refuse to hire or employ or to bar or to discharge or require to retire, unless justified by lawful considerations other than age, from employment such individual or to discriminate against such individual in compensation or in terms, conditions or privileges of employment; provided, however, it shall not be an unlawful employment practice to refuse to accept for employment an applicant who has received a notice of induction or orders to report for active duty in the armed forces; provided further that nothing herein contained shall be construed to bar an employer from refusing to accept for employment any person on the basis of sex in those certain circumstances where sex is a bona fide occupational qualification, reasonably necessary to the normal operation of the particular business or enterprise; provided further that nothing herein contained shall be construed to bar an employer from refusing to accept for employment or to promote any person over 70 years of age; provided further that it shall not be an unlawful employment practice for a club exclusively social or fraternal to use club membership as a uniform qualification for employment, or for a religious association or organization to utilize religious affiliation as a uniform qualification in the employment of clergy, religious teachers or other employees engaged in the religious activities of the association or organization, or in following the tenets of its religion in establishing and utilizing criteria for employment of an employee; provided further, that it shall not be an unlawful employment practice to require the retirement of any employee who, for the two-year period immediately before retirement, is employed in a bona fide executive or a high policy-making position, if that employee is entitled to an immediate non-forfeitable annual retirement benefit from a pension, profit sharing, savings or deferred retirement plan, or any combination of those plans, of the employer of that employee which equals in the aggregate at least $27,000. 00; and provided further that an employer may restrict employment to citizens of the United States where such restriction is required by federal law or is otherwise necessary to protect the national interest.

The provisions of subsections a. and b. of section 57 of P.L.2003, c. 246 (C.34:11A-20), and the provisions of section 58 of P.L.2003, c. 246 (C.26: 8A-11), shall not be deemed to be an unlawful discrimination under P.L.1945, c. 169 (C.10:5-1 et seq.).

For the purposes of this subsection, a "bona fide executive" is a top level employee who exercises substantial executive authority over a significant number of employees and a large volume of business. A "high policy-making position" is a position in which a person plays a significant role in developing policy and in recommending the implementation thereof.

b. For a labor organization, because of the race, creed, color, national origin, ancestry, age, marital status, domestic partnership status, affectional or sexual orientation, disability or sex of any individual, or because of the liability for service in the Armed Forces of the United States or nationality of any individual, to exclude or to expel from its membership such individual or to discriminate in any way against any of its members, against any applicant for, or individual included in, any apprentice or other training program or against any employer or any individual employed by an employer; provided, however, that nothing herein contained shall be construed to bar a labor organization from excluding from its apprentice or other training programs any person on the basis of sex in those certain circumstances where sex is a bona fide occupational qualification reasonably necessary to the normal operation of the particular apprentice or other training program.

c. For any employer or employment agency to print or circulate or cause to be printed or circulated any statement, advertisement or publication, or to use any form of application for employment, or to make an inquiry in connection with prospective employment, which expresses, directly or indirectly, any limitation, specification or discrimination as to race, creed, color, national origin, ancestry, age, marital status, domestic partnership status, affectional or sexual orientation, disability, nationality or sex or liability of any applicant for employment for service in the Armed Forces of the United States, or any intent to make any such limitation, specification or discrimination, unless based upon a bona fide occupational qualification.

d. For any person to take reprisals against any person because that person has opposed any practices or acts forbidden under this act or because that person has filed a complaint, testified or assisted in any proceeding under this act or to coerce, intimidate, threaten or interfere with any person in the exercise or enjoyment of, or on account of that person having aided or encouraged any other person in the exercise or enjoyment of, any right granted or protected by this act.

e. For any person, whether an employer or an employee or not, to aid, abet, incite, compel or coerce the doing of any of the acts forbidden under this act, or to attempt to do so.

f. (1) For any owner, lessee, proprietor, manager, superintendent, agent, or employee of any place of public accommodation directly or indirectly to refuse, withhold from or deny to any person any of the accommodations, advantages, facilities or privileges thereof, or to discriminate against any person in the furnishing thereof, or directly or indirectly to publish, circulate, issue, display, post or mail any written or printed communication, notice, or advertisement to the effect that any of the accommodations, advantages, facilities, or privileges of any such place will be refused, withheld from, or denied to any person on account of the race, creed, color, national origin, ancestry, marital status, domestic partnership status, sex, affectional or sexual orientation, disability or nationality of such person, or that the patronage or custom thereat of any person of any particular race, creed, color, national origin, ancestry, marital status, domestic partnership status, sex, affectional or sexual orientation, disability or nationality is unwelcome, objectionable or not acceptable, desired or solicited, and the production of any such written or printed communication, notice or advertisement, purporting to relate to any such place and to be made by any owner, lessee, proprietor, superintendent or manager thereof, shall be presumptive evidence in any action that the same was authorized by such person; provided, however, that nothing contained herein shall be construed to bar any place of public accommodation which is in its nature reasonably restricted exclusively to individuals of one sex, and which shall include but not be limited to any summer camp, day camp, or resort camp, bathhouse, dressing room, swimming pool, gymnasium, comfort station, dispensary, clinic or hospital, or school or educational institution which is restricted exclusively to individuals of one sex, from refusing, withholding from or denying to any individual of the opposite sex any of the accommodations, advantages, facilities or privileges thereof on the basis of sex; provided further, that the foregoing limitation shall not apply to any restaurant as defined in R.S.33:1-1 or place where alcoholic beverages are served.

(2) Notwithstanding the definition of "public accommodation "as set forth in subsection l. of section 5 of P.L.1945, c. 169 (C.10:5-5), for any owner, lessee, proprietor, manager, superintendent, agent, or employee of any private club or association to directly or indirectly refuse, withhold from or deny to any individual who has been accepted as a club member and has contracted for or is otherwise entitled to full club membership any of the accommodations, advantages, facilities or privileges thereof, or to discriminate against any member in the furnishing thereof on account of the race, creed, color, national origin, ancestry, marital status, domestic partnership status, sex, affectional or sexual orientation, disability or nationality of such person.

In addition to the penalties otherwise provided for a violation of P.L.1945, c. 169 (C.10:5-1 et seq.), if the violator of paragraph (2) of subsection f. of this section is the holder of an alcoholic beverage license issued under the provisions of R.S.33:1-12 for that private club or association, the matter shall be referred to the Director of the Division of Alcoholic Beverage Control who shall impose an appropriate penalty in accordance with the procedures set forth in R.S.33:1-31.

g. For any person, including but not limited to, any owner, lessee, sublessee, assignee or managing agent of, or other person having the right of ownership or possession of or the right to sell, rent, lease, assign, or sublease any real property or part or portion thereof, or any agent or employee of any of these:

(1) To refuse to sell, rent, lease, assign, or sublease or otherwise to deny to or withhold from any person or group of persons any real property or part or portion thereof because of race, creed, color, national origin, ancestry, marital status, domestic partnership status, sex, affectional or sexual orientation, familial status, disability, nationality, or source of lawful income used for rental or mortgage payments;

(2) To discriminate against any person or group of persons because of race, creed, color, national origin, ancestry, marital status, domestic partnership status, sex, affectional or sexual orientation, familial status, disability, nationality or source of lawful income used for rental or mortgage payments in the terms, conditions or privileges of the sale, rental or lease of any real property or part or portion thereof or in the furnishing of facilities or services in connection therewith;

(3) To print, publish, circulate, issue, display, post or mail, or cause to be printed, published, circulated, issued, displayed, posted or mailed any statement, advertisement, publication or sign, or to use any form of application for the purchase, rental, lease, assignment or sublease of any real property or part or portion thereof, or to make any record or inquiry in connection with the prospective purchase, rental, lease, assignment, or sublease of any real property, or part or portion thereof which expresses, directly or indirectly, any limitation, specification or discrimination as to race, creed, color, national origin, ancestry, marital status, domestic partnership status, sex, affectional or sexual orientation, familial status, disability, nationality, or source of lawful income used for rental or mortgage payments, or any intent to make any such limitation, specification or discrimination, and the production of any such statement, advertisement, publicity, sign, form of application, record, or inquiry purporting to be made by any such person shall be presumptive evidence in any action that the same was authorized by such person; provided, however, that nothing contained in this subsection shall be construed to bar any person from refusing to sell, rent, lease, assign or sublease or from advertising or recording a qualification as to sex for any room, apartment, flat in a dwelling or residential facility which is planned exclusively for and occupied by individuals of one sex to any individual of the exclusively opposite sex on the basis of sex;

(4) To refuse to sell, rent, lease, assign, or sublease or otherwise to deny to or withhold from any person or group of per-

sons any real property or part or portion thereof because of the source of any lawful income received by the person or the source of any lawful rent payment to be paid for the real property; or

(5) To refuse to rent or lease any real property to another person because that person's family includes children under 18 years of age, or to make an agreement, rental or lease of any real property which provides that the agreement, rental or lease shall be rendered null and void upon the birth of a child. This paragraph shall not apply to housing for older persons as defined in subsection mm. of section 5 of P.L.1945, c. 169 (C.10:5-5).

h. For any person, including but not limited to, any real estate broker, real estate salesperson, or employee or agent thereof:

(1) To refuse to sell, rent, assign, lease or sublease, or offer for sale, rental, lease, assignment, or sublease any real property or part or portion thereof to any person or group of persons or to refuse to negotiate for the sale, rental, lease, assignment, or sublease of any real property or part or portion thereof to any person or group of persons because of race, creed, color, national origin, ancestry, marital status, domestic partnership status, familial status, sex, affectional or sexual orientation, disability, nationality, or source of lawful income used for rental or mortgage payments, or to represent that any real property or portion thereof is not available for inspection, sale, rental, lease, assignment, or sublease when in fact it is so available, or otherwise to deny or withhold any real property or any part or portion of facilities thereof to or from any person or group of persons because of race, creed, color, national origin, ancestry, marital status, domestic partnership status, familial status, sex, affectional or sexual orientation, disability or nationality.

(2) To discriminate against any person because of race, creed, color, national origin, ancestry, marital status, domestic partnership status, familial status, sex, affectional or sexual orientation, disability, nationality, or source of lawful income used for rental or mortgage payments in the terms, conditions or privileges of the sale, rental, lease, assignment or sublease of any real property or part or portion thereof or in the furnishing of facilities or services in connection therewith;

(3) To print, publish, circulate, issue, display, post, or mail, or cause to be printed, published, circulated, issued, displayed, posted or mailed any statement, advertisement, publication or sign, or to use any form of application for the purchase, rental, lease, assignment, or sublease of any real property or part or portion thereof or to make any record or inquiry in connection with the prospective purchase, rental, lease, assignment, or sublease of any real property or part or portion thereof which expresses, directly or indirectly, any limitation, specification or discrimination as to race, creed, color, national origin, ancestry, marital status, domestic partnership status, familial status, sex, affectional or sexual orientation, disability, nationality, or source of lawful income used for rental or mortgage payments or any intent to make any such limitation, specification or discrimination, and the production of any such statement, advertisement, publicity, sign, form of application, record, or inquiry purporting to be made by any such person shall be presumptive evidence in any action that the same was authorized by such person; provided, however, that nothing contained in this subsection h., shall be construed to bar any person from refusing to sell, rent, lease, assign or sublease or from advertising or recording a qualification as to sex for any room, apartment, flat in a dwelling or residential facility which is planned exclusively for and occupied exclusively by individuals of one sex to any individual of the opposite sex on the basis of sex;

(4) To refuse to sell, rent, lease, assign, or sublease or otherwise to deny to or withhold from any person or group of persons any real property or part or portion thereof because of the source of any lawful income received by the person or the source of any lawful rent payment to be paid for the real property; or

(5) To refuse to rent or lease any real property to another person because that person's family includes children under 18 years of age, or to make an agreement, rental or lease of any real property which provides that the agreement, rental or lease shall be rendered null and void upon the birth of a child. This paragraph shall not apply to housing for older persons as defined in subsection mm. of section 5 of P.L.1945, c. 169 (C.10:5-5).

i. For any person, bank, banking organization, mortgage company, insurance company or other financial institution, lender or credit institution involved in the making or purchasing of any loan or extension of credit, for whatever purpose, whether secured by residential real estate or not, including but not limited to financial assistance for the purchase, acquisition, construction, rehabilitation, repair or maintenance of any real property or part or portion thereof or any agent or employee thereof:

(1) To discriminate against any person or group of persons because of race, creed, color, national origin, ancestry, marital status, domestic partnership status, sex, affectional or sexual orientation, disability, familial status or nationality, in the granting, withholding, extending, modifying, renewing, or purchasing, or in the fixing of the rates, terms, conditions or provisions of any such loan, extension of credit or financial assistance or purchase thereof or in the extension of services in connection therewith;

(2) To use any form of application for such loan, extension of credit or financial assistance or to make record or inquiry in connection with applications for any such loan, extension of credit or financial assistance which expresses, directly or indirectly, any limitation, specification or discrimination as to race, creed, color, national origin, ancestry, marital status, domestic partnership status, sex, affectional or sexual orientation, disability, familial status or nationality or any intent to make any such limitation, specification or discrimination; unless otherwise required by law or regulation to retain or use such information;

(3) (Deleted by amendment, P.L.2003, c. 180).

(4) To discriminate against any person or group of persons because of the source of any lawful income received by the person or the source of any lawful rent payment to be paid for the real property; or

(5) To discriminate against any person or group of persons because that person's family includes children under 18 years of age, or to make an agreement or mortgage which provides that the agreement or mortgage shall be rendered null and void upon the birth of a child. This paragraph shall not apply to housing for older persons as defined in subsection mm. of section 5 of P.L.1945, c. 169 (C.10:5-5).

j. For any person whose activities are included within the scope of this act to refuse to post or display such notices concerning the rights or responsibilities of persons affected by this act as the Attorney General may by regulation require.

k. For any real estate broker, real estate salesperson or employee or agent thereof or any other individual, corporation, partnership, or organization, for the purpose of inducing a transaction for the sale or rental of real property from which transaction such person or any of its members may benefit financially, to represent that a change has occurred or will or may occur in the composition with respect to race, creed, color, national origin, ancestry, marital status, domestic partnership status, familial status, sex, affectional or sexual orientation, disability, nationality, or source of lawful income used for rental or mortgage payments of the owners or occupants in the block, neighborhood or area in which the real property is located, and to represent, directly or indirectly, that this change will or may result in undesirable consequences in the block, neighborhood or area in which the real property is located, including, but not limited to the lowering of property values, an increase in criminal or anti-social behavior, or a decline in the quality of schools or other facilities.

l. For any person to refuse to buy from, sell to, lease from or to, license, contract with, or trade with, provide goods, services or information to, or otherwise do business with any other person on the basis of the race, creed, color, national origin, ancestry, age, sex, affectional or sexual orientation, marital status, domestic partnership status, liability for service in the Armed Forces of the United States, disability, nationality, or source of lawful income used for rental or mortgage payments of such other person or of such other person's spouse, partners, members, stockholders, directors, officers, managers, superintendents, agents, employees, business associates, suppliers, or customers. This subsection shall not prohibit refusals or other actions (1) pertaining to employee-employer collective bargaining, labor disputes, or unfair labor practices, or (2) made or taken in connection with a protest of unlawful discrimination or unlawful employment practices.

m. For any person to:

(1) Grant or accept any letter of credit or other document which evidences the transfer of funds or credit, or enter into any contract for the exchange of goods or services, where the letter of credit, contract, or other document contains any provi-

sions requiring any person to discriminate against or to certify that he, she or it has not dealt with any other person on the basis of the race, creed, color, national origin, ancestry, age, sex, affectional or sexual orientation, marital status, domestic partnership status, disability, liability for service in the Armed Forces of the United States, or nationality of such other person or of such other person's spouse, partners, members, stockholders, directors, officers, managers, superintendents, agents, employees, business associates, suppliers, or customers.

(2) Refuse to grant or accept any letter of credit or other document which evidences the transfer of funds or credit, or refuse to enter into any contract for the exchange of goods or services, on the ground that it does not contain such a discriminatory provision or certification.

The provisions of this subsection shall not apply to any letter of credit, contract, or other document which contains any provision pertaining to employee-employer collective bargaining, a labor dispute or an unfair labor practice, or made in connection with the protest of unlawful discrimination or an unlawful employment practice, if the other provisions of such letter of credit, contract, or other document do not otherwise violate the provisions of this subsection.

n. For any person to aid, abet, incite, compel, coerce, or induce the doing of any act forbidden by subsections l. and m. of section 11 of P.L.1945, c. 169 (C.10:5-12), or to attempt, or to conspire to do so. Such prohibited conduct shall include, but not be limited to:

(1) Buying from, selling to, leasing from or to, licensing, contracting with, trading with, providing goods, services, or information to, or otherwise doing business with any person because that person does, or agrees or attempts to do, any such act or any act prohibited by this subsection; or

(2) Boycotting, commercially blacklisting or refusing to buy from, sell to, lease from or to, license, contract with, provide goods, services or information to, or otherwise do business with any person because that person has not done or refuses to do any such act or any act prohibited by this subsection; provided that this subsection shall not prohibit refusals or other actions either pertaining to employee-employer collective bargaining, labor disputes, or unfair labor practices, or made or taken in connection with a protest of unlawful discrimination or unlawful employment practices.

o. For any multiple listing service, real estate brokers' organization or other service, organization or facility related to the business of selling or renting dwellings to deny any person access to or membership or participation in such organization, or to discriminate against such person in the terms or conditions of such access, membership, or participation, on account of race, creed, color, national origin, ancestry, age, marital status, domestic partnership status, familial status, sex, affectional or sexual orientation, disability or nationality.

10:5-13.   Remedies; filing complaint; prosecution of suit in Superior Court

Any person claiming to be aggrieved by an unlawful employment practice or an unlawful discrimination may, personally or by an attorney-at-law, make, sign and file with the division a verified complaint in writing which shall state the name and address of the person, employer, labor organization, employment agency, owner, lessee, proprietor, manager, superintendent, or agent alleged to have committed the unlawful employment practice or unlawful discrimination complained of and which shall set forth the particulars thereof and shall contain such other information as may be required by the division. Upon receipt of the complaint, the division shall notify the complainant on a form promulgated by the director of the division and approved by the Attorney General of the complainant's rights under this act, including the right to file a complaint in the Superior Court to be heard before a jury; of the jurisdictional limitations of the division; and any other provisions of this act, without interpretation, that may apply to the complaint. The Commissioner of Labor, the Attorney General, or the Commissioner of Education may, in like manner, make, sign and file such complaint. Any employer whose employees, or some of them, refuse or threaten to refuse to co-operate with the provisions of this act, may file with the division a verified complaint asking for assistance by conciliation or other remedial action.

Any complainant may initiate suit in Superior Court under this act without first filing a complaint with the division or any municipal office. Upon the application of any party, a jury trial shall be directed to try the validity of any claim under this act specified in the suit. All remedies available in common law tort actions shall be available to prevailing plaintiffs. These remedies are in addition to any provided by this act or any other statute. Prosecution of such suit in Superior Court under this act shall bar the filing of a complaint with the division or any municipal office during the pendency of any such suit.

At any time after 180 days from the filing of a complaint with the division, a complainant may file a request with the division to present the action personally or through counsel to the Office of Administrative Law. Upon such request, the director of the division shall file the action with the Office of Administrative Law, provided that no action may be filed with the Office of Administrative Law where the director of the division has found that no probable cause exists to credit the allegations of the complaint or has otherwise dismissed the complaint.

A party to an action based upon a violation of this act shall mail a copy of the initial pleadings or claims, amended pleadings or claims, counterclaims, briefs, and legal memoranda to the division at the same time as filing such documents with the Office of Administrative Law or the court. Upon application to the Office of Administrative Law or to the court wherein the matter is pending, the division shall be permitted to intervene.

10:5-14. Investigation of complaint; attorney general's duties

After the filing of any complaint, the Attorney General shall cause prompt investigation to be made in connection therewith and advise the complainant of the results thereof. During the period beginning with the filing of such complaint and ending with the closure of the case or 45 days from the date of a finding of probable cause, the Attorney General shall, to the extent feasible, engage in conciliation with respect to such complaint. Neither the Attorney General nor any officer or employee of the division shall disclose any conversation between the Attorney General or a representative and the respondent or a representative at such conference, except that the Attorney General and any officer or employee may disclose the terms of a settlement offer to the complainant or other aggrieved person on whose behalf the complaint was filed.

10:5-14.1. Enforcement of act; summary proceedings

At any time after the filing of any complaint the Attorney General may proceed against any person in a summary manner in the Superior Court of New Jersey to compel compliance with any of the provisions of this act, or to prevent violations or attempts to violate any such provisions, or attempts to interfere with or impede the enforcement of any such provisions or the exercise or performance of any power or duty thereunder.

10:5-14.1a. Penalties; disposition

Any person who violates any of the provisions of the "Law Against Discrimination," P.L.1945, c. 169 (C.10:5-1 et seq.), shall, in addition to any other relief or affirmative action provided by law, be liable for the following penalties:

a. In an amount not exceeding $10,000 if the respondent has not been adjudged to have committed any prior violation within the five-year period ending on the date of the filing of this charge;

b. In an amount not exceeding $25,000 if the respondent has been adjudged to have committed one other violation within the five-year period ending on the date of the filing of this charge; and

c. In an amount not exceeding $50,000 if the respondent has been adjudged to have committed two or more violations within the seven-year period ending on the date of the filing of this charge. The penalties shall be determined by the director in such amounts as he deems proper under the circumstances and included in his order following his finding of an unlawful discrimination or an unlawful employment practice pursuant to section 16 of P.L.1945, c. 169 (C.10:5-17). Any such amounts collected by the director shall be paid forthwith into the State Treasury for the general purposes of the State.

10:5-27. Fair construction; other laws not affected; procedure herein, while pending, exclusive; other remedies

The provisions of this act shall be construed fairly and justly with due regard to the interests of all parties. Nothing contained in this act shall be deemed to repeal any of the provisions of the Civil Rights Law [FN1] or of any other law of this State relating to discrimination because of race, creed, color, national origin, ancestry, marital status, affectional or sexual orientation, disability, nationality or sex or liability for service in the Armed Forces of the United States; except that, as to practices and acts declared unlawful by section 11 of this act, [FN2] the procedure herein provided shall, while pending, be exclusive; and the final determination therein shall exclude any other action, civil or criminal, based on the same grievance of the individual concerned. Nothing herein contained shall bar, exclude or otherwise affect any right or action, civil or criminal, which may exist independently of any right to redress against or specific relief from any unlawful employment practice or unlawful discrimination. With respect only to affectional or sexual orientation, nothing contained herein shall be construed to require the imposition of affirmative action, plans or quotas as specific relief from an unlawful employment practice or unlawful discrimination.

10:5-27.1. Attorneys fees

In any action or proceeding brought under this act, the prevailing party may be awarded a reasonable attorney's fee as part of the cost, provided however, that no attorney's fee shall be awarded to the respondent unless there is a determination that the complainant brought the charge in bad faith. If the complainant's case was initiated by a housing authority on behalf of a tenant for a violation of paragraph (4) of subsection g. or paragraph (4) of subsection h. of section 11 of P.L.1945, c. 169 (C.10:5-12) and the complainant prevailed, reasonable costs, including attorney fees, of the housing authority may be assessed against a nonprevailing respondent. If the complainant's case was presented by the attorney for the division and the complainant prevailed, the reasonable costs, including attorney fees, of such representation may be assessed against a nonprevailing respondent.

APPENDIX H
NEW JERSEY CIVIL RIGHTS ACT

This act provides protection in addition to that provided by the Law Against Discrimination. It applies to violations of any rights provided under state or federal statutes or constitutions.

TITLE 10
CIVIL RIGHTS
CHAPTER 6
CIVIL RIGHTS ACT

10:6-1.   New Jersey Civil Rights Act

This act shall be known and may be cited as the "New Jersey Civil Rights Act."

10:6-2.   Civil actions for rights violations

a. If a person, whether or not acting under color of law, subjects or causes to be subjected any other person to the deprivation of any substantive due process or equal protection rights, privileges or immunities secured by the Constitution or laws of the United States, or any substantive rights, privileges or immunities secured by the Constitution or laws of this State, the Attorney General may bring a civil action for damages and for injunctive or other appropriate relief. The civil action shall be brought in the name of the State and may be brought on behalf of the injured party. If the Attorney General proceeds with and prevails in an action brought pursuant to this subsection, the court shall order the distribution of any award of damages to the injured party and shall award reasonable attorney's fees and costs to the Attorney General. The penalty provided in subsection e. of this section shall be applicable to a violation of this subsection.

b. If a person, whether or not acting under color of law, interferes or attempts to interfere by threats, intimidation or coercion with the exercise or enjoyment by any other person of any substantive due process or equal protection rights, privileges or immunities secured by the Constitution or laws of the United States, or any substantive rights, privileges or immunities secured by the Constitution or laws of this State, the Attorney General may bring a civil action for damages and for injunctive or other appropriate relief. The civil action shall be brought in the name of the State and may be brought on behalf of the injured party. If the Attorney General proceeds with and prevails in an action brought pursuant to this subsection, the court shall order the distribution of any award of damages to the injured party and shall award reasonable attorney's fees and costs to the Attorney General. The penalty provided in subsection e. of this section shall be applicable to a violation of this subsection.

c. Any person who has been deprived of any substantive due process or equal protection rights, privileges or immunities secured by the Constitution or laws of the United States, or any substantive rights, privileges or immunities secured by the Constitution or laws of this State, or whose exercise or enjoyment of those substantive rights, privileges or immunities has been interfered with or attempted to be interfered with, by threats, intimidation or coercion by a person acting under color of law, may bring a civil action for damages and for injunctive or other appropriate relief. The penalty provided in subsection e. of this section shall be applicable to a violation of this subsection.

d. An action brought pursuant to this act may be filed in Superior Court. Upon application of any party, a jury trial shall be directed.

e. Any person who deprives, interferes or attempts to interfere by threats, intimidation or coercion with the exercise or enjoyment by any other person of any substantive due process or equal protection rights, privileges or immunities secured by the Constitution or laws of the United States, or any substantive rights, privileges or immunities secured by the Constitution or laws of this State is liable for a civil penalty for each violation. The court or jury, as the case may be, shall determine the appropriate amount of the penalty. Any money collected by the court in payment of a civil penalty shall be conveyed to the State Treasurer for deposit into the State General Fund.

f. In addition to any damages, civil penalty, injunction or other appropriate relief awarded in an action brought pursuant to subsection c. of this section, the court may award the prevailing party reasonable attorney's fees and costs.

APPENDIX I
PENSION FREQUENTLY ASKED QUESTIONS

SP-0710-0604

Fact Sheet #71

A PUBLICATION OF THE NEW JERSEY DIVISION OF PENSIONS AND BENEFITS

Benefits Under the Domestic Partnership Act

All Pension Funds and the State Health Benefits Program

Chapter 246, P.L. 2003, the Domestic Partnership Act, establishes certain rights and responsibilities for domestic partners in the State of New Jersey. The law also extends public pension and State Health Benefits Program (SHBP) benefits to same-sex[1] domestic partners of State employees and retirees and permits local governmental employers to extend those same domestic partner benefits to their employees and retirees.

This fact sheet deals only with the pension and SHBP benefits extended by Chapter 246. It does not address the broader rights and responsibilities covered by the law nor does it cover questions of eligibility for a domestic partnership since they are outside of the scope of the Division of Pensions and Benefits.

ELIGIBILITY

Under Chapter 246 a domestic partner is defined for pension and SHBP benefits eligibility as a person of the same sex to whom the employee or retiree has entered into a domestic partnership and received a New Jersey *Certificate of Domestic Partnership* through application to a local registrar.

The Domestic Partnership Act applies to any **State employee** or **State retiree** who has obtained a New Jersey *Certificate of Domestic Partnership* (or a valid certification from another jurisdiction that recognizes same-sex domestic partners, civil unions, or similar same-sex relationships). A **State employee** includes employees of the executive, judicial, and legislative branches paid through Centralized Payroll, employees of Rutgers University, UMDNJ, NJIT, and the State colleges and universities, and employees of the Palisades Interstate Park Commission, the NJ Building Authority, the State Library, the Waterfront Commission of NY Harbor, and the Commerce and Economic Growth Commission. A **State retiree** is any retiree from one of the above mentioned employers.

The Domestic Partnership Act applies to eligible employees and retirees of local public entities **only if** the governing body adopts the benefit by resolution or ordinance (see Adoption by Local Public Entities, below). The local public employee or retiree must also obtain a New Jersey *Certificate of Domestic Partnership* from the State of New Jersey (or a valid certification from another jurisdiction that recognizes same-sex domestic partners, civil unions, or similar same-sex relationships).

Note: Residents of another state may obtain a New Jersey *Certificate of Domestic Partnership* from any New Jersey local registrar as long as one of the partners is a member of a New Jersey administered pension system. If necessary, a *Certificate of Pension Membership* form can be used by out-of-state residents to provide the documentation needed to obtain a New Jersey *Certificate of Domestic Partnership*.

Adoption by Local Public Entities

In order for the Domestic Partnership Act to apply to the employees/retirees of a local public entity, the entity's governing body must pass a resolution or ordinance extending the domestic partner benefit and file it with the Division of Pensions and Benefits. The decisions to provide pension and/or SHBP benefits to domestic partners are separate and distinct decisions that must be made by the governing body.

The law gives the employer the option to extend, or not extend, the domestic partner benefit to its employees and retirees. However, if the employer wishes to provide domestic partner *pension* benefits, it must do so for **all** its employees and retirees in all of the pension funds in which it participates.

PENSION BENEFITS

The Domestic Partnership Act adds a same-sex domestic partner to the definition of spouse, widow,

---

[1] The law specifically states that the pension and health benefits provisions of the law <u>do not</u> apply to opposite-sex domestic partners because they could obtain those benefits by exercising the option of marriage.

Fact Sheet #71

SP-0710-0604

A PUBLICATION OF THE NEW JERSEY DIVISION OF PENSIONS AND BENEFITS

and widower to the **State component** of the Public Employees' Retirement System (PERS), Teachers' Pension and Annuity Fund (TPAF), Police and Firemen's Retirement System (PFRS), State Police Retirement System (SPRS), and Judicial Retirement System (JRS), so that the domestic partner is treated in the same manner as a spouse. The law allows **local employers** to apply the same changes through action of its governing body.

PERS and TPAF Members

For the **PERS** and **TPAF**, the only benefit added by this law is that for Accidental Death. An eligible domestic partner will now be able to receive a pension benefit if the employee died by accident in the performance of his or her duty while at work. Regular PERS and TPAF retirements are not impacted since retirees can already name anyone as a joint and survivor beneficiary of their pension benefit. The Internal Revenue Service (IRS) does, however, restrict who a member can name as a beneficiary under Options 2, A, and B. Under Options 2 and A, a member cannot name a non-spouse beneficiary who is more than 10 years younger than the member; under Option B, the beneficiary cannot be more than 19 years younger. Additionally, a survivor's benefits from an Accidental Disability retirement or accidental line-of-duty death going to a domestic partner would be subject to federal tax. This is not the case when a survivor's benefit is paid to a spouse.

PFRS and SPRS Members

For the **PFRS** and **SPRS**, the statutory survivor's benefit, provided upon the death of the employee or retiree, will be able to go to a same-sex domestic partner under this law in the same manner as is now done for a spouse. Additionally, if a surviving partner is receiving a PFRS or SPRS survivor's benefit (with the exception of a survivor of an Accidental Death in the line of duty) and subsequently marries or establishes a new same-sex domestic partnership[2], the survivor will lose the pension benefit.

JRS Members

For the **JRS**, the statutory survivor's benefit, provided upon the death of the employee or retiree, will be able to go to a same-sex domestic partner under this law in the same manner as is now done for a spouse. Additionally, if a surviving partner is receiving a JRS survivor's benefit, and subsequently marries or establishes a new same-sex domestic partnership[2], the survivor will lose the pension benefit.

If a judge wishes to also select a joint and survivor retirement option, the IRS restrictions for Options 2, A, and B mentioned above under the PERS and TPAF would apply.

Other Pension Funds

The Domestic Partnership Act does not extend any domestic partner *pension* benefits to members of the Alternate Benefit Program, the Consolidated Police and Firemen's Pension Fund, the Prison Officers' Pension Fund, or the Volunteer Emergency-Worker's Survivors Pension.

STATE HEALTH BENEFITS PROGRAM COVERAGE

Coverage under the SHBP for same-sex domestic partners is available to any State employee, State retiree, an eligible employee or retiree of a local public entity **if** the governing body adopts the benefit by resolution (see Adoption by Local Public Entities, above). The eligible employee or retiree must obtain a New Jersey *Certificate of Domestic Partnership* (or a valid certification from another jurisdiction that recognizes same-sex domestic partners, civil unions, or similar same-sex relationships) and attach a photocopy of the *Certificate of Domestic Partnership* to the *SHBP Enrollment Application.*

Note: While the law states that local public employers who participate in the SHBP have the option of providing health benefit coverage to domestic partners, it does not offer that option to public employers who do not participate in the SHBP.

---

[2] Note that the establishment of a heterosexual domestic partnership will not cause the loss of the survivor's benefit because the pension and health benefits portions of the law do not apply to heterosexual couples.

SP-0710-0604

Fact Sheet #71

A PUBLICATION OF THE NEW JERSEY DIVISION OF PENSIONS AND BENEFITS

Enrolling a Domestic Partner When an Employee

An employee must qualify for the domestic partner benefit by being a State employee or an employee of a SHBP-participating local employer who has adopted a resolution to extend domestic partner benefits. You then have 60 days from the date that you obtain your *Certificate of Domestic Partnership* to add an eligible domestic partner to your SHBP coverage. To add a new domestic partner, you must file an *SHBP Enrollment Application* with your employer and include a photocopy of your *Certificate of Domestic Partnership*. You may also add dependent children of your domestic partner at this time **provided they also qualify as your dependents** (see Enrolling Dependent Children below).

If you do not add your domestic partner or other eligible dependent children when first eligible, you must wait until the next regular SHBP open enrollment period.

Retiree SHBP Coverage

State retirees, and retirees of a SHBP-participating local public entity that has adopted domestic partner SHBP coverage by resolution, may cover a domestic partner in retirement provided that the retiree meets the requirements of the Domestic Partnership Act **and** all other requirements for eligibility in the Retired Group of the SHBP. See Fact Sheet #11, *Enrolling in the State Health Benefits Program When You Retire*, for more information.

Note: While some education and local PFRS retirees receive SHBP coverage paid — in-full or in-part — by the State, these retirees were not State employees and are not considered State retirees. Therefore, the eligibility of a domestic partner of an education or local PFRS retiree for SHBP coverage remains based on the actions of the governing body of the retiree's former employer. If the employer participates in the SHBP with its active employees and the governing body passes a resolution to extend the domestic partner health benefits to its employees and retirees, the retirees of that employer will be able to add an eligible domestic partner to their SHBP coverage.

Enrolling Dependent Children

The children of your domestic partner can be added as dependents under your SHBP coverage **only if** they are single, under the age of 23, live with you, **and are dependent upon you for support.** You will have to file an *Affidavit of Dependency* when you add them to your coverage.

The Cost of Domestic Partner Coverage

The Member & Spouse level of coverage will also be used for an employee and domestic partner. The premium rate for Member & Spouse and Member & Domestic Partner coverage will be the same. If the employee also has children enrolled for coverage, then the Family level of coverage will include the domestic partner at the same cost as if a spouse were covered.

TAXATION OF SHBP BENEFITS FOR DOMESTIC PARTNERS

The federal Internal Revenue Code (IRC) allows an employer to provide certain benefits to its employees on a tax-exempt basis. Those benefits can also be extended to spouses and dependents of an employee on the same tax-exempt basis. The IRC, however, does not recognize a domestic partner in the same manner as a spouse and does not automatically recognize a domestic partner as a dependent for tax purposes. Therefore, your employer may have to treat the domestic partner SHBP benefit as taxable to you and withhold federal income, Social Security, and Medicare taxes on its value. **This is also true if you are a retiree and are receiving employer- or State-paid health benefits coverage. If you add a domestic partner to your coverage, you should expect to receive a *Form W-2* and have to pay federal income, Medicare, and Social Security taxes on the imputed value of the domestic partner benefit.** Similarly, since the domestic partner's coverage is a federally taxable benefit, an employee who participates in the State's Tax$ave (IRC Section 125) Premium Option Plan, or another employer's Section 125 plan, cannot make pre-tax payments for the cost of a domestic partner's coverage. Pre-tax dollars may still be used to pay for the employee's portion of the cost of his or her own and dependent children's coverage (see Certifying a Partner's Dependent Status on page 4).

Fact Sheet #71

SP-0710-0604

A PUBLICATION OF THE NEW JERSEY DIVISION OF PENSIONS AND BENEFITS

The domestic partnership benefit is not subject to New Jersey State income tax. If you live outside of New Jersey, you should check with your State's tax agency to determine if the domestic partner benefit is subject to state taxes.

Determining the Imputed Income

The SHBP has no previous claims experience with domestic partners and, therefore, no basis on which to determine the true cost of domestic partner coverage. Until the SHBP can develop several years of claims experience with domestic partners, we will use the cost for Single coverage in determining the imputed value of SHBP coverage. The imputed income for federal tax withholding purposes will be the full cost of Single coverage for the plan in which the employee or retiree is enrolled less any amount the employee/retiree pays towards the cost of the domestic partner's coverage.

Example 1: A State employee with Single coverage in NJ PLUS, the Employee Prescription Drug Plan, and the Dental Expense Plan adds a domestic partner to the coverage of all three plans. The domestic partner benefit is a federally taxable benefit. The biweekly imputed income for the NJ PLUS and Employee Prescription Drug Plan, for which there is no employee premium charge, is the full cost of Single coverage, or $131.75 and $47.32, respectively. The biweekly imputed income for the Dental Expense Plan, for which the employee does premium share, is $13.48. This is the full cost of Single coverage, $18.48, minus the amount that the employee has paid for the domestic partner coverage, $5.00 (the difference between the employee share for Single coverage, $9.24, and for Member & Spouse/Domestic Partner coverage, $14.24). The total biweekly imputed income attributable to domestic partner coverage for this employee is $192.55, the sum of the imputed incomes for all three plans.

Example 2: A State retiree with State-paid Single with Medicare retired SHBP coverage in the Traditional Plan adds a domestic partner to the plan. The domestic partner benefit is a fed-

erally taxable benefit. The monthly imputed income for the Traditional Plan is the full cost of Single with Medicare coverage, $376.21, minus the premium sharing amount that the employee pays for the domestic partner coverage, $94.06 (the difference between the retiree share for Single with Medicare coverage, $94.05, and for Member & Spouse/Domestic Partner with Medicare coverage, $188.11). Therefore, the total monthly imputed income attributable to domestic partner coverage for this retiree is $282.15.

Example 3: An employee of a local employer with Single coverage in the Traditional Plan adds a domestic partner to the coverage. The employer also requires its employees to pay the full cost of dependent coverage. Since the employee, rather than the employer, pays the full cost of the domestic partner's coverage (the $545.95 monthly dependent cost of Member & Spouse/Domestic Partner coverage), the employee will have no imputed income for this benefit and no additional tax liability.

Certifying a Partner's Dependent Status

If a domestic partner can meet the Internal Revenue Service's definition of a dependent for tax purposes, found in Section 152 of the IRC, the employer does not have to treat the domestic partner coverage as a taxable benefit. The requirements for dependent status are not easily met and are strictly enforced by the IRS. If an employee wants to claim a dependency exemption for a domestic partner, all five of the following dependency tests must be met:

- The member of the household or relationship test,
- The citizen or resident test,
- The joint return test,
- The gross income test, and
- The support test.

See Internal Revenue Service *Tax Topic 354 - Dependents* for additional information on dependent status for federal tax purposes.

The IRS has stated in private letter rulings that an employer can rely on an employee's written certifi-

SP-0710-0604

Fact Sheet #71

A PUBLICATION OF THE NEW JERSEY DIVISION OF PENSIONS AND BENEFITS

cation that the dependent meets the IRS tests for dependency. An employee or retiree can provide certification that a domestic partner meets the Internal Revenue Code criteria for a dependent in one of several ways:

- State employees paid through Centralized Payroll can submit the *Employee Tax Certification — Domestic Partner Benefit* form to certify their partner's dependent status.

- Employees of other employers should see their employer's Human Resources Officer or Benefits Administrator to determine how tax dependent certification should be provided.

- Retirees can submit the *Employee Tax Certification — Domestic Partner Benefit* form to certify their partner's dependent status.

Since an individual's situation can change, an employee or retiree who files a certification stating that the domestic partner meets the IRS definition of dependent will be required to file a new certification every calendar year to continue that same tax treatment of the benefit.

Employees or retirees may also wish to consult with a professional tax advisor or contact the Internal Revenue Service directly at 1-800-TAX-1040 or over the Internet at: *www.irs.gov*.

This fact sheet has been produced and distributed by:
New Jersey Division of Pensions and Benefits • PO Box 295 • Trenton, New Jersey 08625-0295
(609) 292-7524 • TDD for the hearing impaired (609) 292-7718
URL: http://www.state.nj.us/treasury/pensions • E-mail: pensions.nj@treas.state.nj.us
This fact sheet is a summary and not intended to provide total information.
Although every attempt at accuracy is made, it cannot be guaranteed.

APPENDIX J
SHBP APPLICATION

HA-0700-0704q

COMPLETING THE NJ STATE HEALTH BENEFITS PROGRAM APPLICATION
STATE EMPLOYEE GROUP
QUICK REFERENCE

- **To change your primary care physician** (PCP) with NJ PLUS or your HMO, **or your dentist** with your DPO, contact your health or dental plan directly. **DO NOT COMPLETE THIS FORM JUST TO CHANGE YOUR PRIMARY CARE PHYSICIAN OR DENTIST.**

- **To enroll** for the first time complete all sections of the application with the exception of section 6.

- **To change health plans only** complete sections: 1, 2a and 2b (if enrolling in an HMO or NJ PLUS be sure to list your primary care physician's identification number), 5 (listing all eligible dependents), and 7.

- **To change dental plans only** complete sections: 1, 4a and 4b (if enrolling in a DPO be sure to list the name of your dentist or his/her identification number), 5 (listing all eligible dependents), and 7.

- **To change coverage level** (adding/deleting dependents) complete sections: 1, 2a and 2b, 3a and 3b, 4a and 4b, 5 (listing all eligible dependents), 6 (listing why you are changing coverage level), and 7.

- **To add a dependent** complete sections: 1, 2a and 2b, 3a and 3b, 4a and 4b, 5 (listing all eligible dependents), 6a, and 7.

- **To terminate/decline coverage** complete sections: 1, 2a and/or 3a and/or 4a (as applicable), and 7. If you are declining enrollment for yourself or any or all of your eligible dependents because of other group health insurance coverage, you may in the future be able to enroll yourself and/or your eligible dependents in a SHBP medical plan, provided that you request enrollment within 60 days after your other group health coverage ends.

SECTION 1 - EMPLOYEE INFORMATION

This section must be completed in its entirety each time an application is submitted. The employee enrolling or enrolled in the plan completes this section.

SECTION 2 - MEDICAL COVERAGE

2a. Check only one box indicating in which medical plan you wish to be enrolled. If you do not want medical coverage or wish to cancel coverage, check the appropriate box.

2b. If you are electing coverage, check the level of coverage desired.

NOTE: A Domestic Partner is defined for eligibility in the SHBP, by Chapter 246, P.L. 2003, as a person of the same sex to whom you have entered into a domestic partnership and received a *Certificate of Domestic Partnership* from the State of New Jersey (or a valid certification from another jurisdiction that recognizes same-sex domestic partners, civil unions, or similar same-sex relationships). If covering a Domestic Partner as a dependent, you must attach a photocopy of the *Certificate of Domestic Partnership* to this application.

SECTION 3 - PRESCRIPTION DRUG COVERAGE

3a. Check only one box. If you do not want prescription drug coverage or wish to cancel coverage, check the appropriate box.

3b. If you are electing coverage, check the level of coverage desired. (if selecting Member & Domestic Partner coverage, see note in 2b above).

SECTION 4 - DENTAL COVERAGE

4a. Check only one box indicating in which dental plan you wish to be enrolled. If you do not want dental coverage or wish to cancel coverage, check the appropriate box.

4b. If you are electing coverage, check the level of coverage desired. (if selecting Member & Domestic Partner coverage, see note under 2b above).

NOTE: Once you decline or cancel Medical, Prescription Drug, or Dental coverage, enrollment is not normally permissible until the next open enrollment period or if other coverage is lost and proof of loss is provided (HIPAA).

SECTION 5 - DEPENDENT INFORMATION

Only eligible dependents may be listed. Completion of this section is essential for proper enrollment. Be sure dependents listed agree with the level of coverage selected in sections 2b, 3b, and 4b. List the name, date of birth, gender, and Social Security number of the family members you wish to be covered under the plan. An eligible spouse is an individual to whom you are legally married. An eligible domestic partner is an individual of the same-sex with whom you have entered into a domestic partnership (see note in instructions for Section 2, above). If you have listed a child that is an adopted child, foster child, stepchild, legal ward, or has a different last name than the employee, proof of dependency is required (contact your payroll/personnel representative for an *SHBP Affidavit of Dependency* form). If you have more than 4 eligible dependent children, attach a separate application and complete Sections 1, 5, and 7. For all dependents, include the NJ PLUS or HMO Primary Care Physician identification number and/or the dentist's name or identification number. All dependents must have this information listed. Refer to the NJ PLUS, HMO, or DPO directory for this information or call the health or dental plan directly.

NOTE: If you are deleting dependents, do not list them in this section. Refer to section 6b and 6c.

SECTION 6 - TYPE OF ACTIVITY

6a. If you are adding a dependent, check the appropriate box and indicate the event date.

6b. If you are deleting a dependent spouse or domestic partner, check reason and indicate the event date.

6c. If you are deleting a dependent child, indicate the event date, list the child's Social Security number, and give reason.

6d. For other changes, check the appropriate box and give reason.

SECTION 7 - EMPLOYEE CERTIFICATION

You must read the Employee Certification statement, **sign it, and date the application.**

Misrepresentation: Any person that knowingly provides false or misleading information is subject to criminal and civil penalties.

EMPLOYER CERTIFICATION

Must be completed by your employer before submitting the application to the SHBP. The Certifying Officer should:

    1) Verify the employee's eligibility;

    2) Verify that the application is legible and completed in its entirety;

    3) Verify that the employee's selected plans and coverage levels are appropriate; and

    4) Complete the Employer Certification section in its entirety.

By signing this application the employer certifies that the information presented is true to the best of their knowledge.

NEW JERSEY STATE HEALTH BENEFITS PROGRAM APPLICATION - STATE EMPLOYEE GROUP Division of Pension and Benefits, P.O. Box 299, Trenton, NJ 08625-0299   HA-0700-0704

1. EMPLOYEE INFORMATION - This section must be filled out completely. Please print or type.

Social Security Number

Last Name   Title (Jr., Sr., etc.)

First Name   MI

Street Address (Include Apartment #)

City   State

ZIP Code + 4   Date of Birth (mm/dd/yy)   Gender (M/F)

Status:
☐ -Single   ☐ -Married   ☐ -Domestic Partnership   ☐ -Divorced   ☐ -Widowed

Are you transferring from another SHBP participating employer?   ☐ Yes   ☐ No
If yes, name of employer:

(Area Code) Home Telephone Number

5. DEPENDENT INFORMATION - List only eligible dependents (see reverse).

☐ Spouse ☐ Domestic Partner

Last Name	First Name	MI	Date of Birth (mm/dd/yy)	Gender	Social Security Number

Children

6. TYPE OF ACTIVITY (complete only if requesting changes to existing coverage)

6a. ADDITION OF DEPENDENT
☐ Marriage - Date (mm/dd/yy)
(Copy of Marriage Certificate required)
Former Name
☐ Domestic Partner - Date (mm/dd/yy)
(Copy of Certificate of Domestic Partnership required)
☐ Birth of Child   ☐ Adoption/Guardianship - proof required
Date of Event (mm/dd/yy)

6b. DELETION OF SPOUSE OR DOMESTIC PARTNER
☐ Separation   ☐ Divorce   ☐ Death   ☐ Termination of Domestic Partnership
Date of Event (mm/dd/yy)

6c. DELETION OF CHILD
☐ Deletion of Child - Date of Event (mm/dd/yy)
Child's Name

6d. OTHER CHANGES
☐ Change in last name only
(List former name)
☐ Change in Soc. Sec. # (Attach a copy of Social Security card)
(List former Soc. Sec. #)
☐ Change in Birth Date (Attach copy of birth certificate)
(List name and correct date)
☐ Other - give reason below (i.e., address change, dependent returns
from military service)

2. MEDICAL COVERAGE

2a. EMPLOYEE SELECTION
☐ I wish to be covered under NJ PLUS.
Enter your NJ PLUS Primary Care Physician's ID#   [0 0 0 0 0]
☐ I wish to be covered under an HMO.
Name of HMO   HMO#
Enter your HMO Primary Care Physician's ID#
☐ I wish to be covered under the Traditional Plan.
☐ I am changing medical plans only.
From   to
☐ I elect to waive medical coverage in any medical plan (see instructions).

2b. LEVEL OF COVERAGE
☐ Single   ☐ Member and Spouse   ☐ Parent and Child(ren)
☐ Family   ☐ Member and Domestic Partner (see instructions)

3. PRESCRIPTION DRUG COVERAGE

3a. EMPLOYEE SELECTION
☐ I wish to be covered.
☐ I elect to waive prescription drug coverage.

3b. LEVEL OF COVERAGE
☐ Single   ☐ Member and Spouse   ☐ Parent and Child(ren)
☐ Family   ☐ Member and Domestic Partner (see instructions)

Dependent's NJ PLUS or HMO Primary Care Physician ID#

4. DENTAL COVERAGE

4a. EMPLOYEE SELECTION
☐ I wish to be covered under the Dental Expense Plan (Traditional).
☐ I wish to be covered under a Dental Plan Organization (DPO)
Name of DPO   DPO#
Name of Dentist or ID#
☐ I am changing dental plans only.
From   to
☐ I elect to waive dental coverage in any dental plan (see instructions).

4b. LEVEL OF COVERAGE
☐ Single   ☐ Member and Spouse   ☐ Parent and Child(ren)
☐ Family   ☐ Member and Domestic Partner (see instructions)

Name of Dependent's Dentist or ID#

7. EMPLOYEE CERTIFICATION
I certify that all the information supplied on this form is true to the best of my knowledge. I understand that if I waive my right to coverage at this time, enrollment is not normally permissible until the next scheduled open enrollment or if other coverage is lost and proof of loss is provided (HIPAA). I also understand that there is no guarantee of continuous participation by medical or dental service providers, either doctors/dentists or facilities in the NJ PLUS, HMO, or DPO plans. If either my physician/dentist or medical/dental center terminates participation in my selected plan, I must select another doctor/dentist or medical/dental center participating in that plan to receive the "in-network" benefit. I authorize any hospital, physician, dentist, or health care provider to furnish my medical/dental plan or its assignee with such medical/dental information about myself or my covered dependents as the assignee may require.

Misrepresentation: Any person that knowingly provides false or misleading information is subject to criminal and civil penalties.

Employee Signature   Date Completed

DIVISION USE ONLY

Effective Dates: Event Reason:
H
P

EMPLOYER CERTIFICATION
To Be Completed By Employer

Employer Name:
Payroll #   Union Code (Rx) Only
(State Biweekly)
Location # (State Monthly Only)
10/12 month employee

MEMBER ACTION
☐ New Enrollment
☐ Return from   Date Employment Began (mm/dd/yy)   ☐ Transfer
☐ Leave of Absence

Signature of Certifying Officer
Telephone #   Date Mailed

Natural (N)
Adopted (A)
Foster (F)
Step (S)
Legal Ward (L)
See Instructions

APPENDIX K
AFFIDAVIT OF DEPENDENCY

HB-0063-0199

State of New Jersey – Division of Pensions and Benefits
New Jersey State Health Benefits Program
PO Box 299, Trenton, New Jersey 08625-0299

Affidavit of Dependency

_____   _____   _____
Name of Employee   Social Security #   Name of Employer–Location #

To enable the Division of Pensions and Benefits to determine the eligibility of the dependent child(ren) listed on my Health Benefits application for coverage in the New Jersey State Health Benefits Program, I state the following with respect to the child(ren) listed below:

RELATIONSHIP (check one)	**RESIDENCE** (check one)	**FINANCIAL SUPPORT** (check one)
☐ my child(ren)	☐ live(s) with me	☐ substantially dependent on me for support and maintenance
☐ my stepchild(ren)	☐ do(es) not live with me _Legal documentation required with affidavit_	☐ not substantially dependent on me for support and maintenance
☐ Other _____ _____ _Legal documentation required with affidavit_	☐ Other _____ _____ _Legal documentation required with affidavit_	

Name(s) of Child(ren)
Please Print

Last Name	First Name	Date of Birth Month-date-year	Social Security #
_____	_____	_____	_____
_____	_____	_____	_____
_____	_____	_____	_____
_____	_____	_____	_____
_____	_____	_____	_____

I certify that the statement and information submitted above is correct.

_____   _____
Print Full Name   _Date_

_____   _____
Address   _Work Phone #_

_____
Signature (must be the same name as printed above)

State of _____, County of _____,

Sworn and subscribed before me this _____ day of _____, _____.

My Commission expires _____, _____.

Signature of Notary Public _____

Official Title _____

201

HB-0063-0199

Affidavit of Dependency Instructions

When must an Affidavit of Dependency be filed?

- For all stepchildren (must live with the employee), foster children, guardianship cases (including grandchildren, nieces, nephews, etc.) and wards when first listed for coverage.

- For newly adopted children when added to existing employee coverage.

- When the last name of the child differs from the last name of the employee.

- On parent-child(ren) contracts when the employee is divorced or single.

When must legal papers or court documentation be provided with the Affidavit of Dependency?

- For all adopted children, foster children, guardianship cases and wards.

- When the dependent child(ren) does (do) not live with the employee.

What constitutes acceptable documentation?

- A copy of the court decree that establishes the relationship between the employee and the dependent. In the case of a divorce, the copy need only contain those pages of the decree that identify the court, the employee and the dependent, the requirement for support, and the signature page.

- A copy of the custody agreement (the document placing the child in your home) from the placement agency.

What should I do with this form?

- If your situation requires an Affidavit of Dependency, complete the form and have your signature notarized.

- If legal documentation is required, attach a copy to the completed Affidavit.

- If you are an active employee, deliver the Affidavit and any legal documentation *to your employer.* If you are a retiree or on COBRA, return the form to the Division of Pensions and Benefits at the following address:

State of New Jersey
Division of Pensions and Benefits
Health Benefits Bureau
PO Box 299
Trenton, NJ 08625-0299

APPENDIX L
SHBP AND NON-SHBP RESOLUTIONS

HB-0688-0504

STATE OF NEW JERSEY
DEPARTMENT OF THE TREASURY
DIVISION OF PENSIONS AND BENEFITS
NEW JERSEY STATE HEALTH BENEFITS PROGRAM
PO Box 299
Trenton, New Jersey 08625-0299

R E S O L U T I O N

A **RESOLUTION** to authorize participation in the New Jersey State Health Benefits Program Act of the State of New Jersey for Domestic Partnership Coverage in accordance with Chapter 246, P.L. 2003.

BE IT RESOLVED:

1. The _____   _____,
    Name of Employer   NJ SHBP Location Number

    a participating employer in the State Health Benefits Program, hereby elects to participate in the Domestic Partnership coverage provided by the New Jersey State Health Benefits Act of the State of New Jersey (N.J.S.A. 52:14-17.25 et seq.) and to authorize coverage for all the active and retired employees and their domestic partners thereunder in accordance with the statute and regulations adopted by the State Health Benefits Commission.

2. As a participating employer we will remit to the State Treasury all premiums on account of active and retired employee and dependent coverage and periodic charges in accordance with the requirements of the statute and the rules and regulations duly promulgated thereunder.

3. As a participating employer, we will be responsible for the reporting of active and retired employees' imputed income associated with coverage of domestic partners and will pay all employer federal taxes due on that imputed income.

4. That domestic partnerships must meet the requirements of the Domestic Partnership Act and a *Certificate of Domestic Partnership*, obtained from the State of New Jersey through application to the employee's Local Registrar (or a valid certification from another jurisdiction that recognizes same-sex domestic partners, civil unions, or similar same-sex relationships), must be made available upon request of the employer and/or the State Health Benefits Program.

5. We hereby appoint the _____ to act as
    Title
    Certifying Officer in the administration of this program.

6. This resolution shall take effect immediately and coverage shall be effective as of _____
    Date
    or as soon thereafter as it may be effectuated pursuant to the statutes and regulations.

I hereby certify that the foregoing is a true and correct copy of a resolution duly adopted by the

_____   _____
Corporate Name of Employer   Street Address

on the _____ day of _____, 20_____.   _____
                                                City   State   ZIP Code

_____   _____
Signature   Area Code   Telephone Number

_____
Official Title

HB-0736-0305

STATE OF NEW JERSEY
DEPARTMENT OF THE TREASURY
DIVISION OF PENSIONS AND BENEFITS
NEW JERSEY STATE HEALTH BENEFITS PROGRAM
PO Box 299
Trenton, New Jersey 08625-0299

R E S O L U T I O N

Notice of Domestic Partner Health Benefits Provided by a Non-SHBP Employer

A **RESOLUTION** to notify the New Jersey State Health Benefits Program (SHBP) of the adoption of Domestic Partnership health benefits coverage through a program other than the SHBP in accordance with Chapter 246, P.L. 2003, and N.J.A.C. 17:1-5.5.

BE IT RESOLVED:

1. The _____   _____,
    Name of Employer   County

    hereby resolves to provide health benefit coverage under the Domestic Partnership Act, Chapter 246, P.L. 2003, and N.J.A.C. 17:1-5.5, for all the active and retired employees and their same-sex domestic partners thereunder.

2. Hereby notifies the New Jersey State Health Benefits Program that it is providing domestic partner coverage through a program other than the State Health Benefits Program for all active employees and for any covered retired employees who are not eligible for enrollment in the State Health Benefits Program.

3. Hereby notifies the New Jersey State Health Benefits Program that coverage should be extended to the eligible same-sex domestic partners of any retired employees who are eligible for enrollment in the State Health Benefits Program.

4. Hereby notifies the New Jersey State Health Benefits Program that it has elected to provide the above named benefits in accordance with the statute and regulations adopted by the State Health Benefits Commission.

5. As a non-participating employer, we will notify the New Jersey State Health Benefits Program of any future change or cancelation of our election to provide health benefit coverage under the Domestic Partnership Act in accordance with the requirements of the statute and the rules and regulations duly promulgated thereunder.

6. That domestic partnerships must meet the requirements of the Domestic Partnership Act; that coverage is limited to same-sex domestic partnerships and a *Certificate of Domestic Partnership*, obtained from the State of New Jersey through application to the employee's Local Registrar (or a valid certification from another jurisdiction that recognizes same-sex domestic partners, civil unions, or similar same-sex relationships), must be made available upon request of the employer and/or the State Health Benefits Program.

7. We hereby appoint the _____ to act as
    Title

    Certifying Officer in the administration of this program.

8. This resolution shall take effect immediately and coverage shall be effective as of _____
    Date

    or as soon thereafter as it may be effectuated pursuant to the statutes and regulations.

I hereby certify that the foregoing is a true and
correct copy of a resolution duly adopted by the

_____   _____
Corporate Name of Employer   Street Address

on the _____ day of _____, 20____.   _____
                                                City   State   ZIP Code

_____   _____
Signature   Area Code   Telephone Number

_____
Official Title

APPENDIX M
PENSION BENEFITS RESOLUTION

CP-0695-0504

STATE OF NEW JERSEY
DEPARTMENT OF THE TREASURY
NEW JERSEY DIVISION OF PENSIONS AND BENEFITS
PO Box 295
Trenton, New Jersey 08625-0295

R E S O L U T I O N

A RESOLUTION to recognize same-sex "domestic partners" as eligible dependents for pension purposes only under the Domestic Partnership Act, Chapter 246, P.L. 2003.

BE IT RESOLVED:

1. That the _____ hereby
   Name of Employer
   authorizes participation under the provisions of the Domestic Partnership Act, Chapter 246, P.L. 2003, and agrees to recognize the same-sex domestic partners of employees, as defined by the Act, as eligible for the same dependent benefits as are provided to spouses under the State-administered pension funds.

2. That by agreeing to provide eligibility to same-sex domestic partners, we understand that such eligibility shall apply to same-sex domestic partners of all employees and retirees enrolled in **any and all** of the State-administered pension funds through this employer.

   Please indicate all that apply:

   ☐ Public Employees' Retirement System   Location # _____

   ☐ Teachers' Pension and Annuity Fund   Location # _____

   ☐ Police and Firemen's Retirement System   Location # _____

3. That domestic partnerships must meet the requirements of the Domestic Partnership Act and a *Certificate of Domestic Partnership*, obtained from the State of New Jersey through application to the employee's Local Registrar, must be made available upon request of the employer and/or the Division of Pensions and Benefits.

4. That the effective date of this resolution, that is, the earliest date for which the same-sex domestic partners of employees of this employer will be eligible for benefits will be _____ or as soon thereafter as it may be
   Insert Date
   effectuated pursuant to the statutes and regulations.

5. We hereby appoint and authorize _____
   Title or Individual Name
   to approve all documents required to carry out the intent of this Resolution and to to execute the said documents on behalf of the employer.

I hereby certify that the foregoing is a true and correct copy of a resolution duly adopted by the

| _____ | _____ |
| Corporate Name of Employer | Street Address |

on the _____ day of _____, 20_____

| | _____ |
| | City   State   ZIP Code |

| _____ | _____ |
| Signature | Area Code   Telephone Number |

| _____ | |
| Official Title | |

APPENDIX N
INSURANCE COMPLIANCE

State of New Jersey
DEPARTMENT OF BANKING AND INSURANCE
OFFICE OF THE COMMISSIONER
PO Box 325
TRENTON, NJ 08625-0325

Tel (609) 292-5360

JAMES E. MCGREEVEY
Governor

HOLLY C. BAKKE
Commissioner

BULLETIN NO. 04-08

TO: **ALL NEW JERSEY HEALTH INSURANCE COMPANIES, HOSPITAL SERVICE CORPORATIONS, MEDICAL SERVICE CORPORATIONS, HEALTH SERVICE CORPORATIONS, HEALTH MAINTENANCE ORGANIZATIONS, DENTAL SERVICE CORPORATIONS, DENTAL PLAN ORGANIZATIONS, AND OTHER INTERESTED PARTIES**

FROM: **HOLLY C. BAKKE, COMMISSIONER**

RE: **DOMESTIC PARTNERSHIP ACT, P.L. 2003, c. 246**

The Domestic Partnership Act, P.L. 2003, c. 246 (the Act), enacted on January 12, 2004, requires New Jersey health insurance carriers to <u>offer</u> policyholders the option to elect coverage for <u>same-gender</u> domestic partners of a covered person if the contract permits coverage for eligible dependents and is issued or renewed on or after July 10, 2004. The Department has made a preliminary determination that it is not necessary to promulgate rules to implement the Act at this time. If in the future information is received which indicates that rulemaking may be necessary, the Department will consider proposing rules at that time. The purpose of this Bulletin is to advise carriers of the Department's position concerning certain permissible and prohibited practices for coverage of domestic partners, and to address certain other issues raised by carriers concerning such coverage.

- Carriers may elect to offer opposite gender domestic partner coverage. While the Act does not require that such coverage be offered, it does not prohibit carriers from offering domestic partner coverage that is broader in scope than that required by the Act.

Visit us on the Web at www.njdobi.org
New Jersey is an Equal Opportunity Employer • Printed on Recycled Paper and Recyclable

- Coverage must be offered for children of domestic partners. The intent of the Act is to treat domestic partners of covered persons as spouses for purposes of providing health insurance coverage. Accordingly, if a spouse's natural, adoptive or stepchildren would be covered, the domestic partner's children would also be covered. It is not necessary for the domestic partner to elect coverage in order for the domestic partner's children to be eligible for coverage.

- In the case of employer-provided coverage, carriers must make the required offer of coverage to the employer, and not to the individual covered employees. Employer-provided coverage includes coverage under a group contract between an insurer and an employer or, where permitted, a multi-employer trust or other multi-employer arrangement. Employer-provided coverage may require the employee to contribute some portion or all of the cost of the coverage.

New Jersey's law against unfair discrimination and trade practices in the business of health insurance at N.J.S.A. 17B:30-12.d states that "No person shall make or permit any unfair discrimination between individuals of the same class and of essentially the same hazard in the amount of premium, policy fees, or rates charged for any policy or contract of health insurance or in the benefits payable thereunder, or in any of the terms or conditions of such policy or contract, or in any other manner whatever." Rates for domestic partner coverage must also meet the rating and rate filing requirements applicable to specific carriers and markets, and may not be excessive. Additionally, the stated intent of the Act is to provide eligible domestic partners with health benefits in the same manner as for spouses. Following are certain permissible and prohibited rating practices for coverage of domestic partners:

- Carriers may calculate rates for coverage of domestic partners as if the domestic partner were the spouse of the covered person by using existing rates for coverage of dependents. This method must be used in the small employer market because the Small Employer Health Benefits Law (SEH law) specifies the types of dependent coverage, and does not allow for any variation in rates other than for the type of coverage, age, gender and location.

- Carriers may use separate rating categories for dependent coverage including spouse, and for dependent coverage including domestic partners or children of domestic partners. This method is not permitted in the SEH market. Any rate difference must be reasonably related to the actual or expected difference between claims for spouses and claims for domestic partners. The Commissioner may require an explanation of any such rate difference, or a demonstration that the rate difference is not unfairly discriminatory.

- Carriers may not use a rate factor that increases the total premium under a group contract based only on the availability of domestic partner coverage.

- Carriers may not charge a higher rate for domestic partners on the basis of the cost of modifying administrative systems to accommodate the enrollment or coverage of domestic partners.

- Carriers may not charge rates for domestic partners that are excessive in relation to rates for the coverage of spouses and that would effectively negate the offer of domestic partner coverage mandated by the Act.

Questions concerning this Bulletin should be directed to:

Gale Simon, Assistant Commissioner
Life & Health
NJ Department of Banking & Insurance
P.O. Box 325
Trenton, New Jersey 08625-0325
Email: gsimon@dobi.state.nj.us
FAX: 609-633-0527

5/14/04   /s/ Holly C. Bakke
Date   Holly C. Bakke, Commissioner

inoord/bbdompar

3

APPENDIX O
IRS TOPIC 354 - DEPENDENTS

 Internal Revenue Service IRS.gov

DEPARTMENT OF THE TREASURY

Topic 354 - Dependents

If you want to claim a dependency exemption for a person, all five of the following dependency tests must be met:

1. The member of household or relationship test,
2. The citizen or resident test,
3. The joint return test,
4. The gross income test, and
5. The support test.

However, special rules apply to allow parents to claim the exemption for a kidnapped child in certain circumstances. Refer to Topic 357, *Tax Information for Parents of Kidnapped Children*, for more information.

The first test is the member of household or relationship test. To meet this test, a person must either live with you for the entire year as a member of your household or be related to you. The Form 1040A Instructions and Form 1040 Instructions list all relatives who meet the relationship test. Your spouse is never considered your dependent. A person is not considered a member of your household if, at any time during the tax year, your relationship with that person violates local law. If a person was born or died during the year and was a member of your household during the entire part of the year he or she was alive, the person meets the member of household test.

The second test is the citizen or resident test. To meet this test, a person must be a citizen of the United States, resident alien, or a resident of Canada or Mexico. To find out who is a resident alien, refer to Topic 851, or refer to Publication 519.

The third test is the joint return test. Generally, you are not allowed to claim a person as a dependent if he or she files a joint return. However, you may claim a person who filed a joint return merely to claim a refund of tax. This exception applies if neither the person nor the person's spouse is required to file a return and no tax liability would have existed for either the person or the person's spouse if each had filed a separate return.

The fourth test is the gross income test. Generally, you may not claim as a dependent a person who had gross income of $3,100 or more for 2004. Gross income is all income in the form of money, goods, property, or services that is not exempt from tax. There are two exceptions to the gross income test. If your child is under age 19 at the end of the year, or is a full-time student under the age of 24 at the end of the year, the gross income test does not apply.

The fifth test is the support test. To claim someone as your dependent you generally must provide more than half of that person's total support during the year. A special rule applies to children of divorced or separated parents, or to children of parents who have lived apart at all times during the last six months of the year. Generally, the custodial parent is treated as the person who provides more than half of the child's support. The noncustodial parent can meet this test if the custodial parent releases his or her claim to the exemption on Form 8332 (PDF), or by a substantially similar written statement. Refer to Publication 501, *Exemptions, Standard Deduction, and Filing Information* for more information.

You must include a valid social security number, individual taxpayer identification number (ITIN), or adoption taxpayer identification number (ATIN) for each dependent claimed on your tax return or the exemption will be disallowed. For more information on the ITIN, refer to Topic 857 or refer to Publication 1915 (PDF). For more information on the ATIN, refer to Publication 968, *Tax Benefits for Adoption*.

For more information on dependents, refer to Publication 501, *Exemptions, Standard Deduction, and Filing Information*, and Publication 929, *Tax Rules for Children and Dependents*.

APPENDIX P
EMPLOYEE TAX CERTIFICATION

FH-0703-0105

STATE OF NEW JERSEY
DEPARTMENT OF THE TREASURY
OFFICE OF MANAGEMENT AND BUDGET

EMPLOYEE TAX CERTIFICATION - DOMESTIC PARTNER BENEFIT
TAX YEAR 2005

Employee Name _____

Employee SSN _____   Payroll # _____

Domestic Partner Name _____

Domestic Partner SSN _____

After reviewing the dependency requirements stated below, I hereby certify that my domestic partner qualifies as my tax dependent pursuant to section 152 of the Internal Revenue Code and, consequently, the cost
incurred by the State of New Jersey to provide health benefits coverage to my dependent partner should be
deemed a non-taxable benefit for federal tax purposes.

I fully understand that if conditions change that would cause my domestic partner to no longer qualify as my
tax dependent, I must notify Centralized Payroll of that fact in writing immediately. I acknowledge that failure
to do so could subject me to criminal prosecution for federal tax fraud.

I am also aware that I will be required to file this *Employee Tax Certification - Domestic Partner Benefit* form
prior to the beginning of each tax year in order for Centralized Payroll to continue to treat the domestic partner health benefits as a non-taxable benefit.

DEPENDENCY REQUIREMENTS

To claim your domestic partner as a dependent for tax filing purposes, the following five requirements provided under section 152 of the Internal Revenue Code must be met:

1. Your domestic partner must be a member of your household during the entire taxable year, and
    the relationship between you and the domestic partner must not violate local law.

2. Your domestic partner must receive more than half of his or her support from you. In making
    this determination, the amount you contribute towards your domestic partner's support must
    be compared with the amounts received for support of your domestic partner from all other
    sources, including any amounts supplied by him, or her and including earnings.

3. Your domestic partner must not file a joint tax return with his or her spouse for the tax year in
    which you are claiming the domestic partner as a dependent.

4. Your domestic partner must have gross income less than the exemption deduction amount of
    $3,200.

5. Your domestic partner must be a U.S. citizen, a U.S. national, or a resident of the U.S., Canada,
    or Mexico at some time during the calendar year in which you are claiming the domestic part-
    ner as a dependent.

Before making this certification, we strongly suggest that you consult with a tax advisor to determine whether
you may claim your domestic partner as a dependent for tax purposes.

Signature _____   Date _____

RETURN THIS SIGNED FORM TO YOUR PAYROLL OFFICER

APPENDIX Q
RETIREE TAX CERTIFICATION

FH-0704-0105

STATE OF NEW JERSEY
DEPARTMENT OF THE TREASURY
DIVISION OF PENSIONS AND BENEFITS
PO Box 295, Trenton, NJ 08625-0295

RETIREE TAX CERTIFICATION - DOMESTIC PARTNER BENEFIT
TAX YEAR 2005

Retiree Name _____

Retiree Address _____

Retiree SSN _____ Retirement Number _____

Domestic Partner Name _____

Domestic Partner SSN _____

After reviewing the dependency requirements stated below, I hereby certify that my domestic partner qualifies as my tax dependent pursuant to section 152 of the Internal Revenue Code and, consequently, the cost incurred by the State of New Jersey to provide health benefits coverage to my dependent partner should be deemed a non-taxable benefit for federal tax purposes.

I fully understand that if conditions change that would cause my domestic partner to no longer qualify as my tax dependent, I must notify Financial Section of the Division of Pensions and Benefits of that fact in writing immediately. I acknowledge that failure to do so could subject me to criminal prosecution for federal tax fraud.

I am also aware that I will be required to file this *Retiree Tax Certification - Domestic Partner Benefit* form prior to the beginning of each tax year in order for the Division of Pensions and Benefits to continue to treat the domestic partner health benefits as a non-taxable benefit.

DEPENDENCY REQUIREMENTS

To claim your domestic partner as a dependent for tax filing purposes, the following five requirements provided under section 152 of the Internal Revenue Code must be met:

1. Your domestic partner must be a member of your household during the entire taxable year, and the relationship between you and the domestic partner must not violate local law.

2. Your domestic partner must receive more than half of his or her support from you. In making this determination, the amount you contribute towards your domestic partner's support must be compared with the amounts received for support of your domestic partner from all other sources, including any amounts supplied by him, or her and including earnings.

3. Your domestic partner must not file a joint tax return with his or her spouse for the tax year in which you are claiming the domestic partner as a dependent.

4. Your domestic partner must have gross income less than the exemption deduction amount of $3,200.

5. Your domestic partner must be a U.S. citizen, a U.S. national, or a resident of the U.S., Canada, or Mexico at some time during the calendar year in which you are claiming the domestic partner as a dependent.

Before making this certification, we strongly suggest that you consult with a tax advisor to determine whether you may claim your domestic partner as a dependent for tax purposes.

Signature _____ Date _____

RETURN THIS SIGNED FORM TO THE DIVISION AT THE ADDRESS SHOWN ABOVE

APPENDIX R
HOSPITAL COMPLIANCE OPINION LETTER

State of New Jersey
DEPARTMENT OF HEALTH AND SENIOR SERVICES
PO BOX 360
TRENTON, N.J. 08625-0360

JAMES E. McGREEVEY
Governor

www.state.nj.us/health

CLIFTON R. LACY, M.D.
Commissioner

July 2, 2004

TO: Hospital Chief Executive Officers

FROM: Marilyn Dahl, Deputy Commissioner,
            Health Care Quality and Oversight

RE: Compliance with the Domestic Partnership Act
            P.L. 2003, c. 246 (corrected)

P.L. 2003, c. 246, codified in pertinent part at <u>N.J.S.A.</u> 26:8A-1 through 12, and elsewhere in Title 26 of the New Jersey Statutes,[1] herein referred to as the Act, will become effective July 10, 2004. Essentially, the Act requires that all persons in domestic partnerships should be entitled to certain rights and benefits that are accorded to married couples under the laws of New Jersey, <u>including visitation rights for a hospitalized domestic partner and the right to make medical or legal decisions for an incapacitated partner.</u>[2] This bulletin is intended to provide guidance for hospital staff seeking to comply with the Act.

INTRODUCTION

The specific provisions pertaining to the Act's application within the hospital setting can be somewhat complex. In the discussion that follows, we have highlighted certain areas of the Act's application. We have also attached, for your reference, pertinent excerpts from the Act, *i.e.*, the statutory definition of "domestic partnership," and certain forms which will be issued by local registrars in order to indicate official recognition of domestic partnerships pursuant to the Act, *i.e.*, the Affidavit of Domestic Partnership and the Certificate of Domestic Partnership.

EMERGENCY MEDICAL SITUATIONS

The Act contains a special provision pertaining to, "emergency medical situation(s)." Specifically, it requires that in such situations, a hospital must treat an individual claiming to be a domestic partner of the affected patient as an immediate family member, (1) for purposes of accompanying the patient while being transported to

---

[1] Specifically, <u>N.J.S.A.</u> 26:2H-12.22, 26:8-4, 26:8-17, 26:8-23 through 25; 26:8-48, 26:8-51, 26:8-55, 26:8-60, 26:8-62 through 64, 26:2H-32, 26:2H-57 through 58, 26:5C-12, 26:6-50, 26:6-57 through 58.1, and 26:6-63.
[2] <u>N.J.S.A.</u> 26:8A-2(d).

the hospital and, (2) for purposes of visiting the partner who is a hospital patient. This requirement applies even if the individual and the affected patient have not filed an Affidavit of Domestic Partnership, so long as one or both of the partners have "advise(d) the emergency care provider that the two persons have met the other requirements for establishing a domestic partnership as set forth in section 4 of P.L. 2003, c. 246 (N.J.S.A. 26:8A-4)."

With regard to the term, "emergency medical situation," it would be advisable to consult with your counsel in order to arrive at an interpretation which is consistent with the requirements of EMTALA as well as of N.J.A.C. 8:43G-12.7.

PROOF OF DOMESTIC PARTNERSHIP IN A NON-EMERGENCY SITUATION

The Act explicitly states that, "[a]ny health care or social services provider…or other individual or entity **may** treat a person as a member of a domestic partnership, notwithstanding the absence of an Affidavit of Domestic Partnership filed pursuant to this Act." P.L. 2003, c.246 (N.J.S.A. 26:8A-6(d)) (emphasis added). Thus, although in an "emergency medical situation" the hospital **must** accept an individual's representation that he/she and his/her partner satisfy the requirements of domestic partnership set forth in the Act, in a non-emergency situation, the hospital **may** accept such a representation. Conversely, in the non-emergency medical situation the hospital may refuse to accept such a representation, instead requiring the production of an Affidavit of Domestic Partnership or a Certificate of Domestic Partnership, or both. We advise that you seek input from your counsel to develop a policy consistent with existing hospital policy related to immediate family members.

RIGHTS AFFORDED BY THE ACT

The Act explicitly affords domestic partners the following rights within the hospital setting:

(1) Visitation rights,
(2) Right to be designated as health care representative in a proxy directive,
(3) Right to consent to disclose records of deceased,
(4) Right to consent to a post-mortem and necroscopic examination,
(5) Right to consent to a gift of all or part of a body,
(6) Right to consent to an organ donation.

MEDICAL OR LEGAL DECISIONS

Hospitals have sought clarification as to whether the Act affords domestic partners the right to make medical or legal decisions for an incapacitated partner in the absence of a proxy directive naming the domestic partner. Although the Act does not explicitly grant such a right, note that the legislative findings section of the Act, states, in pertinent part that, "[a]ll persons in domestic partnerships should be entitled to certain rights and benefits that are accorded married couples under the laws of New Jersey, including, … visitation rights for a hospitalized domestic partner and the right to make medical or legal decisions for an incapacitated partner…" P.L. 2003, c. 246, Section 2 (N.J.S.A. 26:8A-2) (emphasis added).

The Department is inclined to view the more general provision within the legislative findings as lending support to the idea of granting a domestic partner the authority to make medical or legal decisions for an incapacitated partner in the absence of a proxy directive, especially in light of the fact that even prior to the Act, N.J.A.C. 8:43G-4.1 recognizes the authority of the "patient's next of kin or guardian or [person designated] through an advance directive, to the extent authorized by law" to give informed consent. It would be advisable to consult with your counsel in order to arrive at an interpretation which is consistent with the requirements of N.J.A.C. 8:43G-4.1.

CONCLUSION

It is essential that hospitals draft well defined and well reasoned policy and procedures regarding domestic partners in both emergency and non-emergency situations. It is also important that such policy and procedures address the full range of rights afforded domestic partners under the Act consistent with the rights and benefits that are accorded married couples under the laws of New Jersey.

See attachments.

APPENDIX S

INHERITANCE TAX WAIVER FORM L-8

Form L-8
(9-04)

STATE OF NEW JERSEY
DEPARTMENT OF THE TREASURY
DIVISION OF TAXATION
Individual Tax Audit Branch
Transfer Inheritance and Estate Tax
50 Barrack Street - PO Box 249
Trenton, New Jersey 08695-0249
(609) 292-5033

AFFIDAVIT AND SELF-EXECUTING WAIVER
(Bank Accounts, Stocks, Bonds, and Brokerage Accounts)

Decedent's Name_____ Decedent's S.S. No. _____/_____/_____
(Last)   (First)   (Middle)

Date of Death (mm/dd/yy) _____/_____/_____ County of Residence _____ Testate ☐ Intestate ☐

To be used ONLY when the assets listed on the reverse side are passing to a member of one of the following groups, either by contract, survivorship, the decedent's will or the intestate laws of this state.

1. Surviving spouse where the decedent's date of death is on or after January 1, 1985,
2. Child, stepchild, legally adopted child, or issue of any child or legally adopted child (includes a grandchild and a great-grandchild but not a step-grandchild or a great-stepgrandchild) where the decedent's date of death is on or after July 1, 1988,
3. Parent and/or grandparent where the decedent's date of death is on or after July 1, 1988,
4. Surviving domestic partner where the decedent's date of death is on or after July 10, 2004 and the partnership was entered into in New Jersey; AND
5. The beneficiary succeeds to the assets by contract or survivorship or the property is specifically bequeathed to said beneficiary, or the property was not specifically bequeathed but ALL heirs at law by intestacy or ALL beneficiaries under the will are described in numbers 1 thru 4 above.

If there are ANY assets passing to ANY beneficiary other than a member of the class listed above, a complete Transfer Inheritance Tax Return must be filed in the normal manner listing all assets in the estate including any which were acquired under an affidavit or waiver and all beneficiaries.

This form may not be used if any portion of the asset passes into a trust or passes pursuant to a disclaimer.

In the case of a surviving domestic partner in order for this form to be used a copy of the Certificate of Domestic Partnership issued by the local registrar bearing the seal of the State of New Jersey must be attached.

If the decedent died after December 31, 2001, in addition to the criteria listed above, this form may only be used if the decedent's taxable estate plus adjusted taxable gifts as determined pursuant to the provisions of the Internal Revenue Code in effect on December 31, 2001 does not exceed $675,000 (Line 3 plus Line 4 on 2001 Federal Estate Tax Form 706).

Although this form may be used when the decedent's taxable estate plus adjusted taxable gifts does not exceed $675,000, a New Jersey Estate Tax Return must be filed if the decedent died after December 31, 2001 and his/her gross estate plus adjusted taxable gifts as determined pursuant to the provisions of the Internal Revenue Code in effect on December 31, 2001 (Line 1 plus Line 4 on 2001 Federal Estate Tax Form 706) exceeds $675,000.

The decedent's gross estate under the provisions of the Internal Revenue Code includes but is not limited to real estate wherever located, stocks, bonds, bank accounts whether held in the name of the decedent individually or jointly, individual retirement accounts, pensions, annuities, life insurance policies whether paid to a beneficiary or the estate and transfers intended to take effect in possession or enjoyment at or after death. The decedent's taxable estate is determined under the provisions of the Internal Revenue Code by subtracting allowable deductions (includes property passing to a surviving spouse or charity) from the gross estate. Adjusted taxable gifts under the provisions of the Internal Revenue Code includes certain transfers made prior to the decedent's death which are not included in the taxable estate.

I have listed the beneficiaries on the reverse of this page. I hereby request the release of the property listed on the reverse of this page and certify that this form is completed in accordance with all the filing requirements set forth above.
State of New Jersey
County of _____ ss.

_____ being duly sworn, deposes and says that the foregoing statements are true to the best of his/her information or belief.

Subscribed and sworn before me this

_____ day of _____, _____

_____   _____
            Notary Public   Executor / Administrator / Joint Tenant

                                                _____
                                                Social Security or Federal Identification Number

                                                _____
                                                Street Address

                                                _____
                                                Town/City   State   Zip

The bank, trust company, association, other depository, transfer agent, or organization releasing the above assets should have thoroughly instructed the Affiant as to the contents of this form of affidavit and self-executing waiver. The original of this affidavit must be filed by the releasing institution within five business days of execution with the Division of Taxation, Individual Tax Audit Branch - Transfer Inheritance and Estate Tax, 50 Barrack Street, PO Box 249, Trenton, NJ 08695-0249. The affiant should be given a copy.

_____   _____
  Name of Institution Accepting Affidavit   Address

By_____

- See Reverse Side for Schedules and Instructions - This Form May Be Reproduced

TO BE VALID THIS FORM MUST BE FULLY COMPLETED

Description of Property	Market Value at Date of Death	This Column For Division Use

Name of Beneficiary	Relation to Decedent

If the decedent died testate, and the asset listed above do not pass by contract or survivorship, <u>a complete copy of the last will and testament, separate writings and all codicils thereto must be submitted</u>.

In the case of bank accounts be sure to list the name of the institution, title of the account and BALANCE as of the DATE OF DEATH.

In the case of stocks be sure to include the name of the company, manner of registration and the number of shares. Bonds should include the name of the issuer, manner of registration, date and face value.

A separate affidavit is required for each institution releasing assets.

RIDERS MAY BE ATTACHED WHERE NECESSARY

APPENDIX T
INHERITANCE TAX WAIVER FORM L-9

09/04

L-9

AFFIDAVIT OF RESIDENT DECEDENT REQUESTING REAL PROPERTY TAX WAIVER(S)

**STATE OF NEW JERSEY
DEPARTMENT OF THE TREASURY
INDIVIDUAL TAX AUDIT BRANCH
TRANSFER INHERITANCE & ESTATE TAX
PO BOX 249
TRENTON, NEW JERSEY 08695-0249**

(609) 292-5033

Forward this form to the Division of Taxation at the address listed above.
This form is not a waiver and is not to be filed with the County Clerk.

L-9	**RESIDENT DECEDENTS ONLY**	L-9
		9/04

Decedent's Name: _____
(Last)   (First)   (MI)

Decedent's SS No. _____ Date of Death (mm/dd/yy) _____ County of Residence _____

This form may be used only when all beneficiaries are Class "A", there is no New Jersey Inheritance or Estate Tax and there is no requirement to file a tax return.

For decedents dying after December 31, 2001 this form may be used only if the decedent's gross estate plus adjusted taxable gifts for Federal estate tax purposes under the provisions of the Internal Revenue Code in effect on December 31, 2001 does not exceed $875,000. The decedent's gross estate plus adjusted taxable gifts consisted of the following:

A. Real estate wherever located (Full Market Value) . . . . $_____

B. Stocks and bonds whether held individually or jointly . . . . $_____

C. Bank accounts whether held individually or jointly . . . . $_____

D. Individual Retirement Accounts . . . . $_____

E. Pensions and Annuities . . . . $_____

F. Life insurance policies whether paid to a beneficiary or to the estate . . . . $_____

G. Transfers intended to take effect in possession or enjoyment at or after death . . . . $_____

H. Other . . . . $_____

I. Gross Estate (Total A thru H) (Line 1 of 2001 Federal Estate Tax Form 706) . . . . $_____

J. Adjusted Taxable Gifts (Line 4 of 2001 Federal Estate Tax Form 706) . . . . $_____

M. Total (I plus J) . . . . $_____

IF THE TOTAL (LINE M) IS GREATER THAN $675,000, DO NOT PROCEED. THIS FORM MAY NOT BE USED. A NEW JERSEY ESTATE TAX RETURN MUST BE FILED.

List all transfers made by the decedent within three years of date of death:

Date	Transferee/Beneficiary	Relationship	Property Transferred	Value

Description of New Jersey Real Estate		Full Assessed Value for Year of Death	Full Market Value at Date of Death
Street and Number			
Municipality	County		
Lot	Block		
Owner(s) of Record: (if decedent owned a fractional interest state how held and fractional value thereof).			
Amount of Mortgage Balance (if any) $			
Street and Number			
Municipality	County		
Lot	Block		
Owner(s) of Record: (if decedent owned a fractional interest state how held and fractional value thereof).			
Amount of Mortgage Balance (if any) $			

RIDERS MAY BE ATTACHED WHERE NECESSARY

Beneficiaries State Full names of all who have an Interest in the Estate (vested, contingent, operation of law, transfer, etc.)	Relationship to the Decedent	Interest of Beneficiary in the Estate

Deponent further states the following schedule contains the names of all beneficiaries who predeceased the decedent.

Name	Date of Death	Domicile at Death

If this form is not fully and properly completed and/or it does not have the required attachments, it will be returned. Did you remember to:

☐ Use the current version of this form.

☐ Answer all questions.

☐ Fill in the decedent's date of death and social security number.

☐ Attach a copy of letters testamentary or letters of administration.

☐ Attach a copy of the decedent's will, codicils, and any trust agreements.

☐ Attach a copy of the decedent's last full year's Federal income tax return including Schedule A, B, and D.

☐ Fully describe the realty to include the owner of record and the street number, municipality, lot, block, county, and the assessed and market values on the decedent's date of death. If an appraisal was made of the realty, attach a copy. If the realty was held by multiple owners, state the names of the joint owners, their relationship to the decedent and whether the realty was held as tenants in common or as joint tenants with right of survivorship. A tax waiver is not necessary and will not be issued for real property held by a husband and wife as tenants by the entirety in the estate of the spouse dying first.

☐ List all beneficiaries who shared in the estate whether by will, intestacy, trust, operation of the law, transfer intended to take effect in possession or enjoyment at or after death or by transfer within three years of death. Indicate the relationship of each to the decedent and their interest in the estate.

☐ In the case of a surviving Domestic Partner, attach a copy of the stamped Certificate of Domestic Partnership issued by the local registrar bearing the seal of the State of New Jersey. If the domestic partnership was entered into outside this State, this form may not be used.

Complete and Notarize

Mailing Address   Name _____ Phone (____) _____

To Send   Street _____

All Correspondence   City _____ State _____ Zip _____

State of: _____ County of: _____

That _____ being duly sworn, has reviewed the information contained in this form and declares to the best of his/her knowledge it is true, correct, and complete. Deponent authorizes the party listed above to act as the estate's representative and to receive the waiver(s) requested herein.

Subscribed and sworn before me

this _____ day of _____, 20_____   Affidavit of: ☐ Executor   ☐ Administrator   ☐ Joint Tenant

_____   _____
(Signature of Notary Public or Attesting Officer)   Signature of Deponent

INSTRUCTIONS

Form L-9 is an affidavit executed by the executor, administrator or joint tenant requesting the issuance of a tax waiver for real property located in New Jersey which was held by a resident decedent.

Form L-9 may not be used if any of the following conditions exist:

☐ Any asset valued at $500 or more passes to a beneficiary other than the decedent's parents, grandparents, spouse, domestic partner (provided that the relationship was entered into in New Jersey), children, legally adopted children, children's issue, legally adopted children's issue or stepchildren by will, intestacy, trust, operation of the law, by transfer intended to take effect in possession or enjoyment at or after death or by transfer within three years of death.

☐ Where a trust agreement exists or is created under the terms of the decedent's will. In the event that all other conditions for the use of Form L-9 are met and there is no possibility that any portion of the trust assets will pass other than to a Class "A" beneficiary, the Division may give consideration to the issuance of a real estate tax waiver.

☐ The relationship of a mutually acknowledged child is claimed to exist.

☐ A domestic partnership, civil union, or reciprocal beneficiary relationship is claimed to exist and the relationship was entered into in a jurisdiction other than New Jersey.

☐ Where the decedent's date of death is after December 31, 2001 and his/her gross estate plus adjusted taxable gifts for Federal estate tax purposes under the provisions of the Internal Revenue Code in effect on December 31, 2001 exceeds $675,000.

☐ In any instance where there is a New Jersey inheritance or estate tax or a tax return is required to be filed.

This form is not a tax waiver and is not to be filed with the County Clerk.

This competed form and attachments should be forwarded to the NJ Division of Taxation, Inheritance and Estate Tax, PO Box 249, Trenton, NJ 08695-0249.

Additional information pertaining to the use of Form L-9 may be obtained by calling the Inheritance and Estate Tax Section at 609-292-5033.

THIS FORM MAY BE REPRODUCED IN ITS ENTIRETY

APPENDIX U

FAMILY PART CASE INFORMATION STATEMENT

FAMILY PART CASE INFORMATION STATEMENT

Attorney(s):
Office Address
Tel. No./Fax No.
Attorney(s) for:

		Plaintiff,
vs.		
		Defendant.

SUPERIOR COURT OF NEW JERSEY
CHANCERY DIVISION, FAMILY PART
COUNTY

DOCKET NO.
CASE INFORMATION STATEMENT
OF _____

NOTICE: This statement must be fully completed, filed and served, with all required attachments, in accordance with Court Rule 5:5-2 based upon the information available. In those cases where the Case Information Statement is required, it shall be filed within 20 days after the filing of the Answer or Appearance. Failure to file a Case Information Statement may result in the dismissal of a party's pleadings.

PART A - CASE INFORMATION:
Date of Statement_____
Date of Divorce (post-Judgment matters)_____
Date(s) of Prior Statement(s)_____
_____
Your Birthdate_____
Birthdate of **Other Party**_____
Date of Marriage_____
Date of Separation_____
Date of Complaint_____
Does an agreement exist between parties relative to any issue?   [ ] Yes   [ ] No.   If Yes, <u>ATTACH</u> a copy (if written) or a summary (if oral).

ISSUES IN DISPUTE:
Cause of Action_____
Custody_____
Parenting Time_____
Alimony_____
Child Support_____
Equitable Distribution_____
Counsel Fees_____
Other issues [be specific]_____

1. Name and Addresses of Parties:
Your Name   _____
Street Address _____   City_____   State/Zip_____
Other Party's Name _____
Street Address _____   City_____   State/Zip_____

2. Name, Address, Birthdate and Person with whom children reside:
a. Child(ren) From This Relationship

Child's Full Name	Address	Birthdate	Person's Name
_____	_____	_____	_____
_____	_____	_____	_____
_____	_____	_____	_____

b. Child(ren) From Other Relationships

Child's Full Name	Address	Birthdate	Person's Name
_____	_____	_____	_____
_____	_____	_____	_____
_____	_____	_____	_____

Revised Family CIS
Adopted July 28, 2004 to be Effective September 1, 2004

PART B - MISCELLANEOUS INFORMATION:

1. Information about Employment (Provide Name & Address of Business, if Self-employed)
Name of Employer/**Business** _____ Address _____

Name of Employer/**Business** _____ Address _____

2. Do you have Insurance obtained through Employment/Business? [ ] Yes [ ] No. Type of Insurance:
Medical [ ]Yes [ ]No; Dental [ ]Yes [ ]No; Prescription Drug [ ]Yes [ ]No; Life [ ]Yes [ ]No; Disability [ ]Yes [ ]No
Other (explain) _____
Is Insurance available through Employment/Business? [ ] Yes [ ] No Explain:_____
_____

3. ATTACH Affidavit of Insurance Coverage as required by Court Rule *5:4-2* (f) (See Part G)

4. Additional Identification:
Confidential Litigant Information Sheet: Filed   [ ]Yes [ ] No

5. ATTACH a list of all prior/pending family actions involving support, custody or Domestic Violence, with the Docket
   Number, County, State and the disposition reached. Attach copies of all existing Orders in effect.

PART C. - INCOME INFORMATION: Complete this section for self and (if known) for spouse.
                                1. LAST YEAR'S INCOME

	Yours	Joint	Spouse or Former Spouse
1. Gross earned income last calendar (year)	$_____	$_____	$_____
2. Unearned income (same year)	$_____	$_____	$_____
3. Total Income Taxes paid on income (Fed., State, F.I.C.A., and S.U.I.). If Joint Return, use middle column.	$_____	$_____	$_____
4. Net income (1 + 2-3)	$_____	$_____	$_____

ATTACH to this form a corporate benefits statement as well as a statement of all fringe benefits of employment. (See **Part G**)

ATTACH a full and complete copy of last year's Federal and State Income Tax Returns. ATTACH W-2 statements, 1099's,
Schedule C's, etc., to show total income plus a copy of the most recently filed Tax Returns. (See **Part G**)
Check if attached: Federal Tax Return [ ]   State Tax Return [ ]   W-2 [ ] Other [ ]

                          2. PRESENT EARNED INCOME AND EXPENSES

	Yours	Other Party (if known)
1. Average gross **weekly** income (based on last 3 pay periods – ATTACH pay stubs) Commissions and bonuses, etc., are: [ ] included [ ] not included* [ ] not paid to you.	$_____	$_____

*ATTACH details of basis thereof, including, but not limited to, percentage overrides, timing of payments, etc.
  ATTACH copies of last three statements of such bonuses, commissions, etc.

	Yours	Other Party
2. Deductions per **week** (check all types of withholdings): [ ] Federal [ ] State [ ] F.I.C.A. [ ] S.U.I. [ ] Other	$_____	$_____
3. Net average **weekly** income (1 - 2)	$_____	$_____

                    3. YOUR **CURRENT** YEAR-TO-DATE EARNED INCOME
                               Provide Dates: From _____   To _____
1. GROSS EARNED INCOME: $ Number of Weeks_____
2. TAX DEDUCTIONS: (Number of Dependents:)

Adopted 7/28/04 to be Effective 9/1/04   2

a. Federal Income Taxes   a. $_____

b. N.J. Income Taxes   b. $_____

c. Other State Income Taxes   c. $_____

d. FICA   d. $_____

e. Medicare   e. $_____

f. S.U.I. / S.D.I.   f. $_____

g. Estimated tax payments in excess of withholding   g. $_____

h.   h. $_____

i.   i. $_____

TOTAL $_____

3. GROSS INCOME NET OF TAXES $ $_____

4. OTHER DEDUCTIONS   If mandatory, check box

a. Hospitalization/Medical Insurance   a. $_____   [ ]

b. Life Insurance   b. $_____   [ ]

c. **Union Dues**   c. $_____   [ ]

d. 401(k) Plans   d. $_____   [ ]

e. Pension/Retirement Plans   e. $_____   [ ]

f. Other Plans—specify   f. $_____   [ ]

g. Charity   g. $_____   [ ]

h. Wage Execution   h. $_____   [ ]

i. Medical Reimbursement (flex fund)   i. $_____   [ ]

j. Other: j. $_____   [ ]

TOTAL $_____

5. NET YEAR-TO-DATE EARNED INCOME: $_____

NET AVERAGE EARNED INCOME PER MONTH: $_____

NET AVERAGE EARNED INCOME PER WEEK $_____

4. YOUR YEAR-TO-DATE GROSS UNEARNED INCOME **FROM ALL SOURCES [including, but not limited to, income from unemployment, disability and/or social security payments, interest, dividends, rental income and any other miscellaneous unearned income]**

Source	How often paid	Year to date amount
_____	_____	$_____
_____	_____	$_____
_____	_____	$_____
_____	_____	$_____
_____	_____	$_____
_____	_____	$_____
_____	_____	$_____
_____	_____	$_____
_____	_____	$_____

TOTAL GROSS UNEARNED INCOME YEAR TO DATE $_____

5. <u>ADDITIONAL INFORMATION</u>:

1. How often are you paid? _____

2. What is your annual salary? $ _____

3. Have you received any raises in the current year? [ ]Yes [ ]No. If yes, provide the date and the gross/net amount.
    _____

4. Do you receive bonuses, commissions, or other compensation, including distributions, taxable or non-taxable, in addition to your regular salary? [ ]Yes [ ]No. If yes, explain:_____
    _____

5. Did you receive a bonuses, commissions, or other compensation, including distributions, taxable or non-taxable, in addition to your regular salary during the current or immediate past calendar year? [ ] Yes [ ] No If yes, explain and state the date(s) of receipt and set forth the gross and net amounts received: _____
    _____

6. Do you receive cash or distributions not otherwise listed? [ ] Yes [ ] No If yes, explain. _____
    _____

7. Have you received income from overtime work during either the current or immediate past calendar year? [ ]Yes [ ]No If yes, explain. _____

8. Have you been awarded or granted stock options, restricted stock or any other non-cash compensation or entitlement during the current or immediate past calendar year? [ ]Yes [ ]No If yes, explain. _____
    _____

9. Have you received any other supplemental compensation during either the current or immediate past calendar year? [ ]Yes [ ]No. If yes, state the date(s) of receipt and set forth the gross and net amounts received. Also describe the nature of any supplemental compensation received._____
    _____

10. Have you received income from unemployment, disability and/or social security during either the current or immediate past calendar year? [ ]Yes [ ]No. If yes, state the date(s) of receipt and set forth the gross and net amounts received._____
    _____

11. List the names of the dependents you claim:_____

12. Are you receiving any alimony and/or child support? [ ]Yes [ ]No. If yes, how much and from whom?_____
    _____

13. Are you paying or receiving any child support? [ ]Yes [ ]No. If yes, list names of the children, the amount paid or received for each child and to whom paid or from whom received. _____
    _____

14. Is there a wage execution in connection with support? [ ]Yes [ ]No If yes explain._____
    _____

15. Has a dependent child of yours received income from social security, SSI or other government program during either the current or immediate past calendar year? [ ]Yes [ ]No. If yes, explain the basis and state the date(s) of receipt and set forth the gross and net amounts received _____
    _____

16. Explanation of Income or Other Information:
    _____
    _____
    _____
    _____
    _____
    _____
    _____
    _____

PART D - MONTHLY EXPENSES (computed at 4.3 wks/mo.)
Joint Marital Life Style should reflect standard of living established during marriage. Current expenses should reflect the current life style. Do not repeat those income deductions listed in **Part C – 3.**

	Joint Marital Life Style Family, including _____ children	Current Life Style Yours and _____ children
SCHEDULE A: SHELTER		
If Tenant:...	$_____	$_____
Rent..	$_____	$_____
Heat (if not furnished)...............................	$_____	$_____
Electric & Gas (if not furnished).....................	$_____	$_____
Renter's Insurance...................................	$_____	$_____
Parking (at Apartment)...............................	$_____	$_____
Other charges (Itemize)...............................	$_____	$_____
If Homeowner:		
Mortgage	$_____	$_____
Real Estate Taxes **(if not included w/mortgage payment)**...	$_____	$_____
Homeowners Ins **(if not included w/mortgage payment)**...	$_____	$_____
Other Mortgages or Home Equity Loans	$_____	$_____
Heat (unless Electric or Gas).......................	$_____	$_____
Electric & Gas.......................................	$_____	$_____
Water & Sewer.......................................	$_____	$_____
Garbage Removal...................................	$_____	$_____
Snow Removal.......................................	$_____	$_____
Lawn Care..	$_____	$_____
Maintenance...	$_____	$_____
Repairs...	$_____	$_____
Other Charges (Itemize)...............................	$_____	$_____
Tenant or Homeowner:		
Telephone..	$_____	$_____
Mobile/Cellular Telephone...........................	$_____	$_____
Service Contracts on Equipment.....................	$_____	$_____
Cable TV...	$_____	$_____
Plumber/Electrician................................	$_____	$_____
Equipment & Furnishings.............................	$_____	$_____
Internet Charges.....................................	$_____	$_____
Other (itemize).......................................	$_____	$_____
TOTAL	$_____	$_____
SHELTER COMBINED TOTAL	$_____	$_____
SCHEDULE B: TRANSPORTATION		
Auto Payment...	$_____	$_____
Auto Insurance (number of vehicles:)............................	$_____	$_____
Registration, License.................................	$_____	$_____
Maintenance.......................................	$_____	$_____
Fuel and Oil..	$_____	$_____
Commuting Expenses.................................	$_____	$_____
Other Charges (Itemize)...............................	$_____	$_____
TOTAL	$_____	$_____
TRANSPORTATION COMBINED TOTAL	$_____	$_____

SCHEDULE C: PERSONAL..	Joint Marital Life Style Family, including _____children	Current Life Style Yours and _____ children
Food at Home & household supplies............................	$_____	$_____
Prescription Drugs..	$_____	$_____
Non-prescription drugs, cosmetics, toiletries & sundries......	$_____	$_____
School Lunch..	$_____	$_____
Restaurants..	$_____	$_____
Clothing..	$_____	$_____
Dry Cleaning, Commercial Laundry............................	$_____	$_____
Hair Care...	$_____	$_____
Domestic Help..	$_____	$_____
Medical (exclusive of psychiatric)*............................	$_____	$_____
Eye Care*...	$_____	$_____
Psychiatric/psychological/counseling*.........................	$_____	$_____
Dental (exclusive of Orthodontic)*............................	$_____	$_____
Orthodontic*..	$_____	$_____
Medical Insurance (hospital, etc.)*............................	$_____	$_____
Club Dues and Memberships....................................	$_____	$_____
Sports and Hobbies..	$_____	$_____
Camps...	$_____	$_____
Vacations...	$_____	$_____
Children's Private School Costs................................	$_____	$_____
Parent's Educational Costs......................................	$_____	$_____
Children's Lessons (dancing, music, sports, etc.)..............	$_____	$_____
Baby-sitting..	$_____	$_____
Day-Care Expenses..	$_____	$_____
Entertainment...	$_____	$_____
Alcohol and Tobacco..	$_____	$_____
Newspapers and Periodicals....................................	$_____	$_____
Gifts...	$_____	$_____
Contributions...	$_____	$_____
Payments to Non-Child Dependents..........................	$_____	$_____
Prior Existing Support Obligations this family/other families (specify)...	$_____	$_____
Tax Reserve (not listed elsewhere)............................	$_____	$_____
Life Insurance..	$_____	$_____
Savings/Investment..	$_____	$_____
Debt Service (from page 7) (not listed elsewhere).............	$_____	$_____
Parenting Time Expenses..	$_____	$_____
Professional Expenses (other than this proceeding)..........	$_____	$_____
Other (specify)...	$_____	$_____

*unreimbursed only..

TOTAL	$_____	$_____
PERSONAL COMBINED TOTAL	$_____	$_____

Please Note: If you are paying expenses for a spouse and/or children not reflected in this budget, attach a schedule of such payments.

Schedule A: Shelter...	$_____	$_____
Schedule B: Transportation.....................................	$_____	$_____
Schedule C: Personal...	$_____	$_____
Grand Totals..	$_____	$_____

PART E - BALANCE SHEET OF ALL FAMILY ASSETS AND LIABILITIES
STATEMENT OF ASSETS

Description	Title to Property (H, W, J)	Date of purchase/acquisition. If claim that asset is exempt, **state reason and value of what is claimed to be exempt**	Value $ Put * after exempt	Date of Evaluation Mo./Day/ Yr.
1. Real Property				
2. Bank Accounts, CD's				
3. Vehicles				
4. Tangible Personal Property				
5. Stocks and Bonds				
6. Pension, Profit Sharing, Retirement Plan(s) 40l(k)s, etc. **[list each employer]**				
7. IRAs				
8. Businesses, Partnerships, Professional Practices				
9. Life Insurance (cash surrender value)				
10. Loans Receivable				
11. Other (specify)				

TOTAL GROSS ASSETS: $_____
TOTAL SUBJECT TO EQUITABLE DISTRIBUTION: $_____
TOTAL NOT SUBJECT TO EQUITABLE DISTRIBUTION: $_____

STATEMENT OF LIABILITIES

Description	Name of Responsible Party (H, W, J)	If you contend liability should not be considered in equitable distribution, state reason	Monthly Payment	Total Owed	Date
1. Real Estate **Mortgages**					
_____	___	_____	___	___	___
_____	___	_____	___	___	___
_____					
2. Other Long Term Debts					
_____	___	_____	___	___	___
_____	___	_____	___	___	___
3. Revolving Charges					
_____	___	_____	___	___	___
_____	___	_____	___	___	___
_____	___	_____	___	___	___
_____	___	_____	___	___	___
_____	___	_____	___	___	___
_____	___	_____	___	___	___
_____	___	_____	___	___	___
4. Other Short Term Debts					
_____	___	_____	___	___	___
_____	___	_____	___	___	___
5. Contingent Liabilities					
_____	___	_____	___	___	___
_____					

TOTAL GROSS LIABILITIES: $_____
(excluding contingent liabilities)

NET WORTH: $_____
(subject to equitable distribution)

Adopted 7/28/04 to be Effective 9/1/04

PART F - STATEMENT OF SPECIAL PROBLEMS

Provide a Brief Narrative Statement of Any Special Problems Involving This Case: As example, state if the matter involves complex valuation problems (such as for a closely held business) or special medical problems of any family member etc.

I certify that the foregoing information contained herein is true. I am aware that if any of the foregoing information contained therein is willfully false, I am subject to punishment.

DATED: SIGNED: _____

PART G - REQUIRED ATTACHMENTS

CHECK IF YOU HAVE ATTACHED THE FOLLOWING REQUIRED DOCUMENTS

1. A full and complete copy of your last federal and state income tax returns
   with all schedules and attachments. **(Part C-1)**

2. Your last calendar year's W-2 statements, 1099's, K-1 statements.   _____

3. Your three most recent pay stubs.   _____

4. Bonus information including, but not limited to, percentage overrides, timing of payments, etc.; the last three statements of such bonuses, commissions, etc. **(Part C)**   _____

5. Your most recent corporate benefit statement or a summary thereof showing the nature, amount and status of
   retirement plans, savings plans, income deferral plans, insurance benefits, etc. **(Part C)**   _____

6. Affidavit of Insurance Coverage as required by Court Rule 5:4-2(f) **(Part B-3)**   _____

7. List of all prior/pending family actions involving support, custody or Domestic Violence, with the Docket Number, County, State and the disposition reached. Attach copies of all existing Orders in effect. (Part B-5)   _____

8. Attach details of each wage execution (Part C-5)

9. Schedule of payments made for a spouse and/or children not reflected in Part D.   _____

10. Any agreements between the parties.   _____

11. An Appendix IX Child Support Guideline Worksheet, as applicable, based upon available information.   _____